TWENTIETH CENTURY VIEWS

The aim of this series is to present the best
in contemporary critical opinion on major
authors, providing a twentieth century per-
spective on their changing status in an era
of profound revaluation

Maynard Mack, *Series Editor*
Yale University

LAURENCE STERNE

LAURENCE
STERNE

A COLLECTION OF CRITICAL ESSAYS

Edited by

John Traugott

Prentice-Hall, Inc. *Englewood Cliffs, N. J.*

Contents

Contents

Introduction

by John Traugott

It is now so long since critics have talked about Sterne's "triviality" that not only is the issue dead but the critics themselves look "trivial." As for his being "scabby"—the encomium of a contemporary echoed by many worthies since—we like that. The criticism of this volume does not, therefore, beat the dead horses of the past. True, we moderns are always top-lofty about the past—even as we ourselves become old-fashioned and other more modern moderns begin to patronize us. However, the remarkable revaluation of Sterne in recent years has something more in it. We really can claim him, not because of our imaginative superiority but because Sterne was an inexplicable anachronism. Benjamin Lehman, who is himself a marker of the turn of Sterne criticism, said twenty-five years ago, ". . . if *Tristram Shandy* did not exist, we should have to say that its achievement . . . , twenty years after *Pamela*, was not to be imagined. To see what Sterne's achievement really was, is, I believe, only in these last few years possible, in a mind made aware by *The Magic Mountain, Ulysses,* and *Remembrance of Things Past*." We can only wonder at past attitudes towards this great original—he was prurient, eccentric, foolish, maudlin; his work was at best a lumber room from which might be culled dear characters good for an edition called *The Beauties of Sterne*. The last thing critics thought was that he had any integrity. In his own time he was sensational, the first literary lion, always a *poseur,* always Shandy. He has always been read and loved, but somewhat clandestinely after the first clamor, intuitively appreciated but felt to be a not quite satisfactory representative of our high culture.

Thackeray, who despised him, and Coleridge, who though mildly disapproving remains one of Sterne's keenest critics, both recognized a quality in Sterne that a number of the essayists following take as the place to begin. "He is always looking in my face, watching his effect," said Thackeray petulantly; but Coleridge was more philosophical: "I would remark that there is a sort of knowingness, the wit of which depends, first, on the modesty it gives pain to; or secondly, on the innocence and innocent ignorance over which it triumphs; or thirdly, on a certain

1

oscillation in the individual mind between the remaining good, and the encroaching evil of his nature, a sort of dallying with the devil . . . so that the mind has in its own white and black angel the same or similar amusement as may be supposed to take place between an old debauchee and a prude,—she feeling resentment, on the one hand, from a prudential anxiety to preserve appearances and have a character, and, on the other, an inward sympathy with the enemy." With very different evaluations, these are fundamentally twentieth century views of the subversive jester in Sterne; they only distantly suggest, however, a deeper aspect of his art which is the real subject of several of the essays following: his tinkering with reality, confusing fiction and actuality, destroying illusion, making convention conscious, and abolishing cause and effect in time. The mind is its own place, a satanic notion—Sterne's, ours.

The reason for our sympathy is not far to search. We are told that one of the vices of our age is its critical spirit—self-conscious, analytic of art, destructive of substantial "reality," taking nothing on the surface, forever searching out secret meanings. The charge is by now so old-hat that we are willing to be what we are. Curiously, what we are has brought about a remarkable revolution of critical interest in the oddest of eighteenth century novelists. "Nothing odd will do long," said the great neoclassical cham, Samuel Johnson, "Tristram Shandy did not last." And yet of all eighteenth century novelists, the odd one is perhaps for us the liveliest, for can we not find in these generalities about our critical age obvious elements of Sterne's practice? *Self-conscious*—it is abominable, says Tristram, for a man to commend himself, but he will not go out of the world with the conceit of his masterly, unremarked strokes rotting in his head (I,22). *Analytic of art*—two sentences or two scenes of Sterne's cannot go by without his reflecting on the grammar, rhetoric, and logic or the narrative devices by which he got from the one to the other: he has no interest in a willing suspension of disbelief. *Destructive of substantial reality*—simultaneously, a misnamed, crushed-nose baby in his crib and a middle-aged clown, Tristram circles the Visitation table of forty years earlier—still another time—sitting in council on his misnaming, eliciting from each of the doctors his private fantasy concerning Phutatorius's sudden outcry after the hot chestnut has fallen surreptitiously, but by Newton's law of gravity, into his breech. From those secret parts Tristram extracts a dialectic concerning reality, wholly oblivious of Newton's law. *Forever searching out secret meanings*—Sterne is not disturbed that everyone, including himself, has his peculiar rhetoric that organizes his private world. Despite Locke, that is the way men live and love.

By what form is all this to be represented? Not, certainly, by a form subservient to Aristotelian criteria of internal probability. Where are the boundaries between the thing represented and the form and style of its representation? Sterne did not pretend, as do most makers of fictions, that his art imitated some external coherence in things. He wants us to think about the inevitable artificiality of all representation. If men cannot tell their secret organizations of the world from the world itself, the "world" is indeed big with jest. If a creaking door hinge is convertible with the hinge of Walter's fate, what has he or anyone—for we all have our creaking hinges—to do with reality? Not for nothing did Sterne trace his ancestry to Yorick, the king's jester, Hamlet's grinning, chop-fallen void. As Lehman remarks, Yorick is the absolute jester of the imagination, having no lines to say. But Hamlet's anguish is not Sterne's, though the Yorkshire parson, like Hamlet, certainly imagined that the world's absolute meanings were to be found only in the empty eyes of the absolute jester. We today have a technical name for this metaphysics—"absurdity," but in some miraculous way Sterne finds such a reality a reassuring joke. His world, then, is very different from ours: one overwhelming difference is that his love—his sentimentalism—is found and nurtured in the terrible jest of solipsism. How he does it is the wonder of the man and his book. No wonder, though, that the twentieth century has rehabilitated the man and battened on his book as though it were a lifeline to humanity itself. We, naturally, do not wish to be inhuman, and, here, miraculously, is an eighteenth century artist who ignores "nature's simple plan," with its springs and cogs, to discover this fragmentary and solipsistic life of ours. Sterne's books, like our own, parody neoclassical formalism. That his mockery of the tricks of his trade owes something to contemporary stage farce is as obvious in Sterne as in Rabelais; yet Sterne's mockery, unlike the fantasy of farce, is intended to represent everyday experience. Such a technique ends where it begins—with a very special conception of reality. E. M. Forster said that a god called Muddle reigns in the Shandy squiredom. The trouble with such an easy formula is that this Muddle knows perfectly well what he is doing. He has designs upon our minds and sensibilities.

In George Eliot's world, as in Fielding's, our emotional response to characters depends upon their relation to natural law. By any cultural calculation Sterne's interiorized world, with its own laws, is inexplicable. Facilely, critics talk about Sterne's sensationalism as deriving from Locke, but as Jean-Jacques Mayoux points out, Locke did not imagine any such interiorized world as Sterne's. This is not to say that he is in revolt against the sanctions of natural law; he is simply uninterested in them. If he has precepts, they are of benevolism (perhaps a new kind of natural law); yet such precepts are paradoxical, for his world *is* interior. Here, however, we touch the genius of his understanding of life. War, for example, is a stock subject of moralists—killing and suffering and cultural deterioration on one side, and bravery, glory, and selflessness on the other. All this is irrelevant to Sterne. What is relevant is Toby's bowling-green war, a private fantasy, which unwittingly satirizes—according to Walter —Marlborough's parade and prancing. Is Toby really bloodthirsty? The question is irrelevant—literally, he wouldn't hurt a fly, even if he has (we must presume if we want to be irrelevant) killed a number of men. And what about Marlborough? *His* bowling green is larger and his silly game is dangerous. Perhaps Sterne's understanding of the universality of hobbyhorses is the beginning of a new cultural wisdom. The hobbyhorse —in Swift, that pernicious "mind of man when he gives spur and bridle to his thoughts"—has found its benign place as private fantasy which does not impose upon the world. We can love Tobys without being taken in by Marlboroughs.

The dense, substantial, immutable, retributive machinery of the novel of Fielding and, more especially, Richardson, which we call internal probability, suited Sterne's age, as did Newton's simple location of time and space and Locke's location of substance in the object and quality in the subject. The object *is* there; we all have the same time and the same space and know the same qualities. Sterne does not scruple to make all this irrelevant, and, worse, he likes to confuse the boundaries of art and life. And yet for all his hilarious, subversive exhibiting of the privacy of our minds, he seems to recognize some real correspondence of minds (or, more accurately, of sensibilities). Solipsism and sentimentalism— these are the two faces of Sterne's coin. This is the way he defines the fall—as solipsism, and the way he redeems the fallen—by sentimentalism.[1]

[1] "Sentimentalism" is today almost certainly a term of abuse—maudlin self-indulgence. What positive connotations survive are of the "weak-sister" sort—pleasant, dreamy feelings for socially approved connections, like one's mother or dog, and places, like one's "home town." We cannot, however, abandon this damaged word which after all names a concept of very great importance in cultural history, a concept Sterne and other great writers took as fundamental to life. To touch fingertips with this or that pretty woman—one of Yorick's occupations—can be taken as a serious activity. It is a sensory experience that warms the blood and may, indeed, be necessary to survival. From sensory experience one passes easily to sympathy and to understanding. We can define sentimentalism by Sterne's practice: By sensory apprehension of the behavior of other persons, and by comparing that behavior by an association of ideas with our own, we conceive a sympathy with other persons. (Yes, of course, a "hothouse" cultivation of feelings can be a vice—whence the modern pejorative sense of the word "sentimentalism.") Though the phenomenon of sentimentalism in Sterne's age may well be an intuitive development of a new principle of cultural coherence at a time when the

One cannot say he rejects the Newtonian world, but Shandean existence dominates it. Toby's idea, the war on the bowling green, has carried off the sash weight; down crashes the window, as was required by Newton's law, circumcizing (at the very least) young Tristram. What reader does not wince? But somehow the physical horror is irrelevant, so benign is the tone. What happens is only a new set of ideas. Existence does not scruple to mix up mental and physical events; Sterne tells us how we exist.

"Once Sterne turned away from a duration plot and from simply crystallized character," Lehman writes, "he was faced with the greatest problem of all—the problem of an ultimate form which could be raised from the material quite naturally seen and felt, a form which should derive no curve or mass from the selective magnetic force of preconceptions of action and character. A hundred and seventy-five years later, novelists are still seeking solutions for these problems which he first confronted. . . ." While all artists seek to revitalize conventions, Sterne sought to do something rather different—to achieve his own form by making the reader conscious of his violation of conventions. Lehman identified the critical interest we have in Sterne. By now it is commonplace. This being said, we need not assume that Sterne was a rude or naïve modern, that in some putative literary history called, perhaps, "The Development of the Modern Novel," he is a first hesitant step. He achieved his own form.

Recognition of Sterne's revolutionary artistic sophistication came first —oddly but with a certain logic—in Russia, where Viktor Shklovsky and the Formalist literary group of the first years of the Soviet regime took *Tristram Shandy* as virtually an embodiment of their aesthetic. Rejecting at once academic historical criticism and symbolist doctrine that "art is thinking in images," the Formalists saw themselves as scientific investigators whose only radical commitment was that art is art. They naturally set about describing all the devices and techniques of literary form. Later they put formal questions in terms not of historical or social forces but of literary traditions and conventions, much as did Eliot in "Tradition and the Individual Talent." Scorning the notion that "content" is a separable something that can be poured into "form," they took form to be simply the aesthetic experience of the literary object. Art is

---

mystique of Church and State was being rapidly attenuated, self-conscious applications of the concept ranged from the puerile elevation of vague benevolistic feelings to a religious principle to Hume's carefully defined doctrine of sympathy. An understanding of Sterne's peculiar sentimentalism is obviously best acquired by attending his own words.

artificial, without ulterior purpose, sometimes, indeed, without "meaning"—merely for itself. Sterne, whose Anglo-Saxon critics at the time Shklovsky wrote (1921) could think of little but his dubious instruction and helter-skelter form, especially suffered from neoclassical aesthetic prejudices. Shklovsky is a breath of fresh air. (Curiously, Sterne himself, though he jokes about gravity and doing some good for the heads of his readers, certainly thought he was instructing. If Shklovsky's notions have validity, they will be reconciled with the odd kind of instruction Sterne had in mind.) In Shklovsky's view, the problem of finding an ultimate novelistic form without prejudice or preconception—the problem Lehman sees as Sterne's—lies in bringing the reader to a perception of the form itself, of the plot, devices, conventions, rules, by which a writer tries by hook or crook to capture reality. Habitualization, Shklovsky remarked, destroys life—one scarcely knows one's wife; art creates a fresh vision of experience by artificial arrangements that defamiliarize, "make strange" (as Shklovsky puts it) our perceptions. Sterne seemed his man, for in pursuing the ways of art, laying them bare, Sterne is without compassion. Does he not, for example, leave Mrs. Shandy bent grotesquely for an age, her ear to the chink in the door where she had only hoped to hear the meaning of the single word "wife"—"a shrill, penetrating sound"—which had come floating through the door as she passed in the hall? Tristram reflects for a paragraph upon her posture, and for a while longer goes to the kitchen for the affairs there, and then appears to forget her entirely, and then suddenly remembers her, only to forget her again, until finally, long after (and after elaborate reflection on the problems of representation), he allows her to straighten up from her grotesque pose. So it is with all the narrative: Sterne wants the reader to see how he goes about his business, not, ever, to suspend his disbelief and forget the joints and hinges of the structure. The narrative is never finished, either overall or in vignette, because that narrative is never the primary interest. Nor has such dedication time for mere instruction.

The present translation of Shklovsky's essay renders his title *"Tristram Shandy*—a Parodying Novel"*: this title, taken with the charmingly paradoxical conclusion, "that *Tristram Shandy* is the most typical novel in any literature," marks out Shklovsky's point-of-view. Not only does the work's "content" become the perception by the reader of its play with typical fictional forms—"making strange"—but the author's reflection on this parody is the principle of development of the novel. In contrast to the ordinary novel's sequential development (and of course, flashbacks, digressions, and parallel plots are only more complicated varieties of sequential development), Sterne's story moves, as in the example of Mrs.

Shandy's eavesdropping, by conscious reflection on the artistic necessities and difficulties of rendering the experience of various motifs—knots, emasculation, the erotic, hobbyhorses, and more—so that we are reminded that it is the artist who makes a unity, not life. Shklovsky uses a striking figure to show Sterne's achievement, that of a series of cones whose apexes represent in a conventional novel the movement of the story-line and the bases the "fill-in" of motivations and background. In Sterne, however, the bases are the locus of the story, and the apexes, the ultimate effects, are only glanced at, or more often left in a cloud of equivocation. (What, for example, is the upshot of Toby's affair with the Widow? Or Mrs. Shandy's long listening at the chink?)

Among Shklovsky's examples of the novelistic conventions Sterne "makes strange" are the illusion of cause and effect given by a linear time sequence, the simultaneous story or subplot enlarging the scope of the action, the digression for working up suspense, the catching of character in pose or gesture, the discovered manuscript or document to deepen or resolve the action, the ending which knots all actions into a meaningful whole. If *Tristram* ends on a cock and bull story and the *Sentimental Journey* on the lewd implication of bare syntax, the reason is that the very frustration of an Aristotelian "end" forces a synchronic experience of all the actions of these books. Miraculously, Sterne has made all his tricks into a whole composition. *Tristram Shandy's* famous time-shifts illustrate the fiction of fictional time but they also bring together all the motifs and make them interdependent. "—Now this is the most puzzled skein of all— . . . I am this moment walking across the market-place of Auxerre with my father and my uncle Toby, in our way back to dinner—and I am this moment also entering Lyons with my postchaise broke into a thousand pieces—and I am moreover this moment in a handsome pavillion built by Pringello, upon the banks of the Garonne . . . where I now sit rhapsodizing all these affairs" (VII,27). Though this is the single explicit link between Volume VII—the anti-guidebook gallop through France—and the rest of the book, Tristram manages to remind us in a few pages of the continuing weaving of motifs from the novel's substance into the drama of this vital flight from Death. The nervous vitality of a man juggling three different moments of his life, bringing together with gentleness and love and yet ridicule the mad singularity of personalities, the ginger of scatology, the wistful story of Jenny's knowing help in the author's flagging sexuality, and the artist's gallant, amused struggle to get it all down sensibly—this wonderful sense of life while running from Death is one of the larger subjects of the novel as a whole. The artist's mind (and the reader's, for he is made an artist, too) is laid bare. All this means that Sterne's famous associationism is wholly conscious.

Now, Shklovsky's remarks do not, certainly, give an adequate account of *Tristram Shandy*. Though his intention is only to demonstrate certain fundamentals of the novel form as illustrated by Sterne's parodying tactics, his purist aesthetic probably could not in any case reach that grateful sense of life called Shandean. A good many of the essays of this collection suggest that Sterne had a peculiar notion of reality, that his own life is strangely figured in the emotional design of the work, that philosophical and moral implications are insistent. What of his comedy and sentiment? Criticism has many tools and we need not expect that any one critic— accomplished lapidary—will polish off and highlight Sterne for a museum.

Shklovsky's purism, his insistence that art is artificial, without ulterior motive or purpose, does seem to gloss over metaphysical implications that other critics, though accepting his sort of aesthetic analysis, seem compelled to pursue. Are we not, for example, constantly faced with Tristram's paradox that reality can only be represented when one is forever conscious of the artificiality of the representation? All his enforced consciousness of hobbyhorses, poses, actions suspended in time, *double entendres,* suggests, as Mayoux says, that all representation must be parody. It is only a short step then to question whether parody is not the only way we have of communicating our experiences—and perhaps the only way of thinking about them ourselves.

Like Shklovsky, Mendilow has seen that Sterne was obsessed by his perception of the artificiality of art, especially the device of selecting incidents so that life seems to have a cause and effect sequence in time. He wants the reader to see such selection as mere convention, his own experience of life being that only one time, the present, has any reality. The present has all other times at its beck and call because other times can exist only as they are part of present experience. Events, therefore, must be arranged not by sequence in time, but as they make present experience. True, a cannon ball hits Toby in the groin; true, it had a certain trajectory; true, he must retire to Shandy Hall. This is cause and effect but the sequence—beyond its comic absurdity—is of no interest at all to Sterne; what interests him is Toby's hobbyhorse. After all, Toby is able to combine the real events of his military career in King William's reign with the real events of Marlborough's campaigns, and both with his own shenanigans on the bowling green. By Sterne's device of the time-shift all three events become one. Nothing is happening to Toby; he simply is. He is static—until the Widow's venerial eye finds him out. At this point, we would expect in a conventional novel, he will change.

But almost instantly the new event is stylized by parody and we simply don't ask what happens next.

Tristram himself is writing in the years 1759-66 about events which occurred before his birth but which give meaning to all the mistakes of the nights of his conception and birth. Furthermore, the real author is associated with the fictional author, and the narration mixes exterior, historical events with interior, psychic events in a way that makes the novel a set of chinese boxes: a real man, Sterne, recreates himself in salon and novel as Tristram and Yorick, wounds his genitals as Tristram and talks about his impotence in his real-life letters, kills himself as Yorick for the pathos of the thing, suggesting the pathos of his own life. Tristram creates as a part of his own consciousness a set of characters, Toby, Walter, and others, who in their turn, oblivious of their duty to their creator, are making, each one, an idiosyncratic construct of life. One can only touch on the weavings, the ins and outs of this fantastic triumph of art over life. And yet, as Mendilow points out, not the smallest date of *Tristram* but can be fitted into a chronological order. Sterne's clowning includes an incredible feat of juggling events, fictional with real, psychic with physical, so that nothing is amiss. In short, our author wants us to puzzle out and reassemble plot sequences and to be conscious of the reason they must be confused.

As Sterne so elaborately claims, his digressions are not properly digressions, for there is no forward-moving architectonic plot from which to digress. In contrast, the flashback and digressive techniques of the conventional novel have points of departure and return. But in *Tristram* there is no point of reference for the time-shifts. This being so, he need never fill in the reader on what has happened during a time lapse. In effect there is no time lapse. All times must be present time. But the Sternean time-shift becomes a narrative device quite as important as the cause and effect sequence of the conventional novel. It can create drama as one event is set against another; it can create climax, suspense, anticipation, and an effect of living presence. We remember the opening pages of *Tristram* in which all these effects are apparent in one paradoxical instant of disjunctive conjunction between a man who is a universal philosopher and a woman who is a universal blank. "Did ever woman, since the creation of the world, interrupt a man with such a silly question?" (I, 2)—this conundrum starts up the machine. A tease that first traps the reader into active participation, it also sets the theme of cross-accidents and its stylistic corollary of associationism. Always, times-past are made part of time-present, the time of composition. It is time-present that makes us puzzle out some sort of connection of one fragment to another—the sentimental story of Yorick (which is moved through a time sequence straight to a denouement), the comedy of the begetting and the horror of the forceps birth (which set a timeless, reiterative pattern of absurd cross-accidents), the madnesses of the brothers (whose busy ingenuities would seem to be leading to something), the implication by way of the Sorbonne doctor's theology that the great world is quite as mad and inconsequential as this little world of six-miles' galloping space for a spavined horse.

If one accepts the view—Shklovsky's and Mendilow's—that Sterne's "tricks" are not a buffoon's but an artist's, then one is haunted by the personality and metaphysics of this odd provincial who found a joyful energy in sapping the neoclassical repose—as he thought it—of the capital's chams. "I should beg Mr. Horace's pardon," said he. Mayoux, though developing Shklovsky's and Mendilow's views, argues for an inextricable relation of Sterne's personality, thought, and art. Refreshingly, he does not try to rehabilitate the man, as do so many recent critics whose sympathy for Sterne's work and, perhaps, cultural intolerance of sentimentality have led them to attempt an "image" of the man more palatable to our age. They discover that his smut and his sentimentality are only illusions, really Rabelaisian gusto and mockery, a "put-on," of contemporary sentimentalists. Well-meaning as it is, this is the sort of "rehabilitation" that saves the man but kills the artist, for Sterne *is* sentimental, and indeed, as Mayoux and other critics argue, his aesthetic is founded in sentimentality. The originality, and one must say, humanity, of Mayoux's essay is that he accepts what is true, that Sterne was a sentimentalist who liked smut, pornography, and obscenity of a sniggering sort. He then goes on to show the intimate connection of this not-very-elevating taste of Sterne's for smut with his sentimentalism and his art.

Is Sterne's obscenity merely an impish wish to purge the reader of hypocrisy? Doubtless, that is a part of the story, but if Sterne liked to pull the reader's nose with sexual equivocation, is it not also true that his entire treatment of sex has a sickly air? Is it not "sex in the head"?, asks Mayoux, quoting D. H. Lawrence's definition of sexual perversion. His relations with women, the ever-present Kittys and Elizas, appear to have been characterized by this attenuated, mental sort of eroticism. Of course, some scholar may well turn up a bastard or two, but will this alter our view of his personality? It seems obvious that he had an "irresistible penchant," says Mayoux, for the dirty joke told with a leering air of innocence, and this penchant is *not—pace* the critics—Rabelaisian. But the matter is deeper: "Whatever the critics may say, an anguish shows through

those interminable histories of noses, of enormous noses, of noses crushed
to nothing, of accidental circumcision which is taken for castration, of
the wound in the groin . . . coming after Tristram's maladroit conception. All this obstinately draws attention to the difficulty of sexual coupling. . . ." Why defend Sterne from these "sickly" aspects of his personality and art, Mayoux asks, when it would be simpler to recognize
the freedom he discovered in cruel necessity, for is not such freedom the
greatest glory of man? We should admire him for making of his misery
something good, something of genius.

What then did he make of his misery? One of the most important aspects of Stern's writings is that they open themselves constantly to the
reader and invite him—seduce him, rather—to take part. Relations of
complicity—often enough "scabby"—are quickly established with the
reader in every vignette or sequence. This complicity is a sort of voyeur-
ism, engaging the curiosity (or salacity) of an onlooker, for the onlooker
is an integral part of sentimentalism. To this sentimental correspondence
Sterne appeals, almost with desperation, as he develops all the lacunae,
doubts, needs in the passages among his characters, between Tristram
and the characters, and between Tristram and the reader. Thus the mock-
learning, the hobbyhorses, the mad ratiocination, the sexual equivocations are a set of private rooms into which the reader is enticed and
shown his complicity in what is going on behind the closed doors. Sterne
toys with the comic anguish felt in this condition, stripping off layer
upon layer of illusions. How is it, Mayoux asks, that with all his skepticism, pathos, and even—distantly—tragedy, Sterne is in fact so gay? In
his game-playing he found a liberty of expression that existence would
seem to have denied him—and us. Despite the manifest fatalities of life,
from crushed noses to mad metaphysics, despite the illusions, the artist
wins an exhilarating freedom in the very game he plays with reality.
Time and space, cause and effect become toys of the mind, whatever their
relentless war against the body. How often Sterne reminds us that his art
is a stand against death. His dance of life with death becomes an heroic
dodge; by a quick change the jester and sentimentalist becomes a hero.
As Mayoux remarks, Sterne is the irreplaceable individual—and knows it.

He knows that every time we represent our experience of "reality" we
change our experience of it. Then the forms of representation become
the object of other forms of representation, and so on until we contemplate the forms of the forms of the forms. . . . The process is endless, always a struggle, always self-conscious, always big with jest because in the
end always frustrated. Art and life can never be quite disentangled. Here
is one example. Walter has decided upon the magic of the name Tris-

megistus to undo the catastrophe of Tristram's crushed nose. (We remember that the nose figures prominently in Walter's schemata for turning life into art and making a perfect child.) With Toby he starts down the stairs, launching on the first step a formal dissertation on the secret spring of hope within each of us which counterbalances the evils of life, and though he has just worked the name-magic with accompanying rhetoric, he realizes that Chance has its own rhetoric. The drama is cast: Rhetoric, Hope, Magic, Chance will spin the passions to a new catastrophe. Toby says he knows nothing of Chance, and with a rhetorical flourish of his crutch to drive home his point accidentally strikes Walter a terrible blow on the shin. Walter's pleasure in having his point proved by life takes off the agony on his shinbone. Then, freezing the duo upon the stairway, Tristram addresses the reader: there is so much talk between them to be got through that he will never get them downstairs so as to start something new. How will he preserve the unity of time? Nothing to do but violate the rules and forget them—"drop the curtain, Shandy." The characters have their art and so does the narrator, and all are trying to tell how it feels to them to get through the day. Communication seems to involve self-consciousness of communication, a dreadful truth, but somehow in Sterne a good joke; the ingenuity of the thing is the joy.

Mayoux puts the matter well: "From fatal disorder and mechanical incoherence the play of the creative intelligence can make a freedom—the only one that will count in Proust's eyes—the only one that can oppose the drift of things toward death. This interiorized world—the world as image—this is the raw material for the creative spirit, a treasure to draw upon. The liberty to make use of this reality as he wishes fascinates Sterne so much that not only does he draw upon it ceaselessly but he constantly makes himself seen while drawing upon it."

Sterne has always the double aspect of innocent and sophisticate. Time and place and learning float free, without relevance or application until, say, one crushes a nose and wants to make the crushing mean something. Then any thing, any place, any time becomes grist for that mental mill. Innocent, because he will not trade on "inevitable" experience (as does Fielding), but sophisticated, because once the mind begins to turn it makes a most careful artifact. The comparison is not invidious: Fielding's naïveté is an ironic device, purely; Sterne's a fool's natural manner. Everyone is an artist but some are simple and some are infinitely complex. Toby is simple (mad, Locke would say) and Tristram is complex, but in either case the mill of the mind grinds out its artifact, and that artifact is "character." "Character" is a construct (one's figure), not to be confused with "self" (one's inner experience). The latter is nearly unseen in

Sterne's writings, only fleetingly glimpsed. All else is art. While Toby, for example, is marching up and down his bowling green and fabricating odd parts and utensils of the house into culverins and petards, he is all art, simply a "character." His "self" appears fugitively in one moment when the Widow Wadman appears with her curious finger and venerial eye. So Walter—if more complex in his art and therefore more complex in "character." Only in the split second of his fall across the bed upon hearing of his son Bobby's death (and before his hand strays into the chamberpot) does his "self" show through. Similarly, an odd intrusion of "self" into Mrs. Shandy's "character" occurs when she turns pale as ashes as Walter, in an inspiration, describes to her the advantages he has found in a book of cutting open her abdomen and uterus to deliver the new child. And Tristram, the supreme artist, the character who includes all other characters, uses the harlequin's trick of allowing a momentary glimpse of the pathetic, even the tragic, through his wardrobe of quick changes. He makes Death stay for a jest and then skips off in his artfulness to continue his desperate art.

All this means that Sterne's characters, including Tristram, are radically different from those of the modern associationist novelist, who deals first of all with the "self," and only with the "character" as the "self" chooses to fret about it. In Sterne, on the contrary, Tristram's associations are conscious and calculated and his characters though surprising do not change. Sterne's principle of continuity and development, then, cannot be what we today mean by "stream-of-consciousness," the evolution of "self" in the passing currents of the mind.

In this connection, it is time to lay the ghost of Locke, that spook said to be back of all the strange happenings of Sterne's works. Locke's short paragraph on the "association of ideas," intended to account for a species of madness, dangerous and unworthy of our reason (that candle of the Lord)—this "association of ideas" Sterne makes the simple-minded principle of Toby's art. Toby brings all of existence down to a military metaphor. But Locke is turned upside down, for Toby is good and genial, not dangerous and mad. As for Tristram, his associationism has nothing whatever to do with Locke. Tristram is a free man, the complete artist, untrammeled, certainly, by Locke's rules of reasoning. The most important use of Locke, then, is as foil—to show off, to test, to measure the Shandean world where people make their own sense and communicate without clear ideas—not at all as Locke would have them do.

This freedom of the clown-artist has nothing to do, then, with an idiot drift of impressions and memories. Does Tristram create his being in these associations? Obviously not, for though his invention is continually surprising, he does not change, any more than harlequin changes his spots as he invents new *lazzi*. What develops is a history of *the* mind, for Sterne like Locke, whom he admired and fairly destroyed, wanted to write a history of the mind and discover the limits of reason. We may rightly appreciate Sterne's prescience of new worlds to come—one thinks especially of his similarity to Samuel Beckett—but in the rationalistic and calculated purpose of his associations, our author is yet an Augustan. Moreover, though he is not preaching, the habit of preacher is not forgotten. The constant references to rhetorical figures of thought and style remind us that his originality and virtuosity depend upon a consciousness of conventions, the conventions of the novel and other literary forms, of preaching, of the fool character, of sentimentalism. Shklovsky might expand his formula, that *Tristram Shandy* is the most typical novel in any literature, to an even more interesting paradox, that Sterne is the most conventional writer. His point is always that men can make of conventions what they want. Unlike Beckett, however, who sometimes shows men utterly alienated while they speak the same clichés and use the same gestures, Sterne uses the conventions to make us sympathize with the eccentricity which develops from them. A good example is the parade and prancing of warriors, a standard ingredient of literature, and especially the quaint character of the superannuated or invalided old warrior and his eccentric talk. The very parody of military activities in Toby's wars of course breaks through the convention; but not content with that, Sterne has Walter one day accuse his brother of being a war-monger. Toby answers gently that his brother must know that the day in school when they read of Priam's bootless plea for Hector's body he could not eat his dinner. Suddenly we are in the world of sentimentality—we have not, all the same, forgotten the satire, that Toby's idiot game is strangely like that of King William and Marlborough. Walter loves his brother for his crazy art, as do we. At the same time we have an exact measure of the sentiment: it does not embrace real warriors nor does it make of Toby a paragon. One has only to compare Thackeray's Colonel Newcome, who resembles Toby, to see Sterne's original use of the "old warrior" convention. We are all small artists, including the reader, whose fantasies—sexual, self-indulgent, mad—arise from common springs of conduct.

J. B. Priestley's tribute to Sterne's sentimentalism defines precisely its philosophical and artistic weight. The Shandys' rational frustrations, he writes, "deal death to philosophies . . . and call up a horrible vision of humanity as a set of puppets worked on the wires of a few instincts. A satirist loathing his species could have taken such tragi-comical little creatures, each in the separate box of his mind, and made of them a scene or narrative that would have jangled the nerves of a dozen generations. Sterne, however, . . . preserves the balance by emphasizing the kinship of his people. If the Shandys cannot share one another's thoughts, they can share one another's feelings. . . ." Far from being a reproach to him, Sterne's sentimentalism is his greatest glory. His very special discovery of the limits of reason and the uses of sentimentalism marks him out the most original man of his century—whose lifeline we in our century gladly take—but still he shows his origins. In creativity and sentiment Sterne finds the answer to absurdity, though absurdity it is. Can one even go so far as to say that Sterne has adumbrated a new politics, perhaps a wry expression of his whiggish distrust of the mumbo-jumbo of Church and State? In the Shandean world is a mad set of real Yorkshiremen, ordered in real social classes and religions, but without the spine-bending compulsion of conventional society. The politics of sympathy Sterne obviously thought a vast improvement on the old dispensation. Can he be serious, the moralists ask?

Certainly some of Sterne's best critics have taken seriously his pretensions to moral purpose. His reputation for being light-headed Sir Herbert Read [2] puts down to the native English phlegm. Confronted by an author remarkable for his wit, Englishmen, says Sir Herbert, hastily search for strains of foreign blood in his ancestry, preferably droll Irish blood or wickedly witty French blood. Sterne answers admirably to these criteria, having been born in Ireland of a mother who may have had French blood. Sir Herbert even suggests the possibility that the greatest degree of humor is the complement of the greatest degree of religion. To know what is right or wrong in this world one needs a devil in him, a devil—to borrow from Coleridge—of the sort of the medieval mystery play, to measure the hollowness and disproportion and farce of the world. This is the agency of humor, according to Colerdige: "The little is made great and the great little in order to destroy both; because all is equal in contrast with the infinite." Sterne is the very embodiment of the humorist, the man who in his own personality gives us the sense of individual peculiarities together with their foundation in common nature. And is not sensibility a requisite of a sense of humor, that nice perception of disproportions in finite things? Thus Read by this chain comes back to morality, defined, now, as a sensibility to conduct operating within a world of fixed laws.

At least we can agree that in Stern's mind sensibility, humor, and

[2] See bibliography.

morality were closely related. Gardner Stout's introductory essay to his recently published definitive edition of the *Sentimental Journey*[3] especially presses this view. Splenetic and morose travelers miss touching fingertips, and not to touch fingertips would be, it seems, to blaspheme the Great Sensorium of the World. "I pity the man who can travel from Dan to Beersheba, and cry, 'Tis all barren. . . ." In a dance with peasants an allegorical figure called Religion kicks up its heels along with the rest. However, as Stout remarks, Yorick's benevolence is warmed by wine costing two livres a bottle but he has only eight sous for the beggars in Montrieul. Still, Sterne does not satirize sentiment; he merely asks the reader to know himself—which requires a certain irony. One is benevolent but the world is imperfect; the journey is sensible but comic.

One does not quarrel with moralistic interpretations such as Read's and Stout's, for they are founded in the emotional experience of the work, but certain recent academic criticism smells of the lamp in trying to saddle Sterne-the-artist with rules of moral conduct scavenged from deservedly obscure latitudinarians Sterne-the-preacher is said to have had in mind. Further, what explicit moralizing Sterne does in the persons of Tristram and Yorick is always equivocal. Sterne's fun is so often found in equivocation that sharpens sensibility. Yorick, for example, just saves himself from actual adultery in *A Sentimental Journey,* but do we, does the author, care? Adultery would be an alien note, for equivocation about his own motives is Yorick's real subject. And who knows what happened syntactically and morally in the last sentence of the book: "So that when I stretched out my hand, I caught hold of the Fille de Chambre's END OF VOLUME II." The action lies in the sensibility of the syntax. " 'For we trust we have a good conscience.' Trust!" says Mr. Yorick, beginning the sermon. Good conscience, indeed! *That* is Sterne's morality.

"In the *Sermons of Mr. Yorick* rather than in *Shandy,*" writes A. D. McKillop, "we find ourselves established in the world of the eighteenth century didactic novel." Though there are very close stylistic (and indeed, moral) affinities between the sermons and the fiction, neither *Tristram* nor the *Sentimental Journey* is preceptorial. Rather, Sterne's history of the mind teaches us the fate we were born with, the fate of living in the box of our minds and of having to communicate with others, that most delicious and anguishing of human experiences. If we can find out, as Sterne says, that delicacy and concupiscence are likely to be the same affection, we have made a beginning toward understanding Sterne's teach-

---

*See bibliography.

ing. His moral purpose is then truly indistinguishable from the artistic end of the book. The jester who tells us how the world is put together of conventions, hobbyhorses, and mad associations is also the moralist who makes us long for communion under these nerve-jangling conditions.

The Sorbonne doctors argue for "a little squirt" to ensure the flight to paradise of the souls of infants destined to die before birth. Tristram pushes the idea to its ultimate ridiculousness in his proposal for an improvement on the Sorbonne doctors, a plenary and anticipatory baptism administered to all homunculi before consummation. Similar to such mad devices for a foolproof cure for serious maladies like death is Locke's effort to render language pure, unambiguous, direct—foolproof. It is like trying to rectify original sin. Therefore Tristram (i.e., Sterne), considering this human condition of fallibility in language, has invented a machinery of indirection, of flanking attacks and surprise—in short, his *style*—to bridge as well as possible the void in all attempts at communication.

That this devotion of Sterne to his art has a philosophical base is the burden of the essay on Sterne's use of Locke in this collection. Against the fallibility of the human reason, the discovery of which Locke pursued with something near a passion, the philosopher sought to shore a system of determinate language and analysis of ideas. The implications of Locke's position—which Locke did not pursue, or even, perhaps, recognize—lead to an extreme skepticism, as the subsequent work of Berkeley and Hume makes clear. Sterne also, in his odd way (which sometimes has surprising affinities with Hume's *Treatise*), discovered the linguistic puzzles in Locke's method. Moreover, Locke's absolute separation of primary and secondary qualities, leaving an unchangeable, unknowable "something" in the object but making everything that we can know subjective (though he would not have conceded this), helped give the head to the larger cultural force of sentimentalism and its variants, sensibility and sensitivity. That this emphasis upon subjectivity founded in sense experience also gave an impetus to the development of sentimentalism seems arguable, but Locke himself never dreamt of all this. Similarly, as we allow a culture its mysterious rivers and surprising confluences, we must also allow to a creative mind like Sterne's its own sources. This is an especially important caution in the case of Sterne simply because to apply the deterministic criteria of literary criticism so prevalent in the academies is to desensitize oneself to his wit, playfulness, and incredible invention. Locke has been entirely too much a factor of critics who treat culture and art as though they were a history of ideas. What we want to know is how cultural forces, including ideas, become material for the peculiar imagination of a particular artist—and undergo, of course, a sea-change.

By odd turns, inevitably, one returns to Sterne the artist, little matter what the critical method. This fact corroborates the conviction of the common reader since Sterne's time—and a reiterated theme of the essays of this volume—that his work somehow makes irrelevant the boundaries of art and life since life itself is in large part art, an idea Tristram constantly implies.

In A. D. McKillop's view, however, the oddments of existence with which Sterne's characters create their private worlds symbolize an objective reality intuited by all men. "We may say," McKillop writes, "that [in Sterne] experience symbolizes or epitomizes reality, as memory epitomizes a span of time, or Hamlet's nutshell includes infinite space . . . The individual experience somehow images in little and simultaneously a moral order and a cosmic order, the world of conscience and consciousness and the world of the microscope and telescope. . . .

"The universe is pictured as a great multiple system, in which sense and spirit, macrocosm and microcosm are linked by allegories and correspondences. . . ." The trivia that might be degrading, ludicrous, or even dangerous become somehow symbolic in Sterne of existence itself. All things—whiskers, buttonholes, green gowns, a falling hat, a hand inadvertently strayed into a chamberpot—have referential value and are the stuff of the universe; moreover, the characters as well as the novelist know it. This network of reference creates the common mind and creates love. Whether we take Sterne's world as purely "absurd" (and the sentimentalism as a desperate effort to fill the void) or as a minute figure of a cosmic order, we are always conscious of the author's will to make us see how all meaning is made—or found—by the individual sensibility. Where a satirist would expose eccentricities as abuses of common sense, Sterne merely takes them as signs of private sense. For this reason, though Sterne pays elaborate attention to pedantry, hostile satire of it is thin. Rather, Tristram asks that we should participate in the Cervantic game in which the absurd becomes sympathetic—in part, certainly, because we recognize in his writings the human fate in dealing with the problem of knowledge. Sterne, Tristram, and Yorick are naïve Cervantic heroes in their attempts to express the inexpressible. Of course we love them for their valiancy against windmills.

But if we today find we can look back to Sterne as a kindred spirit, Sterne himself, D. W. Jefferson shows, looks back—especially in his fun with mad learning—to the "tradition of learned wit" of Rabelais, Donne, Jonson, Shakespeare, Burton, and Swift's circle. In that earlier world before the Enlightenment clarified the works of the Great Mechanick so that men knew their place and the boundaries of sense and nonsense, Rabelais, amused by his own habit of scholastic speculative ingenuity, could have his alter ego, Panurge, spin out an entire cosmic order in support of lending and borrowing. Where Swift turns his reductive fire against mad religious reasonings, Sterne, though paying tribute to Swift, hoping that his Tristram would "swim down the gutter of time with *A Tale of a Tub*," rediscovers certain aspects of that more grateful world of Rabelais. There, unburdened by cold facts, a man could unbridle his reason to pass easily from trivia to the cosmos. Not only Walter but Tristram and even Toby do just this. To pass by Walter's theories, we need only recall Tristram's legalistic, physiological, psychological, and metaphysical fun with the world of that "little gentleman," the homunculus (i.e. the human sperm). But as Mayoux remarks, Sterne, while closer in feeling to the tradition than Swift, could never in his age discover the surprising cosmic correspondences of Rabelais, nor could he sustain Rabelais' appetite. Rather, Sterne uses learned wit to discover paradoxes and contradictions, disjunctions between individual minds, even while each spins its own systems. Though Sterne values the hobbyhorses of his characters, their odd information and benign imaginings of enormous effects from trivial causes, as an aspect of the artful human spirit, he certainly has no sense of an ultimate order that makes Rabelais' movement from serious to flippant, from romance to bawdry so exhilarating and reassuring. Here we come upon that ever-fascinating aspect of literary invention, the recreation by original talent of traditional materials. Sterne's mind grasped and transformed Rabelaisian learned wit— the ingenuities, paradoxes, and systems of intellectual speculation—into his own vision of absurdity and alienation. As Jefferson remarks, Sterne's ability to be at once serious and flippant about sentimentalism would seem to be an aspect of that mental habit of learned wit which passes from the serious to the comic and back. No wonder, then, that Sterne did not satisfy the earnest middle-class readers of novels in the nineteenth century. His gaiety, irreverence, flippancy, absurdity, his stylistic and speculative ingenuities, were then as old-fashioned as they are now modern.

Without forgetting to laugh, we pay tribute with these essayists to the valiant original genius who with such gaiety rides his Cervantic hobbyhorse into the void of the jest, making sure that he has the reader along to share his effrontery. Where Richardson bamboozles us with Clarissa's coffin or some other bric-a-brac of the theater into taking his own sentiment for reality, Sterne's sensibility will never let us rest in sentiment. The sentiment is only as real as the anxiety; both remain. This devilish fool presumes to show us with words about words that reality is never quite there. If Sterne had had his way he would have continued the process until the world's end. When Death knocks at his door, he bids him come again in so gay a tone of careless indifference that Death doubts of his commission. "Now there is nothing in the world I abominate worse than to be interrupted in a story. . . . Had I not better, Eugenius, fly for my life?" Equivocation seems to be life itself. All else is death. "All womankind, continued Trim, love jokes; the difficulty is to know how they choose to have them cut; and there is no knowing that but by trying, as we do our artillery in the field, by letting down their breeches, till we have hit the mark. —I like the comparison, said my uncle Toby, better than the thing itself." Better than the thing itself Sterne likes equivocation. Mankind is such a collection of odd styles, existence such a concatenation of odd events, that equivocation seems to Sterne almost a moral imperative.

*   *   *

The editor regrets that W. B. C. Watkins's essay is far too long to include here in its entirety. Had space permitted, the essays listed in the bibliography by Sigurd Burckhardt, Cyril Connolly, Ernest Lockridge, Edwin Muir, J. B. Priestley, Herbert Read, Gardner Stout, and Virginia Woolf would have been included.

Of Time, Personality, and the Author

by Benjamin H. Lehman

The Life and Opinions of Tristram Shandy, Gent. is full of premonitions of the future of the novel. These indications arose from what might, of course, have been a largely unconscious distrust in Laurence Sterne of the truth-telling power of the novel as written in his day, and their full significance can hardly have been clear to him as the indications were almost certainly dark to his contemporaries. For the distrust, of which there are abundant satiric evidences, was the inevitable response made by the perfect naturalness of Sterne's psyche to the unreality of even the great novels of Richardson and Fielding. It reveals itself deeply by his concern with being-in-time as distinguished from duration by the clock, with personality as more inclusive than "character," with activity rather than action, and with the relation of the author to his material. Each of these concerns raised a problem, and the art of prose fiction was young and there were as yet no tried solutions for any one of them. Most noteworthy of all, once Sterne turned away from a duration plot and from simply crystallized character, he was faced with the greatest problem of all—the problem of an ultimate form which could be raised from the material quite naturally seen and felt, a form which should derive no curve or mass from the selective magnetic force of preconceptions of action and of character. A hundred and seventy-five years later, novelists are still seeking solutions for these problems which he first confronted and, however benefited by a fuller science of psychology and a truer physics, can hardly be said to have found satisfactory solutions, though Proust and Joyce and Thomas Mann have reared memorable visions of reality by attacking the problems boldly. The way of Richardson and Fielding was no blind alley, one admits, as—were there no other evidence —*War and Peace* alone would prove. But that work is a triumph of un-

"Of Time, Personality, and the Author: A Study of *Tristram Shandy*" by Benjamin H. Lehman. From *Studies in the Comic, University of California Studies in English*, Vol. VIII, No. 2 (Berkeley, 1941), pp. 233-50. Copyright © 1941 by the Regents of the University of California. Reprinted by permission of the author and the University of California Press.

rivaled creative power over the limitations of a form, a triumph more readily achieved after a century of exploring possibilities, even though it solved part of the problem of the relation of the author to its material by introducing the essay commentary in the manner of Fielding. To assert within those limitations as much truth about the world, to evoke as notable a reality in the late 1750s when Sterne began to write *Tristram Shandy*, would have been an unimaginable feat. Or perhaps not, given the peculiarly right and sufficiently powerful imagination. For indeed if *Tristram Shandy* as we have it did not exist, we should have to say that that achievement also, twenty years after *Pamela*, was not to be imagined.

To see what Sterne's achievement really was, is I believe only in these last years possible, in a mind made aware by *The Magic Mountain, Ulysses,* and *The Remembrance of Things Past.* In its author's time and for long after, *Tristram Shandy* seemed only a most singular work, engaging and diverting, the beneficiary of a quality largely called style, bawdy and touching by turns, the bizarre emanation of irregular genius. In due course, it came to be regarded as a heap of verbal talus at the base of a tall hypothetical cliff—the book that Sterne would have written had he lived another hundred years—from which were to be excavated a few extremely vital figures known as Uncle Toby, Mrs. Shandy and Walter Shandy, Trim and the Widow Wadman, along with a pretty badly damaged outhouse or two with which a world that held its nose contrived to become very familiar. And in due course the academics let themselves loose on the book. Taking at the foot of the letters, in wrong meaning probably, the word "rhapsodical" which Sterne in a Chapter 13 unluckily applied to his work, they called it a huge improvisation for the display of characters and sentiments, a huge miscellany, a patchwork of extracts (a certain Dr. John Ferriar having published in 1812 his ferretings out of Rabelais, Beroalde de Verville, Bouchet, Bruscambille, Scarron, Swift, Burton, Bacon, Blount, Montaigne, Bishop Hall—to name a few). One called it a "picaresque of the intellect," and Saintsbury drew on his second language, the first having given out, and called it a "fatrasie." They measured the book by its predecessors and successors; it was "a travesty of the regular novel, the main lines of which had been so carefully drawn and the theory so ably expounded by Fielding." They described it in terms of other things instead of describing it in terms of itself; it was "a mere caricature of the novel" compared with "the serious works of fiction" which preceded it. They judged it as though Richardson or a clergyman —how Sterne denied that!—had written it and they found it unmoral and dirty; they judged it as though Jane Austen had written it and found it gave too little space to "characters"; they judged it as though Emily

Brontë had written it and found it wanting in passion and poetry. To be sure, they spoke of its humor, but they did not describe that humor or find humor an informing as well as infusing quality. They seemed rather amazed at Sterne's success in creating such insistently lively characters. But not for long, for they were drawn away to trace the footprints of sentimentality which caught their eye, and, finding that, however it might be in *A Sentimental Journey,* here those tracks confused their definition of that word, they took their position again behind the cropped hedges of what they called style. Not all, but most, thus. And not one of the academic critics, at any rate, positively attempted to discover the precocious work of art with an ascertainable specific gravity, qualities of its own, understood in terms of the implied first principles of its imagined cosmos. That to do so is now easier than it formerly was, I have allowed. And I shall venture to describe, as simply as I can, what I see when I raise *Tristram Shandy* in my mind.

First of all *Tristram Shandy,* although it is comedy, is a serious work, and it is serious throughout. The most tangential laughter, viewed in relation to the whole, proves to be very serious indeed. It is always, however adroitly the fact may be covered, a philosophic laughter. In some senses of the word Laurence Sterne was, of course, not a philosopher. He had little or no feeling for great ideas, great ways of life, or for great spirits dedicated to such ways of life, inspired by such ideas; or at most such feeling as he had was passive, perhaps released in fireside hours over the fortunes of Gargantua and Pantagruel and of Don Quixote. Any explicit insights derived from philosophy so understood arise by the way in Tristram Shandy and are often, it may be always, borrowed. Yet of philosophy in another sense, every paragraph carries the weight and the lift. Philosophy considered as the wisdom of acceptance after recognition, understood as the mental climate of an imagination served by a true eye and deeply imbued with a reverence for reality, discovered in "the naked temper of a merry heart"—this philosophy the book is not only made of but is enveloped in as in an atmosphere.

For Sterne, the stark reality lay there in the world, to be seen. And he had no blinding prudence like that congruence with commercial class morality against which only unguessed genius betrayed Richardson into greatness. Sterne was as wise as Fielding and a hundred times less conventional, for where Fielding only asserted that the earthy exists Sterne conjured it into visibility. As wise—the whole book bears witness—and a thousand times more truthful. Beneath the title of *Tom Jones* I read a phantom subtitle: Virtue Rewarded. The virtue is not Pamela's virtue; it is forthright honesty, robust and most simple. Fielding changed the subject, but he did not give up the delimiting pattern. But for Sterne's profoundly natural psyche no copybook maxim could serve as a philosophy of even a fragment of life, the less could it serve to give shape to a picture of the world. To his eye, life was a complicated activity in its basis, indescribably more complicated by the overlay of institutions and by the inadequacy of all mediums of communication, particularly of language since there is not one language but as many as there are grades of perception and fields of culture: Uncle Toby and Trim can communicate in words, but not Uncle Toby and Walter Shandy; Trim and Bridget can communicate in words, but not Uncle Toby and the Widow Wadman. For Sterne, the world is contingency incarnate. Anything and everything may be upset by thoroughly but irrelevantly motivated chance. If chance sometimes advances a clean line of action, it more often impedes it or carries it on a tangent; and if chance often takes the form of a falling window or a shot in the groin, it is because to Sterne's implacable eye the procreative and the erotic and their instruments are highlighted in the stark reality of the world. The choice lying, as a philosopher of our day says, between a mask and a fig leaf, Sterne's psyche chose the mask. The mask laughs, and there are large apertures for free seeing. He will not observe in terms of any prudence whatsoever or any convention, least of all the clerical convention which he has long since seen through. To a friend who had read some manuscript pages of *Tristram Shandy* and thought that coming from a clergyman they showed "a Forgetfulness of his Character," he replied "that an attention to his Character would damp his Fire and check the Flow of his Humor, and that if he went on, and hoped to be read, he must not look at his Band or his Cassock."

The function of laughter in Sterne is corrective, naturally, but not of abuses which may be reformed. His laughter is not to make life more tolerable by tinkering at the minutiae of behavior; it strikes deeper than that, perhaps as deep as a design Rebecca West has observed in Joyce's *Ulysses*. In humanity there is an inherent, incongruous, and pain-making force that bids it aspire, and this force must be restrained. Dream and ambition do not coincide with reality. The iridescent bubble of human vanities must be pricked. Aspiration must be reminded of its earthy origin. To do this, in futile atempt to prevent Fate, was to be the chief motive of Leopold Bloom in our own day, and to do so was the ironic, the dreadful function of the jester in Elizabethan tragedy, as Rebecca West has reminded us. Yorick the Parson (read Laurence Sterne) was descended from the greatest and purest jester of them all, who, having no lines to say, exists as the absolute jester of the imagination. Those reminders that we are "mortal men, mortal men" that once set the table on a roar have ceased in the world, Sterne tells us in a sentence of quiet bite. The post of jester had "for near two centuries . . . been totally abolished, as altogether unnecessary, not only in that court, but in every other court of the Christian world." Clearly Sterne thought it time to revive the post, in the Christian world if not in the court.

Yet life, though Sterne's intelligence made nonsense of it since it could not make sense, was good if guarded by the jest. Though the world was not in truth susceptible of those patterns of single lines converging on a point that Richardson and Fielding traced, for which they assumed the purity of aspiration and the success of their several kinds of purity, it was nonetheless susceptible of significant report, admitted of account. The incongruous and the inconsistent, the contingent, all the diverse doing and being, though it could come to nothing, had something in it—a vitality masquerading oddly. And that something was good. The temper of Yorick's heart was a naked temper; but the heart consented, it was a merry heart. Sterne said so, himself.

Yorick Sterne had also a head, and he had read many books. He read Locke. Newton and Hobbes he knew at some distance. But he had read Locke, was at home with his conceptions, never ceased praising him. Out of Hobbes and in strict analogy to the Newtonian physics, on the principle that all knowledge starts from the reception of sensations, Locke had developed the laws of association of impressions and ideas. Man's whole mental and conscious life no less than his body was one with the natural order. But the picture of the outer world was not in the outer world, where the stimuli that provoked it lay; it was in the consciousness and the unconsciousness. Since therefore all that man can know was mind-made and not actual, all principles of morality were imposed on the natural order by the idea-association process of the mind. As laid down in a hundred directions, they did not consist with the reality, because man's dreams and hopes and the fossils of old institutions and procedures got associated into the reality patterns and falsified them. Incidental to his main concerns, flicking at weed heads as he passed, Sterne satirized—to take an instance—the scholastic methods which still survived in religion and in philosophy and did not consist with reality. But as he moved un-impeded on his main objective, which was the rendering of reality without moral or formal preconception, it was the implications of other phases of Locke's thought that grew more fruitful for him.

First of all, personality existed and manifested itself in Time; association of ideas and communication took place in Time. But Time is not a single mode, as Thomas Mann in our day never tires of demonstrating. Since it is a condition of consciousness, it is measured on two and perhaps more clocks, quite differently paced. "In our computations of time we are . . . used to minutes, hours, weeks, and months," says Tristram, but—the implication goes on—some ancient essence in us is aware of time only by the intensity and fullness of being, as we may suppose the clockless animals are aware of it, as we ourselves show we are when by saying we have had a very good time we mean we have had no sense of time at all. Something like this Walter Shandy one day tried to explain to his brother. In reply "You puzzle me to death" cried my Uncle Toby, who was as profoundly and truly animal as any man can ever have been, and lived at ease in the Time world he could not understand when it was explained. For him the hours, weeks, months did not exist; for Walter Shandy they existed as matter for preconceived reflection on the folly of preconception, qualified by a suspicion that there is a worth in Toby's honest ignorance—" 'twere almost a pity to exchange it for a knowledge."

For Tristram himself clock duration constitutes an element in a problem. The outward aspect of the events in his story did in fact take place as the sun moved through successive positions; but not their significance to the reporting, the shaping consciousness. " 'Tis a point settled . . . that provided he keeps along the line of his story,—an author may go backwards and forwards as he will . . ." Into his work he says, "two contrary motions are introduced . . . and reconciled, which were thought to be at variance with each other. In a word, my work is digressive, and it is progressive too—and at the same time." These digressions, which are only incidentally satiric of the suspense techniques of straight story-telling, make progress because Sterne is reporting the associational life as well as the physical life of Tristram Shandy; what is digression under the aspect of clock time (the physical life) is progression under the aspect of being time (the associational life): we learn why people acted or spoke as they did, because Tristram remembers in order that he may know. Its effect is to give a truer account of the world perceived than any other, as is the effect in Proust. Is not *The Remembrance of Things Past* one immense digression into the mind's life, while the physical hand suspends a madeleine over a cup of tea? Just as everything in that work goes on in the mind of Moi, the reporter, so in Sterne's work everything goes on in the mind of Tristram.

The point is that Tristram is a figure in the novel, not a mere projection of Sterne. He has a nature and a quality of his own. In a sense nothing happens to him, certainly no events that can be laid end to end and called an action. Yet he observes everything and reflects on everything, even if often the reflection is implicit in the report. His mind is in continuous activity, under the dominance of its own laws. There is no selection and ordering in terms of an issue raised by an impermanent or local morality, nor in terms of a falsifying line of action called a plot. The activity goes on, whether forward or backward, by the associational relevance of the apparently irrelevant, by fixing on the illusive, the evanescent, the indefinable which engage that mind and which it contrives to report by suggestion. And if, sometimes, led by who shall say what sensation-association, it hops as unfollowably as a flea, we have simply to admit that Tristram's mind was like that, Sterne saw it thus. And it is so true to nature that we can often not tell what it is about, just as we cannot tell what nature is about. The trouble with Sterne's predecessors, he cannot have failed to see, was that they made segments of life too ordered and too intelligible to be true accounts, connections too simply clear to be credible. And, so viewed, *Tristram Shandy* is a deep-laid criticism of the novels of Richardson and Fielding.

Tristram is a figure in the story, but he is considerably less a personality than the other figures. The character through whom a world is seen invariably lacks the high visibility of other figures in a novel: he can only see out of himself, can never see round himself. And even compared with other notable creations in the same predicament, say the Moi in Proust, Tristram is vague, because Sterne seeking to solve a problem of presentation did not understand the importance of clearly detaching himself at all points from that projection of himself that he calls Tristram. But even here Sterne accomplishes a profound truthfulness to nature. Though there is a sense in which any individual is more real to himself than other people are—in his awareness of his own sensations and stream of consciousness—there is another sense in which he is less real—in his awareness of how he himself, were he someone else, would strike his own senses, move as an object in his own stream of consciousness. And it is this second kind of awareness to which all readers are habited by their practice in living, and because of this find themselves more imaginatively responsive to the objectively reported, the subjectively suggested figures. Yet apart from all these considerations, Tristram lacks the undeniable reality of Uncle Toby, in a special sense and on quite special grounds.

Sterne was, in the naked temper of his merry heart, in an exceptional position. Whatever the parson's actual nature and situation (and it was such that he could write the sermons, the letters, and *A Sentimental Journey*, also), this part of himself that his psyche chose to project was so closely in league with nature that Tristram appears to have escaped the realizing touch of isolation. Each of the other figures, deeply and greatly different as they are, shows itself shut up in its own world. No matter how warm their animal fellow feeling, at best they understand one another only by fits and starts. A pervasive loneliness is at the core of each, as in life itself. But Tristram understands them all, and the power of imagination that makes that possible dissolves the loneliness in him, makes him by so much less real to us because nothing in our own experience has prepared us to imagine him.

With that characteristic of being locked up in their own individualities as basis, Uncle Toby, Trim, Mrs. Shandy, Yorick, and the rest grow to something beyond characters in a book; they become personalities in a universe authentic and large enough to sustain them. Their actions are characteristic of their quality, but, more than that, those actions have something of the habitual about them. And like real people the figures show themselves in different aspects to various people. Tom Jones, for example, and Pamela turned the same characteristics to everyone, and whatever particular expressiveness appeared, very slightly if at all conditioned the continuously dominant aspect. The result is a definable inflexible monotony of being, giving finally an effect of narrowness, of specialization. Trim with Bridget, Uncle Toby with the Widow Wadman, Walter Shandy with Mrs. Shandy, though they remain completely themselves, do, like people in life, refocus themselves when they leave one another to join their ladies. Uncle Toby, for instance, knows he does not understand his brother's harangues, even when he does not say so; but in the benign female warmth, importing illusions of humane interest within the widow's person, he does not even wonder if he has caught the drift: he is suffused with well-being and that is enough. So that afterward he suffers a sort of violence in his gentleness when the Corporal lays bare the truth, and because he cannot quickly refocus for Trim he says to gain time, "Let us go to my brother Shandy's." There is a flux in the continuity of these figures which makes them living personalities, like the greatest in literature, rather than vivified characters in a book.

Things happen to them, but they also happen to things. They do not mature in their own natures but they grow in reality in our minds, as we see them a-being. And see them we do. Are Sophia Western's matchless eyes as tangible—visible—as the Widow Wadman's?

> I protest, Madam, said my Uncle Toby, I can see nothing whatever in your eye.
> It is not in the white; said Mrs. Wadman: my Uncle Toby looked with might and main into the pupil—
> [Writes Tristram thereupon:] Now of all the eyes which ever were created —from your own, Madam, up to those of Venus herself, which certainly

were as venereal a pair of eyes as ever stood in a head—there never was an eye of them all, so fitted to rob my Uncle Toby of his repose, as the very eye, at which he was looking—it was not, Madam, a rolling eye—a romping or a wanton one—nor was it an eye sparkling—petulant or imperious—of high claims and terrifying exactions, which would have curdled at once that milk of human nature, of which my Uncle Toby was made up—but 'twas an eye full of gentle salutations—and soft responses—speaking—not like the trumpet stop of some ill-made organ, in which many an eye I talk to, holds coarse converse—but whispering soft—like the last low accents of an expiring saint—"How can you live comfortless, Captain Shandy, and alone, without a bosom to lean your head on—or trust your cares to?"

It was an eye—

But I shall be in love with it myself, if I say another word about it.

—It did my Uncle Toby's business.

Set in that great space between Venus in an implied act of life and a saint in the article of death, between the sound of a trumpet and a soft whisper, in a space filled with activity, with images and calls upon the motor sense—might and main, created, stood, rob, repose, rolling, romping, wanton, sparkling, petulant, imperious, speaking—in that space a pair of eyes are in action above a bosom one can lean one's head on, in front of a brain most inquisitive to know one of Uncle Toby's cares. "It was an eye . . . it did my Uncle Toby's business." The Captain hardly sees those eyes, for all his staring, but those eyes happen to the Captain; and the Captain happens to them, too, and they do not roll, or romp, or sparkle, or wanton—though who can doubt that they have done and will again?—no: they humanely, softly whisper for Uncle Toby.

We have here not an action, stripped bare, but activity richly arrayed in reference, grounded in an instinctive philosophy of living. And this effect of the individual passage is enhanced if we remember the book as a whole, or even if we remind ourselves of its method. The absence of chronology, the seeming want of order that, I believe, justify themselves in the associational mind of a narrator who takes his place within the universe under observation, are discovered at last to be resourceful means of rendering reality. The reader very early identifies himself with the observing reporter, takes on his state of mind and fancies himself moving selectively among the inexhaustible data of experience, prompted by the associations native to that state of mind. That the resulting imagined world has more reality than a stripped and ordered account there is considerable evidence to show.

Perhaps the best and at all events the most appropriate evidence for my purposes here consists of the *Essays of Montaigne* as he set them down compared with an arrangement of these, called *The Autobiography of Michel de Montaigne,* made by Marvin Loewenthal. The appropriateness lies in this: that the *Essays* was a favorite book with Laurence Sterne, that they constitute a Life and Opinions, made in a different temper and by a less personality-haunted talent, in many respects not unlike *Tristram Shandy.* Montaigne set down his Essays, we say, anyhow, that is, as things occurred to him: in writing *Of the Vanitie of Words* there might arise in his mind certain thoughts or impressions on loneliness, and in writing *Of Solitarinesse* there might arise in his mind ideas concerning the impossibility of full communication. His book is the museum piece for the illustration of the action of the associational faculty. From it, Michel de Montaigne emerges as real, as immediate, as rememberable as any man from the past. Now, Loewenthal has "arranged" the Essays: we read duly of parentage, childhood, prime; we learn under the proper heading what Montaigne thought of his diversions, why he traveled. Most of the quotations for which Montaigne fluttered his memory are omitted. The book is cleaned up and doubtless valuable to the impatient curious, though if they have heard the renown of the *Essays* it will baffle or disappoint even them; for it is an inert autobiography and a filing case of cindered opinions. The nature and mode of Montaigne's organism have vanished: the book is ordered but it has no form, it has a shape imposed from without, no living structure; and it affords no significant experience. A great personality has become a character; a being who lived by the clock of a mind, the clock of being that made strange fruitful connections, is measured against a calendar, his ideas by logic instead of by psychologic. That delicate and vital, however erratic, that most revealing relation of the writer to his material has been destroyed. For people who should thus misguidedly apply the techniques of science in space and in time to living entities raised by art, Sterne uttered an early laughing warning. His invention foresaw all such in that expert who timed Garrick's pauses in speaking Hamlet's soliloquy, blind to life in eye and gesture, insensitive to the procession of inner images projected into the theater, because he could spare no attention from his stopwatch, he said, if he was to count seconds and their fractions. And Sterne's invention foresaw all the experts with their procrustean spatial apparatus in that one who measured the angles of *Tristram Shandy* with rule and compass, and found it all out of plumb.

No doubt Laurence Sterne was not, like our contemporaries, conscious of the problem of significant form. But his psyche knew very well what it was about. It was rendering to the imagining reader-mind a material that was at once a fragment and a whole. Like nature, that material does not begin anywhere or end anywhere, or perhaps we should say it does begin anywhere and end anywhere. Where it began and where it ended and by what connections it got from one point to the other was a relative matter, depending on who viewed it and where he stood, depending no less on the frame of reference of the mind in which it was seen.

Relativity is the word. There is a dream—as modern as a famous passage in Anatole France's *Garden of Epicurus*—written by the Parson in his library long before *Tristram Shandy* was begun, discovered by Paul Stapfer, printed in his *Laurence Sterne, sa Personne et ses Ouvrages* in 1870, and accepted by Wilbur Cross as authentic. Sterne had been reading in Fontenelle, and walked in his orchard. In the brilliant summer night, Fontenelle's moon and myriad worlds were above him, and within reach of his hand on any green leaf of his plum trees were nations performing, he says, "actions as truly great as any we read of in the history of Alexander. Their courage, resolution, and patience of pain may be as great as that exhibited by the Macedonian army, nay and even the prize of the contest no way inferior to that which animated the brave Greeks. The possession or conquest of the leaf may gratify as many and as strong desires in them, as that of the Earth in us." Reflecting that time and space are but relative to the size and shape of the brain, he supposes that to the beings of the leaf an hour or a minute may seem as long as four score and ten years to human beings. Then came to memory Addison's paper in which is told of Mahomet's ninety thousand conferences with God "in so small a space of time, that Mahomet at his return found his bed still warm, and took up an earthen pitcher, which was thrown down at the very instant that the Angel Gabriel carried him away, before the water was all spilt." Laurence Sterne then went to bed and had a dream. In it the dreamer was "transported to the blue surface of a luscious plum growing in his favorite tree." "There began to be heard all over the world a huge noise and fragor in the skys, as if all nature were approaching to her dissolution. The stars seem'd to be torn from their orbits, and to wander at random thro' the heavens." Waking, he returned to the orchard; a brisk gale of wind had arisen, some plums had fallen. "I cou'd then no longer doubt how the matter was." In the world of suppositious microscopic beings a cataclysm had occurred. The delicate and strong analogy is made. Sterne could no longer doubt how the matter was; he quotes Pope, "And now a Bubble burst, and now a world." But the Parson in his library at Sutton

moralized, too. "The time will come when the powers of heaven shall
be shaken, and the stars shall fall like the fruit of a tree, when it is shaken
by a mighty wind." Tristram could never have added that last.

His psyche knew very well indeed what it was about. It did not forget
that dream, but for the making of *Tristram Shandy* Sterne would not
moralize, would not "look at his Band and his Cassock." First of all into
exile went the Parson and all his works, save one sermon, which crossed
the Shandy way by such strange fatalities, was given Trim to read, and
was, by Dr. Slop, Walter Shandy, Uncle Toby, and Trim himself, riddled
with profane commentary in which is precipitated all the wayward
revery of all congregations preached at from time's beginning. And into
the book itself went a parson. Parson Yorick is a natural man, a mighty
inversion of all that is properly clerical, not one who blows the bubble
of aspiration, but the descendant of the jester, whose function it is to
discourage delusion in mortals by pricking that bubble. And Yorick dies
in his first appearance—though he will reappear, since the order of experience is not of the calendar, but within a mind—that his function,
defined in him, may be included in the nature of Tristram. This is as it
should be if the materials are to take form in one consciousness, for the
mind of Tristram has wider range, is more acute, and of a subtler habit
of association than Yorick's. It is more *natural*, since it is more inclusive.
And for Tristram, by virtue of his Yorick quality, when a discussion of
abstract interest or ideal content has gone far enough, the earthy will
assert itself, and from the intellectually tenuous or the emotionally over-
wrought, the attention will drop, plummetlike, in a Priapean pun. Or it
may flow out at placid thirty-page length of ribaldry, in Slawkenbergius's
Tale, where symbolic obscenity is carried to the limit, and the point slyly
underlined by the author's name which conceals under its rough German
a series of cloacal and phallic images. Moreover, Yorick has the last words
in the book, coarse words which—spoken especially to Mrs. Shandy—
reaffirm his nature and his function, and reassure us at last by the contrast how much more various a nature, how much more diversified a
function Tristram himself has.

Tristram, who had a way of his own as *A Sentimental Journey* or ten
pages of Sterne's Sermons or of his letters will show, is aware that the
telling of the whole story can end only in infinity, since a year's writing
will hardly serve to get him born. Of that whole, *whenever* he stops, he
will have only a fragment; that fragment can however be a unity of another sort, the criteria being in the consciousness, not in the world of
outer phenomena. *Tristram Shandy* is a unity. The work begins and
closes on the procreative theme and encloses a world of the living activity

that is its consequence. And it suggests experience in other generations. Out of that first begetting sprang this experience of things; out of Obadiah's wife's interesting event will arise a new experience, a different one, unpredictable from anything we have come to know, so profuse and far-flung are the possibilities that lie in wait beyond consciousness.

Of the special experience which is *The Life and Opinions of Tristram Shandy* the constituents are diverse and present themselves in nonsensical phenomenal sequence, in indescribably modified inconsequence, no less than in terms of recognizably chronological cause and effect (as within the neatly drawn incident) and in understandable logic (as in the exploration of a brief state of mind). The great central matters of love and war are exhibited not in their glamorous phases, but in their tawdry aftermaths as demonstrations of that inevitable coming to earth of which Yorick and the jesters continuously warn; and in the last pages the "provision for continuing the race of so great, so exalted and godlike a Being as man" and "the act of killing and destroying a man" are brought in Tristram's mind into a juxtaposition which, seen in the light of these observations, must be heard as a profound and subtle laugh: one of the most breathtaking conclusions in literature. Into that experience called *Life and Opinions of Tristram Shandy* flow all things, from the borrowed matter that almost nonactively passes through the mind to the paper, from that inert stuff to episode and aphorism incomparably enriched in the suggestion they take on before they find place on paper. All of it is presented in a frame of reference of the completest relativity and the completest nonsense, the logical non sequiturs of the associational faculty. Of all, perhaps the most astonishing and the most significant is the fact that Tristram is the son in the flesh of a woman who cannot understand an implication and a man who tortures all reality to fit a hypothesis—Tristram who is the genius of implication and had the intuition to find that reality was its own hypothesis, that if you kept expanding the hypothesis to fit the facts you presently had no hypothesis at all—moral or intellectual or scientific; you had only nature, but nature as perceived by a given mind, with qualities and habits of its own. In a book of truth-telling non sequiturs, this is the greatest non sequitur of all, the final expression in form of the reality of Sterne's world.

Laurence Sterne

by Alan Dugald McKillop

I

The preeminence of Richardson and Fielding in the generation after 1750 gave currency to a superficial distinction between the serious and the humorous novelist. The serious novelist was didactic, and was concerned with wickedness and suffering, heroism and virtue; the humorous novelist, though also concerned with moral standards, dealt with folly rather than wickedness, could enjoy a moral holiday and present manners in a robust and even outrageous way, could take advantage of the distinction between what virtuous people could say and do and what virtuous people could see and hear. This is to be taken as a statement of readers' expectations, not as an accurate description of the novelists themselves. Continuing with this oversimple contrast, we may say that variations on the model of the humorous novel had great success in the third quarter of the century, and that variations on the model of the serious novel had great success in the last quarter. Smollett and Sterne, in different ways, won success by variations on the humorous novel. The serious novel often came to be nicknamed "sentimental"; Sterne was the first to offer a humorous novel which could also be nicknamed "sentimental."

Until recently the English-speaking world has been for the most part merely tolerant of Sterne's humorous and sentimental effects. He has often been taken to be a "Mr. Oddity," and somehow at the same time the arch-sentimentalist. German criticism evolved philosophical conclusions from his combination of humor and pathos, and Coleridge's memorable comments belong here; but in general it has remained for post-Victorian criticism to do justice to Sterne's original genius, and the present generation is showing intense interest in his oblique and complex methods.

"Laurence Sterne." From *The Early Masters of English Fiction* by Alan Dugald McKillop, pp. 182-219. Copyright © 1956 by the University of Kansas Press. Reprinted by permission of the author and the University of Kansas Press. Notes have been shortened or dropped without notice.

Here, even more than with the other novelists, we gain much from an adequate biography—the late Governor Cross has done this great service for both Fielding and Sterne—and we also have the advantage of our own persistent interest in the technique of prose fiction. The age of Joyce, Proust, and Kafka tolerates deviations from plain objective narrative as never before, and this accrues somewhat to the advantage of Richardson and greatly to the advantage of Sterne.

Sterne's work is so highly individual that one is tempted to linger over what Gamaliel Bradford used to call "psychography." The solid English eighteenth century tolerated eccentricity and oddity; it took the stability of institutions for granted, and assumed that the whole system was so well established that it could put up with extreme mannerism in its representatives—the don, the lawyer, the clergyman, the squire, and even the author himself. It was an age of good sense, but it was also an age of harmless play, and in Great Britain at least comedy and satire were not taken to be dangerously subversive. This point is connected with what has been said about the development of a sympathetic attitude toward the humorous character—Sir Roger de Coverley, Parson Adams, Doctor Primrose, Goldsmith's Man in Black, Smollett's Matthew Bramble. In real life Dr. Johnson stood as the incarnation of the idea that a humorist could be a pillar of society; his fundamental views were steady and predictable, his reactions highly unpredictable. It was humor that helped to keep Johnson's Toryism from being "monolithic," as we like to say nowadays. Johnson would not have been flattered by the comparison with Sterne—"nothing odd will last"—but admirers of Johnson's humor, or Goldsmith's, cannot be blind to the side of life Sterne represents. In Sterne the novelist himself becomes the humorist, writing about humorists; the actions of the novelist become unpredictable for the immediate future, like the actions of the characters; whim or impulse is thus raised to the second power, since we must reckon with the unforeseen both in form and content; the novel seems to become disorganized and irresponsible, though this disorganization is apparent rather than real.

We are tempted to find the explanation in the temperament and experiences of Sterne himself: the son of an army officer, he was taken in charge by members of his family, educated at Cambridge, given church livings and eventually a place in the Cathedral Chapter at York. In all this there appears little discipline, no real professional training or steady effort of any kind, no striking down of deep roots. Sterne appears as a clever minor clergyman, depending, like so many people in the eighteenth century, on the good graces of patrons, but not deeply involved or seriously concerned with the quest for favor. He liked to read, write,

paint, converse, hunt a little, farm a little. Dilettante, humorist, virtuoso
—all are words that might apply. He had written some political pieces
for the York newspapers, and developed his informal and flexible style
in letters and sermons; as a member of the "Demoniacs" who met at
John Hall Stevenson's "Crazy Castle" at Sutton-on-the-Sea, he participated
in facetious talk and scribbling inspired by the reading of odd and useless
works, and also, it must be added, by the sophomoric aspiration of the
members to be considered devilishly witty and reckless. The local success
of *A Political Romance,* later called *The History of a Good Warm Watch-
coat* (1759), led to the rapid writing of the first two volumes of *The Life
and Opinions of Tristram Shandy,* published at York by Hinxman in
December, 1759, and in London by Dodsley at the beginning of 1760.
The immediate and prodigious success of this work made Sterne a literary
lion, and he came up to town in March, 1760, and exploited his popularity
by publishing two volumes of sermons in May. *Tristram Shandy* absorbed
much of the rest of his life: Volumes III and IV appeared in January,
1761, V and VI in December, 1761, dated 1762, VII and VIII not until
January, 1765, after a long sojourn in France in quest of health. Volume
IX, in fact and probably in intention the last, appeared in January, 1767;
meanwhile Sterne had again traveled extensively on the Continent, and
the special outgrowth of this tour was *A Sentimental Journey through
France and Italy,* "by Mr. Yorick," brought out in February, 1768, the
sixth and last New Year season marked by one of Sterne's important
publications. Two more volumes of the *Journey* were promised, but
Sterne died a few weeks later.

Sterne's apparently whimsical and erratic ways in *Tristram Shandy*
gave contemporary readers a delightful but not entirely unprecedented
surprise. No one could take literally those famous remarks, "Ask my pen,
—it governs me,—I govern not it" (VI, 6), or, "I begin with writing the
first sentence—and trusting to Almighty God for the second" (VIII, 2),
or the novelist's report that when he is at a loss what to do next a pinch
of snuff, a shave, or a clean shirt will help him out (IX, 13). "A sudden
impulse comes across me—drop the curtain, *Shandy*—I drop it—Strike
a line here across the paper, *Tristram*—I strike it—and hey for a new
chapter!" (IV, 10). He can deliberately propose to insert "a good quantity
of heterogeneous matter," so as to "keep up that just balance betwixt
wisdom and folly, without which a book would not hold together a single
year" (IX, 12); he can assert that he has attained "that necessary equi-
poise and balance, (whether of good or bad) betwixt chapter and chapter,
from whence the just proportions and harmony of the whole work

results" (IV, 25). Effects are carefully calculated, and Sterne looks at his scenes and characters with an artist's eye.

Obviously the work is in part a burlesque, yet it is not the mere mimicking of a serious literary form, with the new novel of Richardson and Fielding being rallied out of its dignity. What happens is that homely and trivial detail as found in the new novel is used in a manner which partakes of the mock-heroic or burlesque tradition and the related tradition of "learned wit." Cervantes had so used the material detail of picaresque episode and the matter picked up by Don Quixote in his reading; Sterne makes similar use of the everyday circumstances of English domestic life, material newly exploited in the developing novel of manners, combining this with details acquired by himself and his characters in reading and in the pursuit of hobbies. Sterne says in one of his letters, referring to a ludicrous episode involving Dr. Slop: "I will reconsider Slops fall & my too Minute Account of it—but in general I am perswaded that the happiness of the Cervantic humour arises from this very thing—of describing silly and trifling Events, with the Circumstantial Pomp of great Ones—perhaps this is Overloaded—& I can soon ease it." [1] But Sterne's real point is that the events are not "silly and trifling." The petty realistic details and the claims of the old learning, the old pompous rhetoric, and the new science are taken to be ludicrous and important at the same time. They can be absurd and significant. The same can be said of feeling or "sentiment"; it is inevitable and admirable, the glory of human nature, but at the same time ludicrous. Remarkable results follow when such attitudes are put into the framework of the didactic novel. *Shandy,* Sterne remarks in reporting one of his sermons, is "a moral work more read than understood." [2]

The straight moralist uses his symbols in a serious and systematic way, and he may believe that his moralizing depends on his pattern and his intention being easily recognized. An impoverished imagination may reduce his symbols to mere signs; Clarissa's coffin, brought into the lodgings where she spends her last days, is as obvious as a skull and crossbones. The satirist like Swift, on the other hand, may intend to degrade or deride the thing symbolized by the use of the symbol. Sterne's mockserious use of detail or episode departs from the facile code of the didactic novelist and also avoids savage satire; he blends the use of a symbol that might be taken as degrading or ludicrous with the assertion of its dignity

[1] *Letters of Laurence Sterne,* ed. L. P. Curtis (Oxford, 1935), p. 77.
[2] *Sermons* (1767), II, 221.

and significance, the implication that the low things of the earth may surpass the great, and the humble things confound the mighty. Here he takes over and alters the device in Swift which Professor Pons calls "the animal myth," [3] with which we may also associate the scheme of the macrocosm and the microcosm. Initial attention centers on the physical detail or object nearest at hand, which may be absurd, homely, trivial, or ignoble, and yet have great referential value.

Hence Sterne's constant attention to gestures, which he takes to be the psycho-physical crossroads of life. Here he elaborates a technique already developed by Defoe and Richardson, and at the same time reminds us, in a variation of the manner of Swift, that man is grotesquely involved with a body. Both Defoe and Richardson had gone some distance in substituting spontaneous gesture for the formal grammar of attitude, and Sterne bases his pantomime on this new realism and enhances its significance. In such a passage as the following we see exactly what Richardson passed on to Sterne: "Mr. Grandison was in the midst of a fine speech, and was not well pleased. He sat down, threw one leg over the knee of the other, hemmed three or four times, took out his snuffbox, tapped it, let the snuff drop thro' his fingers, then broke the lumps, then shut it, and twirled it round with the fore-finger of his right-hand, as he held it between the thumb and fore-finger of the other, and was quite like a sullen boy: Yet, after a while, tried to recover himself, by forcing a laugh at a slight thing or two said in company, that was not intended to raise one" (*Grandison*, II, 2). Richardson realizes the principle stated by Sterne in one of his sermons: "I would sooner form a judgment of a man's temper from his behaviour on such little occurrences of life, as these, than from the more weighed and important actions, where a man is more upon his guard:—has more preparation to disguise the true disposition of his heart." [4] And in *Shandy*: "A man of sense does not lay down his hat in coming into a room,—or take it up in going out of it, but something escapes, which discovers him" (VI, 5). As already appears in Richardson, the minutiae of gesture are built up into action and characterization:

My father thrust back his chair,—rose up,—put on his hat,—took four long strides to the door,—jerked it open,—thrust his head half way out,—shut the door again,—took no notice of the bad hinge,—returned to the table,—plucked my mother's thread-paper out of *Slawkenbergius's* book,—went hastily to his bureau,—walked slowly back, twisting my mother's thread-

[3] E. Pons, *Swift: Les années de jeunesse et le "Conte de Tonneau"* (Strasbourg, 1925), p. 368.

[4] *Sermons* (1769), III, 61.

paper about his thumb,—unbuttoned his waistcoat,—threw my mother's thread-paper into the fire,—bit her satin pin-cushion in two, filled his mouth with bran,—confounded it;—but mark!—the oath of confusion was levelled at my uncle *Toby's* brain,—which was e'en confused enough already,—the curse came charged only with the bran,—the bran, may it please your honours,—was no more than powder to the ball. (III, 41)

Gestures and reactions are intimately associated with unconsidered and trivial objects, the snuffbox, the pin-cushion, the thread-paper, and it turns out that such details are not trivial after all. You can pick them up everywhere, they offer short cuts to reality, and their abundance mocks the set and formal proceedings of mankind:

I hate set dissertations,—and above all things in the world, 'tis one of the silliest things in one of them, to darken your hypothesis by placing a number of tall, opaque words, one before another, in a right line, betwixt your own and your reader's conception,—when in all likelihood, if you had looked about, you might have seen something standing, or hanging up, which would have cleared the point at once—"for what hindrance, hurt, or harm, doth the laudable desire of knowledge bring to any man, if even from a sot, a pot, a fool, a stool, a winter-mittain, a truckle for a pully, the lid of a goldsmith's crucible, an oil bottle, an old slipper, or a cane chair,"—I am this moment sitting upon one. Will you give me leave to illustrate this affair of wit and judgment, by the two knobs on the top of the back of it? (III, 20)

This catalogue from Rabelais (III, 16) savors of random, homely, even gross experience, and of the possibilities of order Sterne finds in such experience. He plays with the idea of random chapters on any topics or objects that may offer—chapters on chapters, on sleep, on whiskers, on chambermaids and buttonholes, green gowns and old hats. Finding topics or objects is a game, like riding a hobbyhorse, "the sporting little filly-folly which carries you out for the present hour—a maggot, a butterfly, a picture, a fiddle-stick—an Uncle Toby's siege—or an *any thing*, which a man makes a shift to get a-stride on, to canter it away from the cares and solicitudes of life" (VIII, 31).

Before we go on to consider the bearing of Sterne's apparently random notations and collectanea on the general plan of his book, we may notice how this method applies to the novel of manners and to his notorious sentimentalism. Some trifling situation or object may be invested with moral and metaphysical meaning, and it is asserted, at least half seriously, that the discovery of such significance is the test of virtue as well as of intelligence. This gives us the context of Corporal Trim's hat or

Uncle Toby's fly. An obvious illustration is the familiar passage in the letters (of doubtful date and provenience, but undoubtedly genuine), often used to illustrate the appearance of the term "sentimental": "One solitary plate, one knife, one fork, one glass!—I gave a thousand pensive, penetrating looks at the chair thou hadst so often graced, in those quiet, and sentimental repasts—then laid down my knife, and fork, and took out my handkerchief, and clapped it across my face, and wept like a child." [5] Here we should notice not only the flood of tears (everybody in the eighteenth century who sheds a tear is called sentimental), but the series of gestures correlated with the physical props—knife, fork, glass, chair, handkerchief—and the importance with which this little system of acts and things is invested. Though Sterne seems to have left no opinion of Richardson on record, he must be indebted to the epistolary novelist's change of scale, his report "written to the moment," his emphasis on the domestic foreground of ordinary life, and his restriction of significant action to family and household. No doubt Sterne, as Cross says, had no use for the "caution and discretion" of Richardson's moral code, but we should not overlook the flexibility of the Richardsonian letter and its concern with minutiae. Both Sterne and Richardson are concerned with the circumstances that envelop things and actions. We do not find in Sterne formally described interiors, but we have details of costume, furniture, and other *impedimenta* given as never before. Restriction of overt and large-scale action is pushed very far; life in city, church, camp, even in the home parish is presented only indirectly in Sterne's network of references. One would have to know the book pretty well to remember that Walter Shandy had been a Turkey merchant in Coleman Street. Sterne even avoids set pictures and extended descriptive narrative in the manner of his master Cervantes. "Now the chapter I was obliged to tear out, was the description of this cavalcade, in which Corporal *Trim* and *Obadiah,* upon two coach-horses a-breast, led the way as slow as a patrole —whilst my uncle *Toby,* in his laced regimentals and tye-wig, kept his rank with my father, in deep roads and dissertations alternately upon the advantage of learning and arms, as each could get the start" (IV, 25). Somewhat similarly, Sterne does not undertake to cover as systematically as Fielding or Smollett the stock themes of eighteenth century satire. Hostile satire, as of Dr. Slop, Didius, and other stupid pedants, is very limited, even though much attention is paid to pedantry. In Sterne's world, John Cowper Powys remarks, "There is no need for any monstrous villainy nor for any egregious hypocrisy such as we are offered in Fielding

⁵ *Letters,* ed. Curtis, p. 11.

and Dickens." It is in the *Sermons of Mr. Yorick* rather than in *Shandy* that we find ourselves established in the world of the eighteenth century didactic novel.

Sterne exuberantly follows the tradition of learned wit, as has been remarked, the tradition found in *A Tale of a Tub* and *The Memoirs of Martinus Scriblerus,* using the *prima facie* content and methods of scholarship for comic purposes. The writer shows exaggerated concern for trifles, displays obscure, minute, and irrelevant erudition with an affected care for accuracy, and sets it forth with an apparatus of formal rhetoric and logic. The curious and studious reader may well be diverted by Sterne's use of Rabelais, Montaigne, Cervantes, Butler, Burton, Bruscambille, Beroalde de Verville, and many others. This has been a fascinating theme for the commentators ever since Ferriar in his *Illustrations of Sterne* (1798) undertook to expose the novelist as a plagiarist. But it is more important to get at the purpose behind all this. The essential step had been taken by Cervantes; all this lore is attributed in one way or another to a comic pedant. Thus we have Walter Shandy's theories, Uncle Toby's military obsessions, and the elaborate lucubrations of Tristram the narrator himself. Such characters, obsessed with a humor or a hobby, are traditional, and traditional also is the implied or expressed presentation of a rational point of view. This point of view might of course be represented by a reasonable character in the story, but, as we have already noted, Cervantes, Marivaux, and Fielding, to name no others, had already brought the narrator into the story and made him serve to some extent as the voice of reason.

But the intervention of the narrator may work in different ways: it may be by the rule of good sense, and be dominated by the strong eighteenth century "decent respect for the opinions of mankind," but it may also have the unpredictability of spontaneous response or impulse. Just as Thackeray called one of his important works *The Book of Snobs. By One of Themselves,* so Sterne might have called *Tristram Shandy* "The Book of Humorists. By One of Themselves." The narrator shows varying attitudes: he may say, "When I seem to be arbitrary, you must nevertheless trust me, for I am really working on a rational plan," or else he may say, "I simply obey my impulses." The narrator in *Shandy* plays the game in both these ways. Fielding's narrator asks for belief in the rational plan, and never makes any serious pretense of flouting it; Sterne's narrator asks for sympathetic participation in the game. Fielding's position is close to the conception of the satirist as the man of plain reason and candor; Sterne's position is close to the conception of the satirist as "the *naïf,* the *ingénu,* the simple heart." [6] The imputation of this attitude to a fictitious character appears in the *Quixote* tradition, and also in what we may call the *Gulliver-Candide* tradition. Such a character must always in a certain sense be defeated or frustrated. Yet Sterne's *ingénu* as novelist cannot be completely defeated, for after all he has written his book—here it is before you in print—and from the outset he hopes, not in vain, for the friendly indulgence and approval of the reader:

> You must have a little patience. I have undertaken, you see, to write not only my life, but my opinions also; hoping and expecting that your knowledge of my character, and of what kind of a mortal I am, by the one, would give you a better relish for the other: As you proceed further with me, the slight acquaintance which is now beginning betwixt us, will grow into familiarity; and that, unless one of us is in fault, will terminate in friendship—*O diem praeclarum!*—then nothing which has touched me will be thought trifling in its nature, or tedious in its telling. Therefore, my dear friend and companion, if you should think me somewhat sparing of my narrative on my first setting out,—bear with me,—and let me go on, and tell my story my own way:—or if I should seem now and then to trifle upon the road,—or should sometimes put on a fool's cap with a bell to it, for a moment or two as we pass along,—don't fly off,—but rather courteously give me credit for a little more wisdom than appears upon my outside:— and as we jog on, either laugh with me, or at me, or in short, do any thing, —only keep your temper. (I, 6)

Parson Yorick is this same *ingénu* as victim, without full privileges of narration and comment; eventually he takes over as narrator in *A Sentimental Journey*. Though Tristram the narrator has his share of pedantry and ingenuousness, he retains a control that can be described as partly rational and partly social; he remains after all in command of the situations in which the other characters and the reader find themselves, in spite of the fact that he professes to be a victim of impulse, to be so busy that he doesn't know how he is going to get from one chapter to another (VIII, 6).

When we combine the miscellaneous of the "learned wit" tradition with the conception of the novelist as *ingénu* going about his business, we find Sterne moving toward the kind of novel that Edouard in Gide's *Les Faux-Monnayeurs* says he would like to write: "I invent the character of a novelist, whom I make my central figure; and the subject of the book, if you must have one, is just that very struggle between what reality offers him and what he himself desires to make of it." He wants to get

[6] See Maynard Mack, "The Muse of Satire," in *Case Memorial Volume* (Ann Arbor, 1952), p. 228.

everything into the book, and yet he must evolve a style, an artistic mode of treatment. He goes on to say, "It is essentially out of the question for a book of this kind to have a plan." He is keeping a notebook preparatory to the work, and it may be that "if I don't succeed in writing the book, it'll be because the history of the book will have interested me more than the book itself—taken the book's place; and it'll be a very good thing." If these ideas were pushed to the limit, Edouard would be identified with the author of *Les Faux-Monnayeurs*, and the notebook would be fully incorporated in and partly identical with the novel. We do not reach these identities in Gide; there is Edouard and there is also the novelist who writes in the third person about Edouard; we have the separate *Journal des Faux-Monnayeurs* beside the book itself. Sterne moves closer to the identification of the novelist in the book with the novelist writing the book. The prehistory of the novel is given largely in the book itself; he does not publish a *Journal de Shandy* alongside of *Shandy*. Though he may talk about planlessness, that is part of his plan, and he knows that when the novelist proposes getting everything into his book what he really has in mind is the discarding of accepted restraints in his selection of points and details, the substitution of another ideal of artistic unity for the conventional one.

II

In telling a story, reporting how life feels, or trying to find the truth, one must begin with experience, with what is actually nearest at the moment, the content of consciousness. Sterne thus professes to write, like Locke, "a history-book . . . of what passes in a man's own mind" (II, 2). What Sterne says at the beginning of the sermon on a good conscience applies to consciousness also: "In other matters we may be deceived by false appearances. . . . But here the mind has all the evidence and facts within herself" (II, 17). Like Locke, he believes that one can somehow pass from the data of immediate experience to the construction of an ordered world, but a world strictly bounded by our limited capacities:

> Can the deepest enquirers after nature tell us, upon what particular size and motion of parts the various colours and tastes of vegetables depend? . . . Nay, have not the most obvious things that come in our way dark sides, which the quickest sight cannot penetrate into; and do not the clearest and most exalted understandings find themselves puzzled, and at a loss, in every particle of matter?
> Go then,—proud man!—and when thy head turns giddy with opinions of thy own wisdom, that thou wouldst correct the measures of the Almighty,—

go then,—take a full view of thyself in this glass;—consider thy own faculties,—how narrow and imperfect;—how much they are checquered with truth and falsehood;—how little arrives at thy knowledge, and how darkly and confusedly thou discoverest even that little as in a glass:—consider the beginnings and ends of things, the greatest and the smallest, how they all conspire to baffle thee;—and which way ever thou prosecutest thy enquiries, —what fresh subjects of amazement, and what fresh reasons to believe there are more yet behind which thou canst never comprehend.—Consider,— these are but part of his ways;—how little a portion is heard of him? Canst thou, by searching, find out God?—wouldst thou know the Almighty to perfection?—'Tis as high as heaven, What canst thou do?—'tis deeper than hell, how canst thou know it? [7]

That Sterne considered this traditional doctrine in line with the findings of Locke is shown by his oft-quoted remark about Locke's philosophy, reported by Suard: "It is a philosophy which never attempts to explain the miracle of sensation; but reverently leaving that miracle in the hands of God, it unfolds all the secrets of the mind; and shunning the errors to which other theories of knowledge are exposed, it arrives at all truths accessible to the understanding." But, since he is a novelist and not a philosopher, he can enjoy the details as they come; he has a "negative capability," as Keats calls it, which is denied to the businesslike epistemologist. Here Sterne is more like an empiricist of the stamp of Bergson or James, and can enjoy a bath in experience. Whatever comes up has the warrant of immediate experience and the importance of an event in human history. The arid data of English empiricism are irradiated with sympathy, and Sterne gives a new reading of the *nihil humani a me alienum puto* of Terence.

With this approach, the humor of a character, fixed though it is, is translated from moment to moment into unpredictable impulses. Every humorist is like Parson Yorick, "as heteroclite a creature in all his declensions" (I, 11), or like Dryden's Zimri in *Absolom and Achitophel*:

> A man so various, that he seem'd to be
> Not one, but all Mankind's Epitome.
> Stiff in Opinions, always in the wrong;
> Was Everything by starts, and Nothing long:
> But, in the course of one revolving Moon,
> Was Chymist, Fidler, States-man, and Buffoon;
> Then all for Women, Painting, Rhiming, Drinking,
> Besides ten thousand Freaks that died in thinking.

[7] *Sermons* (1769), III, 294-95.

The idea applies not only to heteroclites like Yorick and Tristram, but also to Walter Shandy, uniform and systematic though he was in holding to his favorite ideas (I, 19). "As many pictures as have been given of my father, how like him soever in different airs and attitudes,—not one, or all of them, can ever help the reader to any kind of preconception of how my father would think, speak, or act, upon any untried occasion or occurrence of life.—There was that infinitude of oddities in him, and of chances along with it, by which handle he would take a thing,—it baffled, Sir, all calculations" (V, 24). The comedy of humors does not necessarily set a fixed character in the midst of a complex and shifting world; it may reverse that situation, and set a complex and shifting character in the midst of a stupid and static world, and it may apply both situations to a single character. The static humorists in the old sense, like Dr. Slop, are comparatively uninteresting; all Sterne's successful characters show in various ways and degrees this interplay between the flux of the mind and the rigidity of fact and convention, or between the bewildering complexity of the facts and the oversimplifications of mind and temperament.

Under these circumstances, how is one to organize the material of experience and attain the fullest practicable knowledge of people and things? Sterne senses the dramatic value of the problem of knowledge, and uses it in his game. "—My good friend, quoth I—as sure as I am I— and you are you—" "—And who are you? said he.—Don't puzzle me; said I" (VII, 33). The humors of Sterne's characters, his own version of the method of "writing to the moment," and the complexities entailed in a close look at the facts make him keenly aware of the great game of cross-purposes called communication. But he is amused and interested; he may profess to be troubled, but he is not really baffled or discouraged by the threat of skepticism or solipsism. Locke had looked with suspicion on the association of ideas or "mental discourse" as a process that worked against the natural and rational relations of things; and he emphasized judgment, the separation or distinction of ideas, as against wit, the ingenious combination of ideas, though he recognized that in relating ideas for the purpose of forming judgments (practical estimates of probability), both agreements and differences among ideas have to be reckoned with, and this calls for what he terms "sagacity." But the fact remains that Locke's "sagacity" is more pedestrian than Sterne's "wit." Sterne is for taking hold of all clues; he enjoys occult agreements and differences. He is not so random or indiscriminate as he appears to be, but Locke would be hard put to it to find order in his "history-book."

Sterne does not get the general out of the particular, or the external world out of the internal, by an orderly Lockean process. He assumes a great scheme in space and time, and no matter what tricks the point and the instant may play upon us the continuum remains secure. Thus the story of the King of Bohemia and his Seven Castles which Trim begins is never told, but remains a point in the expanse of chronology and geography presented by the successive digressions (VIII, 19). Much attention has been paid to the game Sterne plays with time, his awareness of concurrent separate time-systems, the difference between chronological or clock-time and the feeling of time for the individual, the difference between the time it takes for events to happen and the time it takes for the novelist to write about them. Great discrepancies appear: in immediate experience clock-time is indefinitely extended or shortened; as Toby and Walter descend the stair a chapter may be written for each step (IV, 10); a day in Tristram's life may take a year in the writing of it (I, 14). But these apparent discrepancies are then matched up, the minute and the enormous are paired, or correspond. As a novelist Sterne takes advantage of the situation indicated by the mathematician's definition of an infinite series as one in which any part may be put into one-one correspondence with the whole. The system is timeless in the sense that it transcends any given time-scheme. In other words, Sterne's tricks with time become tricks with space.

We may say that Sterne assumes that experience symbolizes or epitomizes reality, as memory epitomizes a span of time, or Hamlet's nutshell includes infinite space. Reality is not simply built up out of single units; it is contained in the given unit. The individual experience somehow images in little and simultaneously a moral order and a cosmic order, the world of conscience and consciousness and the world of microscope and telescope. The early fragment published by Stapfer, the "Meditation on a Plum Tree," shows Sterne's interest in Fontenelle's conception of the plurality of worlds, his idea of a world in a leaf or the blue of a plum. Lehman and Watkins have recently redirected attention to this important fragment, though chiefly with reference to Sterne's treatment of time. Readers of Miss Nicolson's studies will immediately be able to put the following passage into its context:

It's hard to say whether [*sic*] side of yᵉ prospects strikes yᵉ imagination most; whether yᵉ solar system or a drop of pepper water afford a nobler subject of contemplation; in short whether we owe more to yᵉ Telescope or microscope. On one side infinite Power and wisdom appear drawn at *full extent;* on yᵉ other, in *miniature.* The infinitely *strong and bold Strokes there,* yᵉ infinitely *nice and delicate Touches here,* shew equally in both yᵉ divine hand.

By a different conformation of its senses a Creature might be made to apprehend any given Portion of space, as greater, or less in any Proportion, than it appears to us. This we are assured of from Optics. I doubt not also but by a *different conformation* of yᵉ Brain a Creature might be made to apprehend any given portion of time as longer or shorter in any proportion than it appears to us. Glasses can make an *inch* seem a *mile.* I leave it to future ages to invent a method for making a *minute* seem a *year.*[8]

Here Sterne has a vision of a cataclysm, with the imagery of a poem on the Last Judgment, and awakens to find that the wind has merely blown the plums to the ground. We thus have cosmological grounds for the novelist's change of scale; the infinitely great and the infinitely small are interchangeable and equally important. Walter Shandy expounds the importance of the minute in terms of scientific precision: *"Knowledge,* like matter, he would affirm, was divisible *in infinitum;*—that the grains and scruples were as much a part of it, as the gravitation of the whole world.—In a word, he would say, error was error,—no matter where it fell,—whether in a fraction,—or a pound,—'twas alike fatal to truth, and she was kept down at the bottom of her well as inevitably by a mistake in the dust of a butterfly's wing,—as in the disk of the sun, the moon, and all the stars of heaven put together" (II, 19). Artistic effects too are the results of delicate adjustments and slight touches, the *poco più* and *poco meno* (II, 6). And so Sterne loves miniatures as such; he is fascinated by the idea of the homunculus, or by Uncle Toby's maps and his fortifications on the bowling green. He can think of his own works as miniatures: "I have lusted earnestly, and endeavoured carefully . . . that these little books, which I here put into thy hands, might stand instead of many bigger books" (IV, 22). The traffic goes both ways, from the great to the small or from the small to the great. The mind striking in at any point and picking up connections is working with and toward the significant. Once a point is seized on, it is treated with an excess of method. The famous little vignettes or episodes are carefully wrought to scale, subdivided and rounded out with incrementally repeated detail, in order to give us *multum in parvo.* The incident of Uncle Toby and the fly "is to serve for parents and governors instead of a whole volume upon the subject" of philanthropy (II, 12).

The universe is pictured as a great multiple system, in which sense and spirit, macrocosm and microcosm, are linked by analogies and corre-

[8] "Fragment Inédit" in Paul Stapfer, *Laurence Sterne* (Paris, 1870).

spondences, and also as a great dynamic system to be studied in terms of cause and effect. Causality lends itself to the same kind of play with great and small, the great cause and the trivial effect, the minute cause and the great effect. "Matters of no more seeming consequence in themselves than, 'Whether my father should have taken off his wig with his right hand or with his left,'—have divided the greatest kingdoms, and made the crowns of the monarchs who governed them, to totter upon their heads" (III, 2). Like Fielding, Sterne loves recondite cause-effect relationships, but Fielding follows out a given sequence to a conclusion, whereas Sterne catches impressionistic glimpses of their operation in the field over which attention ranges. The correspondence and causal connection of great and small are briefly expressed in Sterne's apostrophe in *A Sentimental Journey* to the "great great *Sensorium* of the world! which vibrates, if a hair of our heads but falls upon the ground, in the remotest desert of thy creation." The filaments of sensation, impulse, imagination, and sentiment connect microcosm and macrocosm.

The episode of the reception of the news of Bobby's death (V, 2-14) may be summarized to illustrate the principal features of Sterne's method. Walter Shandy is planning details of Bobby's proposed grand tour, with the map before him; he is interrupted first by the servant Obadiah, who wants to go on an errand but can go neither on horse nor on foot, and then by Uncle Toby's report of the letter telling of Bobby's death. Walter then delivers a pompous speech on mortality, taken out of Burton's *Anatomy of Melancholy*; his discourse is misunderstood in different ways by Toby and Mrs. Shandy. The latter, who just happens to be in the passage, plays her usual part of uncomprehending listener, and is left standing at the door for five minutes and seven chapters. Sterne then diagrams the machinery of the family, and extends the concurrent action:

> Though in one sense, our family was certainly a simple machine, as it consisted of a few wheels; yet there was this much to be said for it, that these wheels were set in motion by so many different springs, and acted one upon the other from such a variety of strange principles and impulses, —that though it was a simple machine, it had all the honour and advantages of a complex one,—and a number of as odd movements within it, as ever were beheld in the inside of a *Dutch* silk-mill.
>
> Amongst these there was one, I am going to speak of, in which, perhaps, it was not altogether so singular, as in many others; and it was this, that whatever motion, debate, harangue, dialogue, project, or dissertation, was going forwards in the parlour, there was generally another at the same time, and upon the same subject, running parallel along with it in the kitchen. (V, 6)

This sets the stage for Trim's oration on death and for the contrast with Walter's pedantic periods. In the kitchen, Obadiah's announcement of the death makes the maid Susannah think of Mrs. Shandy's green satin nightgown, which may be given to the servant now that the mistress will be going into mourning (and if the mistress herself should die, the whole wardrobe would follow); the foolish scullion, thinking of her own case of dropsy, says simply, "So am not I"; Obadiah himself thinks that they will have a terrible task stubbing the Ox-moor (the expense of Bobby's education had postponed that project). The gestures and words of Trim's oration—the stick struck perpendicularly on the floor, the dropping of the hat, the question, "Are we not here now, and gone in a moment?" —acquire by incremental repetition and elaborate commentary a significance that Walter's learning never attains. Sterne restates in humorously solemn style the principle of the tremendous trifle: "Now, as I perceive plainly, that the preservation of our constitution in church and state,—and possibly the preservation of the whole world—or what is the same thing, the distribution and balance of its property and power, may in time to come depend greatly upon the right understanding of this stroke of the corporal's eloquence—I do demand your attention" (V, 7). Yet we still remain in a world of "chamber-maids, green-gowns, and old hats" (V, 8), the world of homely objects and simple thoughts. Thus we have in the space of a few chapters concurrent actions which taken together give the impression of depth or extension, interruption and frustration, futile rhetoric, imperfect communication, surprising cause-effect sequences, unpredictable transitions and associations of ideas, trivial physical symbols for great things, and the basic idea of the machine.

The famous digression on digressions will further illustrate how Sterne plans the presentation of his action in space and time. Walter and Toby have been sitting silently for an hour and a half. Walter asks a question, and Toby begins to answer, but Toby's humorous character impels Sterne at this point to state the theory of the English as a humorous people, Toby knocking the ashes out of his pipe the while. Sterne then applies the theory of humors to the whole family, especially to Aunt Dinah, who had married the coachman, and whose case greatly mortified Uncle Toby's modesty. Walter, on the other hand, was constantly referring to Dinah: "The backslidings of *Venus* in her orbit fortified the *Copernican* system, called so after his name; and the backslidings of my aunt *Dinah* in her orbit, did the same service in establishing my father's system, which, I trust, will for ever hereafter be called the *Shandean System,* after his" (I, 21). While Walter talked of Dinah, Toby would whistle *Lillibulero*; Sterne calls this the *Argumentum Fistulatorium,* and discusses its classification in logic. Then he pauses to explain and justify his method of "progressive digression":

> In this long digression which I was accidentally led into, as in all my digressions (one only excepted) there is a master-stroke of digressive skill, the merit of which has all along, I fear, been overlooked by my reader,—not for want of penetration in him,—but because 'tis an excellence seldom looked for, or expected indeed, in a digression;—and it is this: That though my digressions are all fair, as you observe,—and that I fly off from what I am about, as far, and as often too as any writer in Great Britain; yet I constantly take care to order affairs so, that my main business does not stand still in my absence.
>
> I was just going, for example, to have given you the great outlines of my uncle Toby's most whimsical character;—when my aunt Dinah and the coachman came across us, and led us a vagary some millions of miles into the very heart of the planetary system: Notwithstanding all this, you perceive that the drawing of my uncle Toby's character went on gently all the time;—not the great contours of it,—that was impossible,—but some familiar strokes and faint designations of it, were here and there touched in, as we went along, so that you are much better acquainted with my uncle Toby now than you was before.
>
> By this contrivance the machinery of my work is of a species by itself; two contrary motions are introduced into it, and reconciled, which were thought to be at variance with each other. In a word, my work is digressive, and it is progressive too,—and at the same time.
>
> This, Sir, is a very different story from that of the earth's moving round her axis, in her diurnal rotation, with her progress in her elliptic orbit which brings about the year, and constitutes that variety and vicissitude of seasons we enjoy;—though I own it suggested the thought,—as I believe the greatest of our boasted improvements and discoveries have come from such trifling hints.
>
> Digressions, incontestably, are the sunshine;—they are the life, the soul of reading;—take them out of this book for instance,—you might as well take the book along with them;—one cold eternal winter would reign in every page of it; restore them to the writer;—he steps forth like a bridegroom;—bids All hail; brings in variety, and forbids the appetite to fail.
>
> All the dexterity is in the good cookery and management of them, so as to be not only for the advantage of the reader, but also of the author, whose distress, in this matter, is truly pitiable: For, if he begins a digression,—from that moment, I observe, his whole work stands stock-still;—and if he goes on with his main work,—then there is an end of his digression.
>
> —This is vile work.—For which reason, from the beginning of this, you see, I have constructed the main work and the adventitious parts of it with intersections, and have so complicated and involved the digressive and progressive movements, one wheel within another, that the whole machine, in

general, has been kept a-going;—and, what's more, it shall be kept a-going these forty years, if it please the fountain of health to bless me so long with life and good spirits. (I, 22)

The word "machine" gives the clue here: "machine" points to Tristram's body and life, to the structure of the book, to the structure of the universe. Popular thought might conceive of the world and man as a system operated by a few simple forces and springs providentially planned and running with infallible regularity. But, still under Providence, it might emphasize the complexity of the mechanism, as in the following passage from Shaftesbury's "Essay on the Freedom of Wit and Humour":

You have heard it (my Friend!) as a common Saying, that *Interest governs the World*. But, I believe, whoever looks narrowly into the Affairs of it, will find, that *Passion, Humour, Caprice, Zeal, Faction,* and a thousand other Springs, which are counter to *Self-Interest*, have as considerable a part in the Movements of this Machine. There are more Wheels and *Counter-Poises* in this Engine than are easily imagin'd. 'Tis of too complex a kind, to fall under one simple View, or be explain'd thus briefly in a word or two. The Studiers of this *Mechanism* must have a very partial Eye, to overlook all other Motions besides those of the lowest and narrowest compass. 'Tis hard, that in the Plan or Description of this Clock-work, no Wheel or Ballance should be allow'd on the side of the better and more enlarg'd Affections; that nothing should be understood to be done in *Kindness or Generosity;* nothing in *pure Good-Nature* or *Friendship,* or thro any *social* or *natural Affection* of any kind: when, perhaps, the main Springs of this Machine will be found to be either these very *natural Affections* themselves, or a compound kind deriv'd from them, and retaining more than one half of their Nature.

In this optimistic tone, Sterne makes a playful application of the "machine" idea to the structure or "machinery" of his book, and to the events of his story and the actions of his characters. Man is an animal, man is a machine worked by natural forces. The related ideas of animality and mechanism were used for satirical purposes by Swift, for caricature by Smollett, for a brilliant and sympathetic presentation of the human situation by Sterne. All the while, of course, Sterne gets his fun out of the way man is involved in the machinery of the cosmos: "Had Dr. *Slop* beheld *Obadiah* a mile off, posting in a narrow lane directly towards him, at that monstrous rate,—splashing and plunging like a devil through thick and thin, as he approached, would not such a phenomenon, with such a vortex of mud and water moving along with it, round its axis, have been a subject of juster apprehension to Dr. *Slop* in his situation, than the worst of *Whiston's* comets?—To say nothing of the

Nucleus, that is, of *Obadiah* and the coach-horse.—In my idea, the vortex alone of 'em was enough to have involved and carried, if not the Doctor, at least the Doctor's pony quite away with it" (II, 9). The astronomical and physiological references are not incidental or arbitrary ornament, but mean that Sterne's book is about the relation of the little to the great world. Whereas the current physico-theology emphasized simplicity and regularity, Sterne professes to find a just representation of the ordered scheme endlessly intricate and perplexing.

"Progressive digression" thus displays human history as it unfolds in space and time, and as the past fuses with the present and the remote with what is close at hand. The art of digression is the art of presenting coexisting aspects of the totality of experience. Sterne achieves such effects on various scales; he has delicate counterpoint within the episode, with incremental repetition of speech and gesture suspending the moment as a tableau and thus giving us a brief conspectus of concurrent action, and then he will proceed suddenly to far wider ranges of reference. One thinks of the use of time in Proust, with multiple memories radiating from a single impression, but a difference is that the wider reference in Sterne is constructed on a framework of quasi-learned and quasi-scientific matter, instead of being minutely compounded of personal reminiscence. Such a cosmic scheme is recognized in Proust also, but Proust maintains a higher degree of subjectivity and relativity: "When a man is asleep, he has in a circle round him the chain of the hours, the sequence of the years, the order of the heavenly host. Instinctively, when he awakes, he looks to these, and in an instant reads off his own position on the earth's surface and the amount of time that has elapsed during his slumbers; but this ordered procession is apt to grow confused, and to break its ranks." [9] Tristram the narrator and the other characters hark back to the past, and conversely the story may get ahead of itself, but past and present are on the same level; the past is not invested with pathos, and Tristram does not long for his lost childhood, or the old soldiers for their early prime. Another comparison which might help to bring out the scholastic and cosmological side of Sterne would be the program of James Joyce—the Odyssean journey in Dublin, or the all-encompassing dream of H. C. Earwicker. But for Sterne man is not swamped or lost in this universe; the past does not crush him, the future does not threaten, and the infinite spaces do not affright. In this connection it is important to remember that the work of the narrator, the telling of the story, is itself one of the concurrent actions; the

[9] *Remembrance of Things Past, Swann's Way,* trans. Scott-Moncrieff (New York, 1934), I, 4.

writing of the novel is an important part of the action of the novel, and therefore may be taken to be an important event in the history of the world, so that man remains the measure of all things.

At the same time Sterne is so keenly aware of the limitations of formal organization that he identifies systematic thought and scholarship with mere scholasticism and pedantry. It is the great Slawkenbergius who exhausts subjects and offers complete explanations (III, 38). Although Slawkenbergius is Walter Shandy's treasury of universal knowledge, Tristram says (III, 42) that he thinks the best parts of this learned author are the interpolated tales. In Sterne's own practice the incidental tale, episode, or tableau is as good a clue as one can get. But when the great frame of reference is approached in this way, there remains a disparity between the situation at a given time and the conclusion toward which it points or the full meaning which it may convey. Complete realization is never attained on the discursive or rational level. We have what we may call the asymptotic approach, or to borrow a phrase from Aldous Huxley, an everlasting "obstacle race."

In the simplest undertakings there appear insuperable obstacles to getting things done. The author and his characters are constantly being interrupted or distracted by circumstances, accidents, unhappy coincidences, physical conditions, imperfect communications, or the curious workings of their own minds, particularly the strange way in which associations of ideas cut across country. An example may be drawn from the episode of Bobby's death, which has been discussed and analyzed above. Walter Shandy just before he gets the news has been planning the details of Bobby's proposed grand tour.

'Twas a most inauspicious journey; my father having had every foot of it to travel over again, and his calculation to begin afresh, when he had almost got to the end of it, by *Obadiah's* opening the door to acquaint him the family was out of yeast—and to ask whether he might not take the great coach-horse early in the morning and ride in search of some.—With all my heart, *Obadiah,* said my father (pursuing his journey)—take the coach-horse, and welcome.—But he wants a shoe, poor creature! said *Obadiah.*—Poor creature! said my uncle *Toby,* vibrating the note back again, like a string in unison. Then ride the *Scotch* horse, quoth my father hastily.—He cannot bear a saddle upon his back, quoth *Obadiah,* for the whole world.—The devil's in that horse; then take *Patriot,* cried my father, and shut the door.—*Patriot* is sold, said *Obadiah.*—Here's for you! cried my father, making a pause, and looking in my uncle *Toby's* face, as if the thing had not been a matter of fact.—Your worship ordered me to sell him last *April,* said *Obadiah.*—Then go on foot for your pains, cried my father.—I had much rather walk than ride, said *Obadiah,* shutting the door.

What plagues! cried my father, going on with his calculation.—But the waters are out, said *Obadiah,*—opening the door again.

Till that moment, my father, who had a map of *Sanson's,* and a book of the post roads before him, had kept his hand upon the head of his compasses, with one foot of them fixed upon *Nevers,* the last stage he had paid for—purposing to go on from that point with his journey and calculation, as soon as *Obadiah* quitted the room; but this second attack of *Obadiah's,* in opening the door and laying the whole country under water, was too much. —He let go his compasses—or rather with a mixed motion between accident and anger, he threw them upon the table; and then there was nothing for him to do, but to return back to *Calais* (like many others) as wise as he had set out. (V, 2)

In this little study in frustration, as often in his scenes and episodes, Sterne reverses the scheme by which we get confused detail set in the simple framework of a great plan or divinely ordained scheme of things. Instead we get clarity and order in detail, confusion in the total situation. The details are ordered with the clarity and precision of a piece of choreography; the interchange between Walter and Obadiah proceeds by incremental repetition, and we come to a climax in the casting down of the compasses. But in a larger view, the calculation with map and road book is never completed, Obadiah never goes on his errand, and of course Bobby never takes the grand tour. We need hardly be reminded that Walter's plans for Tristram are thwarted at every point. We learn just how it was, according to Walter's theories, that the universe conspired against little Tristram—begotten at the wrong time and subject to unfavorable prenatal influences, his very birth a violation of Walter's obstetrical theories, christened Tristram instead of Trismegistus in direct contradiction of Walter's theories about Christian names, circumcised or worse by the fall of a window-sash (Corporal Trim had taken the weights out to use as field pieces in the game of fortifications).

In spite of overriding obsessions, human ends are infinitely various, but we may say that in *Shandy* the ends are sexual satisfaction, the riding of hobbyhorses, and the full expression of ideas and sentiments. All these entail endless perplexities and an infinity of unfinished business. It is characteristic of Sterne that he is constantly reading sexual meanings into equivocal utterances, and thus attesting man's insistent and unsatisfied interest in the theme. As Professor Work remarks, sexual impotence "hovers like a dubious halo over the head of every Shandy male, including the bull." [10] The most obvious and elaborate though not the

[10] Introduction, *Tristram Shandy* (New York, 1940), p. lx.

best treatment of sex as unfinished business is of course the courtship of
Uncle Toby and the Widow Wadman. But other perplexities of the
brothers Shandy are more engaging. Uncle Toby is involved in endless
intricacies as he tries to tell how he got his wound at the siege of Namur;
his simple purpose and good intentions are entangled in the whole terminology of military engineering. Language interposes itself between a
man and his own good intentions, and between man and man. The
brothers never reach an understanding on intellectual terms. Walter
derides Toby's hobbyhorse with great eloquence and a battery of tech-
nicalities (III, 24); and at the same time he is always trying to impose his
own ideas; on this level the brothers can never get together, whether
Walter is using Latin or English (III, 39). Yet they can meet on the plane
of human sympathy, with gesture and physical circumstance effecting
what words cannot:

> My uncle *Toby* would never attempt any defence against the force of this
> ridicule, but that of redoubling the vehemence of smoking his pipe; in doing
> which, he raised so dense a vapour one night after supper, that it set my
> father, who was a little phthisical, into a suffocating fit of violent coughing;
> my uncle Toby leaped up without feeling the pain upon his groin,—and,
> with infinite pity, stood beside his brother's chair, tapping his back with one
> hand, and holding his head with the other, and from time to time, wiping
> his eyes with a clean cambric hankerchief, which he pulled out of his pocket.
> —The affectionate and endearing manner in which my uncle *Toby* did these
> little offices,—cut my father through his reins, for the pain he had just
> been giving him.—May my brains be knocked out with a battering ram or
> a catapulta, I care not which, quoth my father to himself,—if ever I insult
> this worthy soul more! (III, 24)

A given situation in Sterne is a deadlock which may be broken or resolved in various ways, by an emphatic gesture, an interruption of some
kind, a flash of intuition or sympathy. Sometimes the resolution may run
through a dialogue, as when Trim and Toby communicate, not by exchange of ideas, but by what we may call the antiphonal expression of
feeling; they have only to confirm and echo one another (IV, 4; IV, 18).

Since this is the way "life and opinions" go, this is the way a book
which reproduces the movement of "life and opinions" must go. Perhaps
this is the answer to the question whether *Tristram Shandy* has a plot,
whether the book is finished or not. Certainly there is no single dramatic
resolution of a central situation, as in *Clarissa* or *Tom Jones;* on the
contrary, to the very end there is a postponement or frustration which
illustrates Emerson's remark that comedy is "a non-performance of what
is pretended to be performed, at the same time that one is giving loud

pledges of performance." And yet, though the ostensible or professed end is not realized, the novelist attains his own end; he builds and presents his world. A basic plot device is that unattained possibilities recede; comedy makes a game of this, even extends it to the procedure of the dramatist or novelist himself, perhaps contents itself with a "happy ending," some form of *de facto* arrangement. It is only by strict limitation to the procedure of the novel of manners, as in *Tom Jones* and *Humphry Clinker,* that the novel can avoid being heavily involved in unfinished business. Tragedy, we may say, accepts neither the *de facto* arrangement nor the indefinite postponement of unattained possibilities; it insists on finishing the business by an ultimate adjustment of personality to unattained possibility. Thus the proposed marriage of Lovelace and Clarissa, in its varying degrees of approach to actuality, is on an entirely different level from the troubled courtship and happy wedding of Tom and Sophia, and the voyage of the *Pequod* would have been no ordinary voyage even if the vessel had got back to its home port. The distinction is not always clear-cut, and it sometimes remains uncertain how far we get an ultimate showdown. Does the deathbed repentance of Don Quixote go any deeper than the final discomfiture of Tartuffe? Can we have conventional serious endings as well as conventional happy endings? It is not merely by way of perpetrating a practical joke that Sterne refuses to round things off in the usual way, or if it is a joke, it is too big a one to be merely funny. His frustrations and approximations produce comedy, dramatize the problem of knowledge and communication, show the limitations of formal rhetoric, traditional learning, and scholarship, and even of the new science and of language itself, and thus set forth the general human situation. In some such way as this it seems possible to correlate the form, the purpose, and the content of *Tristram Shandy.* Perhaps we may say that Cervantes had taken the essential step in the construction of Sterne's world when he set up the partnership of Don Quixote and Sancho Panza; these two make their way as best they can in a world of hard discordant fact and persistent illusion, and their working partnership and the only attainable solution of their problems must be on the basis of loyalty, sympathy, and love.

A comparison as to underlying plan with Joyce's *Ulysses* has already been suggested. If, however, we think of Joyce's use of the *Odyssey,* in Eliot's words ("Ulysses, Myth and Order") as "simply a way of controlling, of ordering, of giving a shape and a significance to the immense panorama of futility and anarchy which is contemporary history," the important difference appears that Sterne is lost in no such chaos or wasteland. His disorder gives delight and hurts not, and leads to an inner coherence of vision which does not depend on the arbitrary imposition of a scheme, or on the erection of a great mass of apparatus in the manner of Slawken-bergius. Unlike Joyce, Sterne is never completely carried away by the scheme to which he appears to be playfully committing himself. He did not live in an age when critics were discussing the aesthetic necessity of such a scheme, however arbitrary. Like Cervantes again, he believed that such schemes were made for man, that man as reader should not be completely subjugated or overawed by literary apparatus, flaunt the apparatus as one may while one is playing the game. There is an elaborate centrifugal and complicating movement in Sterne, but there is also a counter-movement toward concentration and simplification. This double movement may be illustrated from the opening of the story. There are so many bypasses and divagations that the life of little Tristram starts before birth and never gets told—it is very difficult to get fairly started away from the *terminus a quo;* but here at the outset there is the converse case of Parson Yorick, so that we begin with a character sketch, a death scene, and an epitaph—a *terminus ad quem.*

It is hard to say whether unity is imposed on *Tristram Shandy* by the function of the narrator, or discovered by the narrator in the great scheme of things. We are here confronted with the problem of knowledge: How much does the knower contribute to what is known? Sterne, as an artist and not a philosopher, is not obliged to answer this question. The narrator is coping with a great system, like Fielding's narrator, but he also enjoys what on the surface appears to be complete liberty. Theoretically he claims the right to start from anything that catches his attention and proceed in any direction. This right, like the convention by which the novelist may claim omniscience and take any point of view, cannot be fully exercised. No artist can use "unchartered freedom"; he must issue himself a charter, if no one else does. The basic assumption in Sterne is that immediate experience, subtle and elusive though it is, can be firmly placed in a general scheme. He would not accept Hume's denial of causal necessity and uniformity, though he is keenly conscious of the difficulty of attaining true knowledge; we have seen that he is close to Locke's position that man can have valid knowledge of a world which is after all much like Newton's. Tristram the narrator is not identical with young Tristram; as narrator he does not keep to the point of view of the child, or write straight "stream of consciousness"; he is the efficient agent of the far-reaching references in time and space; he is both inside and outside the moment; he is not only the knower of English empirical philosophy, but the philosopher who writes with confidence about that knower—a somewhat different matter. The German exponents of romantic irony who imitated Sterne moved beyond him in the direction of pure subjectivity. At the same time Sterne undertakes to relate the individual to his world by the shortcut of sympathy and love, the bonds by which society is held together, and here he is close to the ethics of Hume and Adam Smith.

III

While *Shandy* obviously does not have a plot in the same sense as *Tom Jones,* the fact remains, as Professor Work has pointed out, that we find a coherent time-scheme, two overlapping main actions—the story of the Shandy household and the story of Uncle Toby—and numerous clues planted early in the story, significant to the initiated, pointing forward to themes which are elaborately developed in the later books. In fact, Sterne substitutes for the unilinear cause-effect sequence often called "plot" a very elaborate set of patterns, themes, and symbols which invite comparison with devices used by later novelists, particularly those who practise the kind of psychological notation called "stream of consciousness" writing. As far as technique is concerned, Sterne and the moderns are much alike: there is an attempt to present or suggest firm order behind or alongside of the apparent chaos of the psychological flux. The ultimate views about the dignity of man may be different, but we can still say of *Tristram Shandy* as of *Ulysses* that it is a book in which design is carried to excess.

All this goes with a high degree of flexibility: in our enthusiasm for the discovery of hidden principles of structure or occult balance we must not deny Sterne the pleasure of experimentation or the exercise of numerous options as he goes along. He did not spend all his energy devising a code. The eighteenth century did not think of the novelist as one who wrote for fit audience though few, nor did it want its writers to be cryptic. As it was, Sterne's innovations gave him the reputation of being an incorrigible eccentric. But when an eighteenth century writer speaks of appealing to choice souls or to the elite, he has in mind not a coterie but an audience relatively large in proportion to the whole reading public. James Joyce is said to have remarked that anyone who wishes to understand his works must give all his time to the study of the subject; the age of Sterne could take such a remark only as a monstrous joke, wilder than any Shandean foible, and only the lack of a sense of humor and proportion in contemporary criticism keeps us from taking it in that way too.

The varying reception of successive installments of the story no doubt influenced Sterne's plans. Of Volumes V and VI he wrote while they were in progress: "These two volumes are, I think, the best—I shall write as long as I live, 'tis, in fact, my hobby-horse: and so much am I delighted with my uncle Toby's imaginary character, that I am become an enthusiast." [11] This is the familiar situation in which a fruitful and self-developing interaction is set up between humorous character and episode. Cervantes, Fielding, and Sterne might all have reported the experience as Scott did later: "When I light on such a character as Bailie Jarvie, or Dalgetty, my imagination brightens, and my conception becomes clearer at every step which I take in his company, although it leads me many a weary mile away from the regular road, and forces me to leap hedge and ditch to get back into the route again. If I resist the temptation, as you advise me, my thoughts become prosy, flat, and dull; I write painfully to myself, and under a consciousness of flagging which makes me flag still more; the sunshine with which fancy had invested the incidents departs from them, and leaves everything dull and gloomy." [12] Volumes V and VI, with the "Bobby's death" sequence in the former, and the story of Le Fever in the latter (skilfully introduced in V, 10), come to lay more stress on delicacy of sentiment, less on learned wit. Sterne evidently thought highly of the Le Fever story, and when he tells us Parson Yorick preached a sermon on the subject, writing "Bravo" in the margin, and then crossing it out (VI, 11), we virtually hear the novelist remarking, "A good episode, if I do say it myself." In VI, 20, we have what may perhaps be interpreted as a transition to Toby as the principal character, and certainly in VI, 29, a formal presentation of Toby in a new role. There may be in VI, 25, an intimated intention to carry the story through to Toby's death. Since he has from the beginning been a major character, this is not a violent shift, and of course the themes of the Shandy family and Uncle Toby can run concurrently, yet we get the impression of free modulation and some degree of improvisation. The fact is, when Sterne says he has things planned to the last iota, he is improvising, and when he says he is completely deranged, he is not deranged at all.

The period of Sterne's residence on the Continent from 1762 to 1764 furnishes copy for Book VII, "a laughing good tempered Satyr against Traveling." [13] With death knocking at the door, Tristram, who is here clearly Laurence Sterne, sets out for the Continent. The motto for this book, "Non enim excursus hic ejus, sed opus ipsum est," boldly attempts to justify the new venture by the doctrine of relevant digression. We may

[11] *Letters*, ed. Curtis, p. 143.
[12] Introductory Epistle, *The Fortunes of Nigel.*
[13] *Letters*, ed. Curtis, p. 231.

speculate about the prehistory of the travel plan. Sterne, it appears, had originally thought of sending Tristram on a tour with Lord Noddy's son —a burlesque of the stock account of the grand tour that would lend itself to satire in the Rabelaisian and Scriblerian tradition, and was transformed in true Shandean style. This journey of Tristram's is interwoven with memories of an earlier journey taken by the Shandy group (VII, 27), in which the humors of Walter, Trim, and Toby were elaborately displayed. The plan for the travels of such a group as a device for presenting "occurrences or scrapes" illustrating diverse humors points to something like the plan of Smollett's *Humphry Clinker*. Sterne's experiments with travel narrative offered two possibilities: the account could stand by itself, as eventually in *A Sentimental Journey,* or it could furnish more books for *Tristram Shandy.* As to Book VII, what probably happened was, as Cross suggests, that Sterne had not succeeded in completing the full account of the Uncle Toby-Widow Wadman affair, which, according to the promises made at the end of Book VI, was to occupy the following books; he therefore fell back on a travel narrative already composed in whole or in part as a separate work or loose continuation, used this material as Book VII, and offered what he had written on the Toby-Wadman affair as Book VIII. In order to make the transition from the travels back to Uncle Toby he represents Tristram as writing Books VIII and IX of *Shandy* on a tour through France (VIII, 1; IX, 24).

Up to the end of 1766 Sterne seems to have thought of continuing *Tristram* indefinitely. On July 23, 1766, he wrote: "At present I am in my peaceful retreat, writing the ninth volume of Tristram—I shall publish but one this year, and the next I shall begin a new work of four volumes, which when finish'd, I shall continue Tristram with fresh spirit." [14] The four volumes, of course, would be the projected independent travel narrative, two volumes of which were completed as *A Sentimental Journey.* Nevertheless Professor Booth has recently shown that Book IX of *Tristram* bears unmistakable marks of having been composed as the last.[15] This is not quite the same thing as saying, as Professor Booth does, "that the book which he had completed represented the completion of a plan, however rough, which was present in his mind from the beginning." This plan, according to Booth's very able analysis, was to contradict the promise of *The Life and Opinions of Tristram Shandy* made on the title-page by the specific device of substituting Uncle Toby's campaigns and amours. But of course there are innumerable other ways of *not* telling of Tristram's life and opinions—telling Walter Shandy's, for example, or citing

[14] *Letters,* ed. Curtis, p. 284.
[15] *Modern Philology,* XLVIII (1951), 172-83.

Slawkenbergius. And how, Tristram might ask, can I tell of my life and opinions without tracing the cosmic network, without considering the various systems, domestic, educational, and psychological, of which the homunculus is the focal point? But this playfully philosophical view could be used to justify the introduction of almost anything, including the Uncle Toby story and miscellaneous travel material. The situation was very flexible; in July, 1776, Sterne was not thinking of Volume IX as his last, though it seems that he came to do so within the next few weeks, and he could easily have put more travel material into *Shandy* instead of detaching it as *A Sentimental Journey*.

We are to think of Sterne as writing with his eye on the public, and as eager to find out how his readers would take more travel narrative in the vein of Book VII. The *Journey* depends largely on obvious sentiment and pathos, rather than on the learned wit, grotesque ribaldry, and humor which dominate the Walter Shandy story and figure to some extent in the Uncle Toby story. The *Journey* is less abstruse and at the same time less rich and dense than *Shandy*; it does not undertake so much cross reference to an elaborate scheme, and does not play so many tricks with time, space, and memory. It gives us Sterne's familiar themes, as when he says of his characteristic use of detail in "The Wig": "I think I can see the precise and distinguishing marks of national characters more in these nonsensical *minutiae,* than in the most important matters of state." Even the more complex episodes follow easily traceable lines of association: the fear of the Bastille is associated with the starling's repeated cry, "I can't get out," and the sequence ends with a well planned but conventional apostrophe to the Goddess of Liberty. Then Yorick visualizes a captive in a cell, and bursts into tears. And as he drives to Versailles he fills in the gap with the history of the starling, even to a picture of his own coat of arms with the starling as crest. The famous sentimental episodes in the *Journey* are part of a program to popularize Sterne's methods, to give easy lessons in the Yorick-Shandy vein. Mechanical methods for getting effects, the underlying technical weakness of the Gothic and sentimental tendencies in late eighteenth century fiction, come to the fore. As Yorick visits the grave of the monk of Calais, looks at the snuffbox the monk has given him, and plucks a nettle from the grave, we witness the mechanization of sentiment, the establishment of the sentimental cliché, the side of Sterne that Henry Mackenzie was to imitate in *The Man of Feeling* (1771). In the snuffbox we see a fetish which is to elicit an automatic response, like the ring which Le Fever and his son kiss (*Tristram Shandy,* VI, 7). Geoffrey Tillotson has aptly cited in illustration of this phase of sentimentalism Shenstone's remark that "inanimates, toys, utensils, seem to merit a kind of affection from us, when they have been our companions through various vicissitudes. I have often viewed my watch, standish, snuffbox, with this kind of regard, allotting them a degree of friendship which there are some men who do not deserve." [16] Physical objects and details, as we have seen, play a livelier and more complex role in *Shandy*; they have of course this sentimental and *gemütlich* aspect, but they are also incitements in a comedy of humors, mock-heroic *impedimenta,* symbols of the macrocosm.

How far was this change a deliberate bid for the continuation of public favor? How far does it correspond to changes in Sterne's own feelings and attitudes? These questions have been asked recently; obviously they do not admit of simple answers. Since sentimentalism involves a highly self-conscious and even self-critical attitude toward feeling, it can never be called "sincere" if by that word we mean "simple" or "direct." Concurrently with the *Journey* Sterne wrote the surviving second part of the *Journal to Eliza,* a record of his characteristic literary amour or flirtation with Mrs. Draper in Bombay, the "Bramine." The *Journal* incorporates sections of his correspondence, and manipulates facts and feelings in such a way that it may be considered another exercise in Yorickan fiction; he evidently played with the idea of making literary capital of his amour as he was making literary capital of his travels. He exploits the pathos of his situation in a relatively direct way in the *Journal,* whereas he still operates with his symbols and tableaux in the *Journey.*

Surely Cross was essentially correct in connecting these last phases of Sterne's work with the state of his health. His tuberculosis was not a pose. Professor Putney has recently argued for a complete separation of the *Journey* from Sterne's private life: "Yorick's sentimental pose was adopted in response, not to Sterne's feelings but to popular demand for the pathos at which Sterne excelled." [17] His demonstration that the *Journey* plays up the pathetic vein in *Shandy* is conclusive, but hardly justifies our pronouncing the *Journey* a "hoax." In another important article Putney treats the *Journey* as a subtle exposé of the errors of sentiment, as expounding a gospel of laughter rather than tears.[18] But we are here dealing with a situation that cannot be resolved simply by setting laughter over against tears, or sincerity over against insincerity. The sentimental traveler Yorick, who is indeed different from the Yorick of

[16] *Essays in Criticism and Research* (Cambridge, 1942), pp. 108-9.
[17] "Laurence Sterne: Apostle of Laughter" in *The Age of Johnson* (New Haven, 1949), pp. 159-70.
[18] "The Evolution of *A Sentimental Journey,*" *Philological Quarterly,* XIX (1940).

Shandy, is not a rounded portrait of Sterne, but a comic figure representing at the same time sentimentalism and the ultimate refinement or attenuation of the comedy of humors. This is not to say that the portrayal of such a character intends a mere burlesque of sentiment; the comedy of humors had long been moving toward sympathetic presentation, and Sterne caps the climax by sympathizing with the humorous aspects of his own personality.

Extreme sentiment has this in common with the humors, that it may be taken as a mechanical force getting out of control, and so has its ridiculous side. Sterne realizes this principle, and uses it throughout his work for comic effect, but this does not mean that true sentiment is merely mechanical. He discusses the point in his sermon on the Good Samaritan:

> In benevolent natures, the impulse to pity is so sudden, that, like instruments of music, which obey the touch—the objects which are fitted to excite such impressions work so instantaneous an effect, that you would think the will was scarce concerned, and that the mind was altogether passive in the sympathy which her own goodness has excited. The truth is,—the soul is generally in such cases so busily taken up, and wholly engrossed by the object of pity, that she does not attend to her own operations, or take leisure to examine the principles upon which she acts. So that the Samaritan, though the moment he saw him he had compassion on him, yet sudden as the emotion is represented, you are not to imagine that it was mechanical, but that there was a settled principle of humanity and goodness which operated within him; and influenced not only the first impulse of kindness, but the continuation of it throughout the rest of so engaging a behaviour.[19]

As I have suggested in a discussion of Richardson, we may say that if sentimentalism means the proclamation of the absolute validity of spontaneous feeling, then no one, not even Henry Mackenzie, is a sentimentalist. Richardson and Sterne may be called sentimental in the sense that they seek by more and more refined analysis to bring out affiliations, connections, harmonies, and identities between feeling and reason, or between the true, the good, and the beautiful. They assume a settled system, not a mere chaos or anarchy of feeling. The sentimentalist who goes in for pure feeling is an unhistorical abstraction, like the mythical neoclassicist who is completely subjugated by "reason." The relations between feeling and comedy or tragedy are complex, and we cannot rest content with a classification of "laughing" and "weeping" novelists, or of partisans of sentiment and anti-sentiment.

[19] *Sermons* (1767), I, 60.

While it is pleasant to enjoy Sterne as a rare bird or a *lusus naturae*, we may learn something more of him and his contemporaries by considering his position in relation to the general enterprise of the eighteenth century novelists. One way of understanding that enterprise is to consider the extent to which they claim adequacy for their interpretation of life as lived by the men about them. Such a claim, we feel, should have its limits. The novel of manners must interpret life by using codes, current ethics, and socially approved or disapproved types; and yet such an interpretation must be accompanied by a sense of the intractable and the insoluble. The novelist must admit such a sense without shattering his frame of reference. The frame is solid in Defoe, though the obscure compulsions of the human will beat against it with the persistence of a buzzing fly at a window pane, so that Defoe attains a dogged iteration of remarkable power. Fielding moves into a more complicated social scene, and modestly and rationally but firmly claims the adequacy of the comic point of view, this point of view involving a large tolerance which includes the normal workings of human nature and extreme variations which may be accepted and enjoyed when accompanied with good intentions. But the comedy of manners does not necessarily carry the novelist beyond the established preference for a good sense at once benevolent and rational. Richardson's studies of the divided mind carry him closer to the ultimate mysteries of personality; sometimes he seems to stumble upon such mysteries rather than to seek them; but it should be noted that the fact that he always assigns his commentary to characters writing letters in his story helps to save him from being forced to claim complete adequacy of interpretation at all points, and gives him in *Clarissa* a saving residue of the insoluble that lies at the heart of tragedy. In comparison with Fielding and Richardson, Smollett's claim to adequacy is perfunctory; he gives us, and it is a great achievement, an intensely recorded and heartily realized but not thoroughly examined life. He is at his best when he takes short views. In relation to this whole situation, Sterne's position appears to be highly original and even unique; he shifts to a comic level the claim of interpretive adequacy; by "a sharper specification of the signs of life" and a shift of scale which follows out Richardson's technique, he carries things to a point of complexity which raises anew the question, "What is truth?" In a telling phrase Professor Crane describes Fielding's treatment of Tom Jones as involving a "comic analogue of fear." [20] The phrase "comic analogue of the quest for truth" could perhaps be used as a description of the effect Sterne attains by

[20] "The Plot of *Tom Jones*," *Journal of General Education*, IV (1950), pp. 112-30.

undertaking to give us a picture of the human situation crosshatched with sensation, impulse, and obsession. German criticism, which has made a serious study of Sterne in its own special idiom, long ago set up a contrast between Jean Paul Richter's profound consciousness of the gap between the ideal and the real and the ensuing development of his cosmic irony, and on the other hand Sterne's cheerful acceptance of man's lot.[21] Sterne brilliantly maintains his comic equilibrium; man's predicament is presented along with redoubled assurance that he still "superior walks amid the glad creation," and thus Sterne in his own way continues and elaborates the affirmations of his great contemporaries in prose fiction.

[21] Gertrude Hallamore, *Das Bild Laurence Sternes in Deutschland* (Berlin, 1936).

A Parodying Novel: Sterne's *Tristram Shandy*

by *Viktor Shklovsky*

In this essay I do not propose to analyze Laurence Sterne's novel; I intend to use it merely as an illustration of the general laws of novelistic form, for here Sterne was an extreme revolutionary. His typical method is to proceed by "laying bare" the literary device; form exists for itself and has no ulterior motivation. The difference between Sterne's novel and an ordinary novel is like the difference between a poem of typical sound-orchestration and a futuristic poem in extrarational language. To date, nevertheless, nothing but a few commonplaces has been written about Sterne.

The first impression of a reader who picks up *Tristram Shandy* is that the novel is chaos. The action is interrupted constantly; the author continually retreats or jumps ahead; the basic story, which is hard to find in the first place, is constantly interrupted by lengthy digressions concerning such odd topics as the effect of a nose or a name on character, or conversations about fortifications.

The book seems to begin in the tone of an autobiography, but then it strays to a description of the hero's birth, which is protracted through the intrusion of all sorts of material. The book turns into the description of a single day.

I will not finish that sentence till I have made an observation upon the strange state of affairs between the reader and myself, just as things stand at present—an observation never applicable before to any one biographical writer since the creation of the world, but to myself—and I believe will never hold good to any other, until its final destruction—and therefore, for the very novelty of it alone, it must be worth your Worships' attending to.

I am this month one whole year older than I was this time twelve-month;

"A Parodying Novel: Sterne's *Tristram Shandy*." From *O Teorii Prozy* (Moscow, 1929) by Viktor Shklovsky. The present translation by W. George Isaak, made especially for this collection, includes the whole of Shklovsky's essay except for several illustrations from other novels. An earlier version of 1921, together with other essays of the Formalist group, appears in *Russian Formalist Criticism: Four Essays*, edited and translated by Lee T. Lemon and Marion J. Reis (Lincoln, Neb., 1965). Reprinted by permission of the author.

and having got, as you perceive, almost into the middle of my fourth volume—and no farther than to my first day's life—'tis demonstrative that I have three hundred and sixty-four days more life to write just now, than when I first set out; so that instead of advancing, as a common writer, in my work with what I have been doing at it—on the contrary, I am just thrown so many volumes back—(IV, 13)

But when one begins to examine the structure of the book, one sees, first of all, that this disorder is intentional, that the work possesses its own poetics. It is all according to law, like a painting by Picasso.

In the book everything is displaced and transposed. The dedication turns up after the first two chapters in violation of the conventions of content, form, and place.

The location of the preface is equally unusual. It occurs not in the beginning of the book but in chapter 20 of the third volume. The author's motive for this displacement of the preface is explained there as follows:

All my heroes are off my hands;—'tis the first time I have had a moment to spare,—and I'll make use of it, and write my preface.

The preface is, of course, written with every possible entanglement that wit can devise. But the crowning entanglement of the book is the displacement of chapters 18 and 19 of Volume IX so that they follow chapter 25. Again Sterne states his motivation:

All I wish is, that it may be a lesson to the world,
"to let people tell their stories their own way."

But this displacement of chapters lays bare Sterne's other basic device, the "time-shift," which brakes whatever action may seem to be developing.

In the beginning Sterne tells the anecdote about the interruption of the sexual act (in which Tristram was begot) by Mrs. Shandy's question. The anecdote is devised as follows. Tristram's father sleeps with his wife only on the first Sunday of each month; that same evening he winds up the clock in order to get "out of the way at one time all family concernments, and be no more plagued and pestered with them the rest of the month." As a consequence, an irresistible association of ideas became established in his wife's mind; as soon as she heard the clock being wound up, a totally different matter came to her mind, and the other way around. That is the reason for her question, "Pray, my dear, have you forgotten to wind up the clock?" and the interruption of Tristram's father's activity.

The ancedote is introduced into the work as follows: first reflections about the irresponsibility of parents, then the mother's question without an explanation of its full significance. We think at first that the question interrupted what the father was saying. Sterne plays with our misconception:

—*Did ever woman, since the creation of the world, interrupt a man with such a silly question?* Pray, what was your father saying?—Nothing.

ℍ Then comes the reasoning about the homunculus, embellished by humorous references to its legal rights.

And only several pages later do we get the explanation of the strange punctiliousness of the father's domestic habits.

Thus, we see the functioning of this device of the "time-shift" from the very beginning of *Tristram Shandy*. Causes are given after effects, after deliberately implanted possibilities of false conclusions. It is Sterne's constant device. And the humorous motif of the coitus connected with a certain day of the month appears occasionally in the novel, bringing together the various parts of this work of such skillful intricacy.

One could schematize this matter as follows: let us have a cone symbolize the event, with its apex representing the causal part of the action. In the ordinary novel the tip of the cone touches the line of the action. In Sterne's novel the story runs along the bases of the cones, so that we find ourselves in a swarm of hints.

The poetics of the novel form commonly calls for such "time-shifts"; take, for example, Turgenev's *The Nest of Gentlefolk*, in which the "time-shift" is motivated by Lavretsky's recollection, or Goncharov's dream of Oblomov, or Gogol's *Dead Souls*, where there are unexplained transpositions in Chichikov's childhood and Tientietnikov's upbringing. But in Sterne the matter is different, for *the device is made obvious* throughout the entire work.

Sterne's exposition, his preparation for a character, is always made after we stop short, disconcerted by some strange word or ejaculation of the new actor.

Here, again, we have the device laid bare. In Pushkin's "The Shot" the device of the "time-shift" is also freely used but it is motivated in terms of the narrative. First we see Silvio practicing marksmanship, then we hear about the unfinished duel; then we meet the Count, Silvio's enemy, and learn about the outcome of events. The chronology of the story is presented out of sequence—II–I–III. But we see the motivation for the "time-shift." Sterne, however, simply lays bare his "time-shifts" with no pretense of motivation from the story-line. Manipulations are for their own sake.

> What I have to inform you comes, I own a little out of its due course;—for it should have been told a hundred and fifty pages ago, but that I foresaw then 'twould come in pat hereafter, and be of more advantage here than elsewhere.

Laid bare too is Sterne's device of sewing together the novel from distinct short stories. In general, Sterne seems to manipulate and expose the novel's very structure: formal devices and structural relations made perceptible by violating their ordinary employment make up the very content of the novel. I have already traced several canonical ways of combining short stories into a novel in my essay on *Don Quixote*. Sterne used new methods; or, rather, employing old ones, he *exposed* their conventionality, blew the convention up, played with it.

In an ordinary novel, the intruding story is interrupted by the main plot. If there are two basic stories, or even several, their strands alternate, as in *Don Quixote* where the knight's adventures at the Duke's court alternate with scenes of Sancho Panza's activities as governor. Zelinskij points to something totally different in Homer. Homer never depicts two simultaneous actions. Even when according to the course of events two actions have to occur simultaneously, they are depicted as following one another. Only the activity of one hero and the "abeyance" of another (i.e., his inactivity) can be depicted simultaneously.

Sterne permitted actions to take place simultaneously, but he "parodied" the development of the subplot and the intrusion into it of new material.

The description of Tristram Shandy's birth is the material developed in the first part, occupying many pages, almost none of which are devoted to the account of the birth itself. What is developed, in the main, is the hero's conversation with Uncle Toby.

The development takes place as follows:

> —I wonder what's all that noise, and running backwards and forwards for, above stairs, quoth my father, addressing himself, after an hour and a half's silence, to my uncle *Toby,*—who you must know, was sitting on the opposite side of the fire, smoking his social pipe all the time, in mute contemplation of a new pair of black-plush-breeches which he had got on;—What can they be doing brother? quoth my father,—we can scarce hear ourselves talk.
>
> I think, replied my uncle *Toby,* taking his pipe from his mouth, and striking the head of it two or three times upon the nail of his left thumb, as he began his sentence,—I think, says he:—But to enter rightly into my

uncle *Toby*'s sentiments upon this matter, you must be made to enter first a little into his character, the outlines of which I shall just give you, and then the dialogue between him and my father will go on as well again. (I, 21)

Then begins the reflection on inconstancy, which is so extraordinary that only direct quotation can reproduce it. Tristram recalls:

But I forget my uncle *Toby*, whom all this while we have left knocking the ashes out of his tobacco pipe.

There follows talk about Uncle Toby into which there is inserted the history of Aunt Dinah. But then Tristram remembers:

I was just going, for example, to have given you the great outlines of my uncle *Toby*'s most whimsical character;—when my aunt *Dinah* and the coachman came a-cross us, and led us a vagary some millions of miles . . .

Unfortunately, I cannot reproduce all of Sterne, and so I continue after a large gap:

. . . I have constructed the main work and the adventitious parts of it with such intersections, and have so complicated and involved the digressive and progressive movements, one wheel within another, that the whole machine in general, has been kept a-going;—and, what's more, it shall be kept a-going these forty years, if it please this fountain of health to bless me so long with life and good spirits.

So ends chapter 22; chapter 23 begins:

I have a strong propensity in me to begin this chapter very nonsensically, and I will not baulk my fancy.—Accordingly I set off thus. . . .

And the reader faces more digressions. Chapter 24 begins:

If I was not morally sure that the reader must be out of all patience for my uncle *Toby*'s character . . .

And in a little less than a page begins the description of Uncle Toby's mania, his hobbyhorse. It appears that Uncle Toby, after being wounded in the groin, became absorbed in building toy fortifications.

But finally, in chapter 6 of Volume II Uncle Toby is able to complete the activity he began seven chapters earlier.

. . . I think, replied my uncle *Toby*,—taking, as I told you, his pipe from his mouth, and striking the ashes out of it as he began his sentence;—I think, replied he,—it would not be amiss, brother, if we rung the bell.

This device of intrusion is used by Sterne constantly, and, as is evident in his jocular reminiscences of Uncle Toby, he not only recognizes the

hyperbolic elaborations of his development, but plays with that development. This method is for Sterne the canon. Another example of this sort
of development (and which in its turn is a part of the earlier development
of Uncle Toby) begins in chapter 19 of Volume II:

> . . . I wish, quoth my uncle *Toby,* you had seen what prodigious armies
> we had in Flanders.

But Toby is interrupted by Sterne to begin the development of Walter's
obsessions. Tristram's father is subject to the following idiosyncratic
notions: the grave dangers of pressure upon the infant's head during
labor, the influence of a man's name upon his character (a theme dealt
with in great detail), and the influences of the size of a man's nose upon
his abilities. The "nose" theme is developed with great flourishes, and
following it, after a small interruption, comes the development of the
material involving the curious tales of men with big noses. Most remarkable is the story of Slawkenbergius. Tristram's father knew ten
versions of this tale. The noseology continues until the second chapter
of Volume IV, a digression from the digression.

At the beginning of Volume III the basic story reappears.

> —I *wish,* Dr. *Slop,* quoth my uncle *Toby* (repeating his wish for Dr. *Slop*
> a second time, and with a degree of more zeal and earnestness in his manner
> of wishing, than he had wished it at first)—I *wish,* Dr. *Slop,* quoth my
> uncle *Toby, you had seen what prodigious armies we had in Flanders.*

Developmental material intrudes again; the sentence is repeated a
fourth time, now by Walter, in the next chapter, "What prodigious armies
you had in Flanders"; and again, a fifth time, in chapter 6, "What
prodigious armies you had in Flanders."

The repeated sentence to mark the continuity of a consciously exaggerated set of developmental devices is only one of Sterne's methods. Here
is another:

> The moment my father got up into his chamber, he threw himself
> prostrate across his bed in the wildest disorder imaginable, but at the same
> time, in the most lamentable attitude of a man borne down with sorrows,
> that ever the eye of pity dropped a tear for. (III, 29)

A description of the pose, a typical stylistic device of Sterne's, follows:

> —The palm of his right hand, as he fell upon the bed, receiving his fore-
> head, and covering the greatest part of both his eyes, gently sunk down with
> his head (his elbow giving way backwards) till his nose touched the quilt;—
> his left arm hung insensible over the side of the bed, his knuckles reclining
> upon the handle of the chamber-pot, which peeped out beyond the valance,

—his right leg (his left being drawn up towards his body) hung half over the side of the bed, the edge of it pressing upon his shin-bone. (III, 29)

Mr. Shandy's despair is caused by the fact that his son was delivered with a nose crushed by the man midwife's instrument. And so enters, as I have said, a whole poem on noses. Half a volume further on (IV, 2) we are brought back to the prostrate father.

My father lay stretched across the bed as still as if the hand of death had pushed him down, for a full hour and a half, before he began to play upon the floor with the toe of that foot which hung over the bed-side. . . .

I cannot resist saying a few words about the description of poses in Sterne. Sterne was the first to introduce descriptions of poses into the novel; moreover, these poses are very strangely represented—more precisely, they are *made strange*.

Here is another example:

Brother *Toby*, replied my father, taking his wig from off his head with his right hand, and with his *left* pulling out a striped India handkerchief. . . (III, 2)

And on the next page:

It was not an easy matter in any king's reign, (unless you were as lean a subject as myself) to have forced your hand diagonally quite across your whole body, so as to gain the bottom of your opposite coat-pocket.

This method of describing a pose passes over from Sterne to Leo Tolstoy, though used less obviously and with a psychological motivation.

But to get back to the topic of development. I will give several examples, choosing instances in which orientation toward the fact of development itself as device is obvious; that is, the work's content becomes the perception of form.

What a chapter of chances, said my father, turning himself about upon the first landing, as he and my uncle *Toby* were going down stairs—what a long chapter of chances do the events of this world lay open to us. (IV, 9)

There follow reflections with an erotic turn, about which more later. Sterne continues discussing his method. All of chapter 10 is devoted to reflections on chapters.

Is it not a shame to make two chapters of what passed in going down one pair of stairs? for we are got no farther yet than to the first landing, and there are fifteen more steps down to the bottom; and for aught I know, as my father and my uncle *Toby* are in a talking humour, there may be as many chapters as steps. . . .

For the next three chapters, we have Sterne's effort to get Toby and Walter off the stairs:

> We shall bring all things to rights, said my father, setting his foot upon the first step from the landing. . . . (IV, 11)

> And how does your mistress? cried my father, taking the same step over again. . . . (IV, 12)

> Holla!—you chairman!—here's a sixpence—do step into that bookseller's shop, and call me a "day-tall" critic. I am very willing to give any one of 'em a crown to help me with his tackling, to get my father and my uncle Toby off the stairs to put them to bed. . . . (IV, 13)

The "content" becomes clearly reflection upon the form itself.

This orientation toward form, especially toward its rules and canons, resembles those poems whose only content is how they are put together.

I will give one last example of Sterne's development:

> My mother was going very gingerly in the dark along the passage which led to the parlour, as my uncle *Toby* pronounced the word *wife*.—'Tis a shrill, penetrating sound of itself, and *Obadiah* had helped it by leaving the door a little a-jar, so that my mother heard enough of it, to imagine herself the subject of the conversation: so laying the edge of her finger across her two lips—holding in her breath, and bending her head a little downwards, with a twist of her neck—(not towards the door, but from it, by which means her ear was brought to the chink)—she listened with all her powers:—the listening slave, with the Goddess of Silence at his back, could not have given a finer thought for an intaglio.
>
> In this attitude I am determined to let her stand for five minutes: till I bring up the affairs of the kitchen . . . to the same period. (V, 5)

Six chapters further on she is still at the chink:

> I am a *Turk* if I had not as much forgot my mother, as if Nature had plaistered me up, and set me down naked upon the banks of the river *Nile*. . . . (V, 11)

But even after this recollection a digression follows. The reminder to himself and the reader is necessary only in order to revive the reader's awareness of the "forgotten mother" so as not to allow the consciousness of the developmental process to lapse. Finally, two chapters more, and she is permitted to change her pose. "Then, cried my mother, opening the door . . ."

In the example cited, the development occurs through an insertion of another, parallel story. In contrast to logically sequential development, in such cases in novels time stands still, or is at the very least not taken into account. Shakespeare's subplot scenes are used in this way. They are inserted into the main plot and divert our attention from the passage of time; and even when the subplot dialogue (necessarily involving new *dramatis personae*) lasts only a few minutes, the author finds it possible to continue the main plot (it is to be supposed, without the curtain falling; for there was no curtain in Shakespeare's time) as if hours, or even a night had passed. Sterne, however, made the *device* real by referring to it and gave it a feeling of palpable development through digressive reflections and reminders that his mother continued to stand leaning forward.

It is interesting to trace the role of time in Sterne's work. "Literary time" is sheer arbitrariness; its laws do not coincide with the laws of actual time. When one realizes, for instance, what a multitude of stories and episodes are concentrated into *Don Quixote,* one sees that the flow of actual time is of no material consequence because nightfall or advent of day does not accompany the sequence of events and plays no role in the composition of the work. The arbitrariness of Sterne's "literary time" is conscious and is employed as material for play. Consider chapter 8 of Volume II:

> It is about an hour and a half's tolerable good reading since my uncle *Toby* rung the bell, when *Obadiah* was ordered to saddle a horse, and go for Dr. *Slop,* the man-midwife;—so that no one can say, with reason, that I have not allowed *Obadiah* time enough, poetically speaking, and considering the emergency too, both to go and come;—though, morally and truly speaking, the man perhaps has scarce had time to get on his boots.
>
> If the hypercritic will go upon this; and is resolved after all to take a pendulum, and measure the true distance betwixt the ringing of the bell, and the rap at the door;—and, after finding it to be no more than two minutes thirteen seconds, and three fifths,—should take upon him to insult over me for such a breach in the unity, or rather probability, of time;—I would remind him, that the idea of duration, and of its simple modes, is got merely from the train and succession of our ideas,—and is the true scholastic pendulum,—and by which, as a scholar, I will be tried in this matter, abjuring and detesting the jurisdiction of all other pendulums whatever.
>
> I would, therefore, desire him to consider that it is but poor eight miles from *Shandy-Hall* to Dr. *Slop,* the man-midwife's house;—and that whilst *Obadiah* has been going those said miles and back, I have brought my uncle *Toby* from Namur, quite across all Flanders, into England:—That I have had him ill upon my hands near four years;—and have since travelled him and Corporal *Trim,* in a chariot and four, a journey of near two hundred miles down into Yorkshire;—all which put together, must have prepared the

reader's imagination for the entrance of Dr. *Slop* upon the stage,—as much, at least, (I hope) as a dance, a song, or a concerto between the acts.

If my hypercritic is intractable,—alleging, that two minutes and thirteen seconds are no more than two minutes and thirteen seconds,—when I have said all I can about them;—and that this plea, though it might save me dramatically, will damn me biographically, rendering my book, from this very moment, a professed ROMANCE, which, before, was a book apocryphal:—If I am thus pressed—I then put an end to the whole objection and controversy about it all at once, by acquainting him, that *Obadiah* had not got above three score yards from the stable-yard before he met with Dr. *Slop*. . . .

Of the older conventional devices Sterne uses that of the "discovered manuscript" almost without change. Yorick's sermon is introduced into the novel in this manner. But the reading of the manuscript does not constitute a lengthy digression from the basic story, because it is constantly interrupted, mainly by emotional exclamations. The reading of the sermon continues through two chapters (II, 17-18) but it is considerably extended by means of insertions typical of Sterne.

The reading begins with a description of the corporal's pose; the representation proceeds by means of Sterne's usual device of describing the awkwardness of a pose.

He stood before them with his body swayed, and bent forwards just so far, as to make an angle of 85 degrees and a half upon the plain of the horizon;—which sound orators, to whom I address this, know very well to be the true persuasive angle of incidence. . . .

And then again—

He stood,—for I repeat it, to take the picture of him in at one view, with his body swayed, and somewhat bend forwards,—his right leg from under him, sustaining seven-eighths of his whole weight,—the foot of his left leg, the defect of which was no disadvantage to his attitude, advanced a little,— not laterally, nor forwards, but in a line betwixt them. . . .

The whole description continues for more than a page. The sermon is interrupted by the story about Corporal Trim's brother. Then come the interjected theological protests of the Catholic Dr. Slop and Toby's observations about fortifications.

The reading of the "discovered manuscript" in Sterne is in this manner much more integrated with the novel than in Cervantes. The "discovered manuscript" in *A Sentimental Journey* is also worked up with relish by Sterne. He finds what he supposes to be a manuscript by Rabelais; but the use of the concluding pages as package wrapping leaves the story unfinished, as is usual with Sterne, for the unfinished story, whether motivated or not by the narrative, is part of Sterne's canon. Nothing at all, for example, motivates the conclusion of *Tristram Shandy*; the novel ends with an abrupt interruption of the narrative.

> L—d! said my mother, what is all this story about?—A Cock and a Bull, said *Yorick*—And one of the best of its kind, I ever heard.

So ends also the *Sentimental Journey*:

> . . . so that when I stretched out my hand, I caught hold of the Fille de Chambre's—

Such endings are, of course, distinct stylistic devices varying according to requirements of particular stories. Sterne worked against the background of the adventure novel with its firmly established form and its rule of ending the story with a wedding. That "form" in Sterne's novels is alteration and destruction of accepted form is, then, also evident in their conclusions. It is as if we are forced off balance where we expect to find firm footing. Gogol's "Shponka and his Aunt" represents a similar method of concluding the short story; but in Gogol the conclusion is motivated: the end of the manuscript was lost in the baking of pies; in Sterne it is lost (for no reason at all) in the wrapping of a nosegay. Hoffmann's notes comprising *Kater Murr* also conclude with a motivated absence of an ending, but with the additional complications of a "time-shift" (justified by the mix-up in page order) and with a parallelism.

Sterne introduces Le Fever's story according to the conventional manner. The choice of a teacher is discussed at Tristram's birth. Uncle Toby suggests Le Fever's son, and so begins the inserted narrative *told by the author*.

> . . . Then, brother *Shandy*, answered my uncle *Toby*, raising himself off the chair, and laying down his pipe to take hold of my father's other hand,— I humbly beg I may recommend poor *Le Fever*'s son to you;—a tear of joy of the first water sparkled in my uncle *Toby*'s eye,—and another, the fellow to it, in the corporal's, as the proposition was made;—you will see why when you read *Le Fever*'s story;—fool that I was! nor can I recollect (nor perhaps you) without turning back to the place, what it was that hindered me from letting the corporal tell it in his own words;—but the occasion is lost, —I must tell it now in my own. (VI, 5)

Le Fever's story, a separate unit, then takes over the narrative.

The description of Tristram's journey—later developed, motif by motif, step by step, in the *Sentimental Journey*—constitutes a unit in itself in *Tristram,* but it too is interrupted by the inserted story of the Abbess of Andoüillets (VII, 21).

Now, all this heterogeneous material, laden with lengthy quotations from works of various pedants, would have shredded the novel to bits had it not been held together by the motifs that run through it. No single motif is fully developed and made real; the motifs merely reappear from time to time, and their realization is postponed into an ever-receding future. But their presence throughout the full length of the novel holds its episodes together.

There are several such motifs. One of them is the motif of the knots. It appears as follows. Doctor Slop's bag of obstetrical instruments is tied with several knots.

> . . . 'Tis God's mercy, quoth he, (to himself) that Mrs. *Shandy* has had so bad a time of it,—else she might have been brought to bed seven times told, before one half of these knots could have got untied.

The following chapter begins—

> In the case of *knots,*—by which, in the first place, I would not be under-stood to mean slip-knots,—because in the course of my life and opinions,—my opinions concerning them will come in more properly . . . (III, 10)

There begins a discussion about knots, loops, bows, and so forth without end. In the meantime, Dr. Slop gets his knife and cuts the knot; but through carelessness he cuts his hand. He begins to curse. The elder Shandy, with a "Cervantes-like earnestness," suggests that he curse not haphazardly but according to all rules of fine art, offering as a model the formula for excommunication used by the Catholic Church. Slop accepts the suggestion and reads the formula. The reading takes up two pages. Curious here is the motivation for the introduction of the material required by Sterne for development. Usually such material—medieval learn-ing, which in Sterne's time had already become subject matter for comedy (like dialect inserted in tales about foreigners)—is connected with the figure of Tristram's father and is motivated by his obsessions. In this case the motivation is more complex. The material concerning the christening before the infant's birth and the droll legal quarrel whether or not a mother is related to her son are totally adventitious to the father's character as father.

In chapter 8 of Volume V the motif of the chapter concerning knots and chambermaids reappears.[1] But instead of developing their connec-tion, another chapter is offered concerning chambermaids, green-gowns,

---

[1] Shklovsky errs: the chapter mentions "buttonholes" not "knots."—ED.

and old hats. The question of the knots is not forgotten, however. It reappears again at the very end of the book (IX, 14) in the form of a promise to write a special chapter about knots.

The references to Jenny are another recurrent but passing motif. Jenny appears in the novel as follows.

> . . . —it is no more than a week from this very day, in which I am now writing this book for the edification of the world;—which is March 9, 1759, —that my dear, dear *Jenny*, observing I looked a little grave, as she stood cheapening a silk of five-and-twenty shillings a yard,—told the mercer, she was sorry she had given him so much trouble;—and immediately went and bought herself a yard-wide stuff of ten-pence a yard. (I, 18)

Then Tristram plays with the reader's curiosity about Jenny's relationship to him.

> I own, the tender appellation of my dear, dear *Jenny*,—with some other strokes of conjugal knowledge, interspersed here and there, might, naturally enough, have misled the most candid judge in the world into such a determination against me.—All I plead for, in this case, Madam, is strict justice, and that you do so much of it, to me as well as to yourself,—as not to prejudge or receive such an impression of me, till you have better evidence, than I am positive, at present, can be produced against me:—Not that I can be so vain or unreasonable, Madam, as to desire you should therefore think, that my dear, dear *Jenny* is my kept mistress;—no,—that would be flattering my character in the other extreme, and giving it an air of freedom, which, perhaps, it has no kind of right to. All I contend for, is the utter impossibility for some volumes, that you, or the most penetrating spirit upon earth, should know how this matter really stands.—It is not impossible, but that my dear, dear *Jenny!* tender as the appellation is, may be my child. —Consider—I was born in the year eighteen.—Nor is there any thing unnatural or extravagant in the supposition, that my dear *Jenny* may be my friend.—Friend!—My friend.—Surely, Madam, a friendship between the two sexes may subsist, and be supported without—Fy! Mr. *Shandy:*—Without any thing, Madam, but that tender and delicious sentiment, which ever mixes in friendship, where there is a difference of sex.

The Jenny motif appears again at the end of Volume IV:

> I shall never get all through in five minutes, that I fear—and the thing I *hope* is, that your worships and reverences are not offended—if you are, depend upon it I'll give you something, my good gentry, next year to be offended at—that's my dear *Jenny*'s way—but who my *Jenny* is—and which is the right and which the wrong end of a woman, is the thing to be *concealed*—it shall be told you in the next chapter but one, to my chapter of button-holes,—and not one chapter before.

Again, in Chapter 13 of Volume VII, "I love the Pythagoreans (much more than ever I dare tell my dear Jenny) for their . . . 'getting out of the body, in order to think well.' "

Again, a mention, a quite sentimental one, rare for Sterne, near the end of the book (IX, 8)—I have skipped several:

> I will not argue the matter: Time wastes too fast: every letter I trace tells me with what rapidity Life follows my pen; the days and hours of it, more precious, my dear *Jenny!* than the rubies about thy neck, are flying over our heads like light clouds of a windy day, never to return more—every thing presses on—whilst thou art twisting that lock,—see! it grows grey; and every time I kiss thy hand to bid adieu, and every absence which follows it, are preludes to that eternal separation which we are shortly to make.
> —Heaven have mercy upon us both!
> Now, for what the world thinks of that ejaculation—I would not give a groat. (IX, 9)

It is interesting to consider here the question of sentimentality in general. Sentimentality cannot be the content of art if for no other reason than that art does not have a separable content. The representation of things from the "sentimental point of view" is a special method of representation, similar to their representation from, say, the point of view of a horse (Tolstoy's "Strider") or a giant (Swift).

In its essence art is outside emotion. Remember how in fairy tales humans are thrust into barrels perforated by nails and then rolled down into the sea. In "Tom Thumb" the ogre cuts off the heads of his daughters, and children protest when that detail is skipped. This is not being cruel; this is entering the fairy-tale world. In his *Ritual Songs of Spring*, Professor Anichkov gives examples of spring dance songs. These songs talk about an evil, belligerent husband, about death, about worms— tragic themes; but this is tragedy of the song world. "Blood" in art is not bloody, it rimes with "love"; it is material either for a sound pattern or for an image pattern.

Art is thus without compassion, or outside it, except in those instances when the feeling of commiseration serves as material for an artistic pattern. But even there, in considering the feeling one must consider it from the point of view of composition, just as in trying to understand a motor one must look at the drive-belt as a detail in a machine—from the mechanic's point of view—and not from the point of view of a vegetarian.

Quite naturally, Sterne is also beyond compassion. Here is an example. The older Shandy's son Bobby dies at the moment that the father is considering whether to use a lucky windfall to send his son abroad or to make improvements on the estate.

. . . my uncle *Toby* hummed over the letter. . . . he's gone! said my uncle
Toby.—Where—Who? cried my father.—My nephew, said my uncle *Toby.*
—What—without leave—without money—without governor? cried my father
in amazement. No:—he is dead, my dear brother, quoth my uncle *Toby.*
(V, 2)

Here death is used by Sterne to create a "misunderstanding"—a common fictional device in which two people speak about different things
while thinking that they are talking about the same thing.

But Sterne's own word-play involving death surprises less, or actually
not at all, when it is compared with the father's word-play. For Sterne,
Bobby Shandy's death serves primarily as motivation of the development.

Will your worships give me leave to squeeze in a story between these two
pages? (V, 3)

And a fragment of a letter of condolence from Servius Sulpicius to
Cicero is here inserted. The motivation of this insertion is that it is
spoken by Mr. Shandy himself. There follows a collection of classic
anecdotes on the subject of disdain for death. It is curious that it is
Sterne himself who is talking about Shandy's eloquence.

My father was as proud of his eloquence as Marcus Tullius Cicero could
be for his life, and for aught I am convinced of to the contrary at present,
with as much reason: it was indeed his strength—and his weakness too.—
His strength—for he was by nature eloquent,—and his weakness—for he
was hourly a dupe to it; and provided an occasion in life would but per-
mit him to shew his talents, or say either a wise thing, a witty, or a shrewd
one—(bating the case of systematic misfortune)—he had all he wanted.—A
blessing which tied up my father's tongue, and a misfortune which let it
loose with a good grace, were pretty equal: sometimes, indeed, the misfortune was the better of the two; for instance, where the pleasure of the
harangue was as *ten,* and the pain of the misfortune but as *five*—my father
gained half in half, and consequently was as well again off, as if it had
never befallen him. (V, 3)

Here is evident with extraordinary clarity the difference between actual
"happiness" and "misery" and these when they are treated as artistic
material.

Further on the mother must learn of the son's death. It is done as
follows. While Mrs. Shandy is listening at the door, Sterne creates a
parallel action in the kitchen, and, as I have already shown, exploits
playfully the length of time the poor mother has to remain in her un-
comfortable pose.

At the same time a conversation is going on in the study about the son's death; this conversation threads together the reflections about death in general, and, imperceptibly, after a discussion of the ways ancient learning was disseminated, goes over to Socrates' speech at his trial.

> . . . though my mother was a woman of no deep reading, yet the abstract of Socrates' oration, which my father was giving my uncle *Toby,* was not altogether new to her.—She listened to it with composed intelligence, and would have done so to the end of the chapter, had not my father plunged (which he had no occasion to have done) into that part of the pleading where the great philosopher reckons up his connections, his alliances, and children; but renounces the security to be so won by working upon the passions of his judges.—"I have friends—I have relations,—I have three desolate children,"—says Socrates.—
>
> —Then, cried my mother, opening the door,—you have one more, Mr. *Shandy,* than I know of.
>
> By heaven! I have one less,—said my father, getting up and walking out of the room. (V, 13)

A very important developmental material in Sterne is that in which the erotic is made strange, and Sterne has an extraordinary variety of methods for doing this. (We are used to the phenomenon of treating the erotic in literature by euphemisms.) I shall give several examples of his making the erotic strange, beginning with one that has to do with distinguishing character.

> . . . I am not ignorant that the Italians pretend to a mathematical exactness in their designations of one particular sort of character among them, from the *forte* or *piano* of a certain wind instrument they use,—which they say is infallible.—I dare not mention the name of the instrument in this place;—'tis sufficient we have it amongst us,—but never think of making a drawing by it;—this is enigmatical, and intended to be so, at least *ad populum:*—And therefore I beg, Madam, when you come here, that you read on as fast as you can, and never stop to make any inquiry about it. (I, 23)

Or here is another one—

> Now whether it was physically impossible, with half a dozen hands all thrust into the napkin at a time—but that some one chestnut, of more life and rotundity than the rest, must be put in motion—it so fell out, however, that one was actually sent rolling off the table; and as *Phutatorius* sat straddling under—it fell perpendicularly into that particular aperture of *Phutatorius's* breeches, for which, to the shame and indelicacy of our language be it spoke, there is no chaste word throughout all Johnson's dictionary—let it suffice to say—it was that particular aperture, which in all

good societies, the laws of decorum do strictly require, like the temple of
Janus (in peace at least) to be universally shut up. (IV, 27)

Especially typical of Sterne's playing at the game of "making strange"
the erotic is the episode having to do with Uncle Toby's wound, which
is developed into one of the criss-crossing plot lines of the novel. He is
courted by a widow who wishes to marry him but is not sure whether he
has been made impotent by the wound. Being a woman, she dares not
ask. This impedes the novel's flow enormously, especially since it is involved with the plot line of Trim's amour with Bridget. Sterne says of his
delaying tactics here:

> . . . there is not a greater difference between a single-horse chair and
> madam Pompadour's *vis-à-vis*, than betwixt a single amour and an amour
> thus nobly doubled and going upon all fours, prancing throughout a grand
> drama. (III, 24)

The novel is then constantly interrupted and the narrative emerges
only in the form of hints. Finally, toward the end of Volume VI, the
hints grow denser. But just here the parenthetical travel motif intrudes.
By the end of Volume VII this is exhausted and we return to Toby's
amour:

> I danced it along through Narbonne, Carcasson, and Castle Naudairy, till at
> last I danced myself into Perdrillo's pavillion, where pulling a paper of
> black lines, that I might go on straight forwards, without digressions or
> parenthesis, in my uncle *Toby*'s amours—

And so, in the development of Toby's romance with the Widow Wadman the wound in the groin is introduced as a delaying device because
of the impossibility of a woman's inquiring about it. How this retarda-
tion is worked out in Sterne, I will show by reference to several passages.

After a solemn promise to relate the history of Uncle Toby's love adventures without digression, Sterne retards the action by means of digressions within the digressions tied together by the repetition of one and
the same sentence, "It is with love as with Cuckoldom" (VIII, 2-4).

Then come the metaphorical references to love as a warm cap, love
as a pie (VIII, 11). The history of Widow Wadman's attacks upon Uncle
Toby follows. But the description of these attacks is again interrupted
by Trim's long narration of the "tedious tale" about "The King of
Bohemia and His Seven Castles." This narrative is of the same type as
the one told by Sancho Panza to his master in the night of the adventure
with the fulling mill, when he had tied Rosinante's legs. The story is
constantly interrupted by Uncle Toby's technical military remarks and

comments on style. . . . Like any "shaggy dog" tale it consciously employs the device of delay and must be interrupted by the listener. In this instance it functions to retard the movement of the basic love story. At last, Trim drops the tale of the King of Bohemia and turns to the history of his own love; finally, the Widow Wadman returns again to the scene. It is here that the motif of the wound reappears.

> I am terribly afraid, said widow *Wadman,* in case I should marry him, *Bridget*—that the poor captain will not enjoy his health, with the monstrous wound upon his groin—
>
> It may not, Madam, be so very large, replied *Bridget,* as you think—and I believe besides, added she—that 'tis dried up—
>
> —I could like to know—merely for his sake, said Mrs. *Wadman*—
>
> —We'll know the long and the broad of it, in ten days—answered Mrs. *Bridget,* for whilst the captain is paying his addresses to you—I'm confident Mr. *Trim* will be for making love to me—and I'll let him as much as he will—added *Bridget*—to get it all out of him—(VIII, 28)

Here again new material is introduced, which in this case consists of *realization* of a metaphor, as happens often in Sterne. The *realization,* in this instance, involves taking literally the metaphor "hobbyhorse" (as obsession) and speaking of it as if it were a real horse, and the extrapolation of the metaphor "ass" for a part of the body.

> For my hobby-horse, if you recollect a little, is no way a vicious beast; he has scarce one hair or lineament of the ass about him. (VIII, 31)

Perhaps the origin of this metaphor is St. Francis's reference to his body as "my brother the ass." The metaphor "ass" is also developed and, furthermore, it provides the basis for situations involving misunderstanding. Tristram's father, for example, asks Uncle Toby about his ass. "Well! dear brother Toby, said my father, upon his first seeing him after he fell in love—and how goes it with your Ass?" (VIII, 32) Uncle Toby takes this as a reference to his behind. The details of the subsequent development are interesting. Tristram's father's speech addressed to Uncle Toby is a parody of Don Quixote's words to Sancho Panza on the office of governor. I shall not illustrate the parallel as the Widow Wadman awaits. Uncle Toby and Trim are on the way to her house. Walter Shandy and his wife are following, talking about the forthcoming wedding. Here again appears the recurrent motif about the impotent husband who sleeps with his wife the first Sunday of the month. This motif which opens the novel also concludes it:

> Unless she should happen to have a child—said my mother—
>
> —But she must persuade my brother *Toby* first to get her one—

—To be sure, Mr. *Shandy,* quoth my mother.

—Though if it comes to persuasion—said my father—Lord have mercy upon them.

Amen: said my mother, *piano.*

Amen: cried my father, *fortissimè.*

Amen: said my mother again—but with such a sighing cadence of personal pity at the end of it, as discomfited every fibre about my father—he instantly took out his almanac; but before he could untie it, *Yorick's* congregation coming out of church, became a full answer to one half of his business with it—and my mother telling him it was a sacrament day—left him as little in doubt, as to the other part—He put his almanac into his pocket.

The first Lord of the Treasury thinking of *ways and means,* could not have returned home, with a more embarrassed look. (IX, 11)

I quote this fragment in order to show that the materials introduced into the narrative by Sterne are not arbitrary; each fragment is relevant to some continuous strain in the novel's composition.

Again other diverging strains reappear; the motif of the knots returns (IX, 14). Finally, the motif of the wound. We are plunged, as is usual in Sterne, into the midst of things.

—— *   *   *   *   *   *   *   *   *   *   *   *
*   *   *   *   *   *   *   *   *   *   *   *.
*   *   *   *   *——

—You shall see the very place, Madam; said my uncle *Toby.*

Mrs. *Wadman* blushed—looked towards the door—turned pale—blushed slightly again—recovered her natural colour—blushed worse than ever; which, for the sake of the unlearned reader, I translate thus—

L——d! I cannot look at it—

What would the world say if I looked at it?

I should drop down, if I looked at it—

I wish I could look at it—

There can be no sin in looking at it.

—*I will look at it.* (IX, 20)

But something else happens.

Uncle Toby thinks that the widow is interested in the geographical location where he was wounded and not in the wound's place on his body. And the reader himself is not sure which is involved. Here the aim of the plot-shift is realized—delay.

Trim brings the disappointed widow a map of Namur, where Toby was wounded. Again there occurs a play on the topic of Uncle Toby's wound. Tristram does it in his own person, circling the topic, reflectively. Then comes the famous time-shift. After the 25th chapter of Volume IX come the 18th and 19th. The interrupted action moves forward only with chapter 26.

It was just as natural for Mrs. *Wadman,* whose first husband was all his time afflicted with a Sciatica, to wish to know how far from the hip to the groin; and how far she was likely to suffer more or less in her feelings, in the one case than in the other.

She had accordingly read Drake's anatomy from one end to the other. She had peeped into Wharton upon the brain, and borrowed Graaf upon the bones and muscles; but could make nothing of it.

She had reasoned likewise from her own powers—laid down theorems— drawn consequences, and come to no conclusion.

To clear up all, she had twice asked Doctor *Slop,* "if poor captain *Shandy* was ever likely to recover of his wound—?"

—He is recovered, Doctor *Slop* would say—

What! quite?

Quite: madam—

But what do you mean by a recovery? Mrs. *Wadman* would say.

Doctor *Slop* was the worst man alive at definitions; and so Mrs. *Wadman* could get no knowledge: in short, there was no way to extract it, but from my uncle *Toby* himself.

There is an accent of humanity in an enquiry of this kind which lulls Suspicion to rest—and I am half persuaded the serpent got pretty near it, in his discourse with Eve; for the propensity in the sex to be deceived could not be so great, that she should have boldness to hold chat with the devil, without it—But there is an accent of humanity—how shall I describe it?— 'tis an accent which covers the part with a garment, and gives the enquirer a right to be as particular with it, as your body-surgeon.

—Was it without remission?—

—Was it more tolerable in bed?

—Could he lie on both sides alike with it?

—Was he able to mount a horse?

The matter is finally resolved as follows. Trim speaks about the captain's wound to Bridget, the widow's maid.

. . . and in this cursed trench, Mrs. *Bridget,* quoth the Corporal, taking her by the hand, did he receive the wound which crushed him so miserably *here.*—In pronouncing which, he slightly pressed the back of her hand towards the part he felt for—and let it fall.

We thought, Mr. *Trim,* it had been more in the middle—said Mrs. *Bridget*—

That would have undone us forever—said the Corporal.

—And left my poor mistress undone too—said *Bridget.*

The Corporal made no reply to the repartee, but by giving Mrs. *Bridget* a kiss.

Come—come—said *Bridget*—holding the palm of her left hand parallel
to the plane of the horizon, and sliding the fingers of the other over it, in a
way which could not have been done, had there been the least wart or pro-
tuberance—'Tis every syllable of it false, cried the Corporal, before she had
half finished the sentence. (IX, 28)

It is interesting to compare this hand-symbolism with the method of
erotic euphemism Sterne uses. But a short preliminary observation. For
the actors of the novel this is a way of avoiding crude impropriety, but
for Sterne, from the point of view of artistic construction, this is a method
of making strange this erotic material. It is interesting to observe that
the same device of "hand-symbolism" is found in the coarse folk anecdotes for men, where no rules of propriety exist, and the purpose is, on
the contrary, to be as bawdy as possible. The euphemistic material, the
"hand-symbolism" in particular, functions there as a device for making
strange.

But back to Sterne. It is again necessary to quote extensively.

—'Twas nothing,—I did not lose two drops of blood by it—'twas not
worth calling in a surgeon, had he lived next door to us—thousands suffer by choice, what I did by accident.
. . . The chamber-maid had left no ******* *** under the bed: Cannot you contrive, master, quoth *Susannah*, lifting up the sash with one hand,
as she spoke, and helping me up into the window seat with the other,—
cannot you manage, my dear, for a single time, to **** *** ** ***
******?
I was five years old.—*Susannah* did not consider that nothing was well
hung in our family,—so slap came the sash down like lightning upon us;
—Nothing is left, cried *Susannah*,—nothing is left—for me, but to run my
country.—(V, 17)

She runs to Uncle Toby's house, who, it turns out, is to blame because
his servant Trim removed the weights to cast toy cannons from them.

Again Sterne's usual device: the effects are given before causes. The
occurrence is told by means of "hand-symbolism."

Trim, by the help of his fore-finger, laid flat upon the table, and the
edge of his hand striking a-cross it at right angles, made a shift to tell his
story so, that priests and virgins might have listened to it. . . .

Farther on comes the development of gossip concerning the event,
digressions, discussions about the digressions, etc.

Father Shandy having learned about the accident runs to his son—
with a book—and begins to talk about circumcision in general. Inter-

esting here is Sterne's parody on motivations behind parenthetical material.

> . . . *Obadiah* [was] enabled to give him a particular account of it, just as it had happened.—I thought as much, said my father, tucking up his night-gown;—and so walked up stairs.
>
> One would imagine from this—(though for my own part I somewhat question it)—that my father before that time, had actually wrote that remarkable chapter in the *Tristra-paedia,* which to me is the most original and entertaining one in the whole book;—and that is the *chapter upon sash-windows,* with a bitter Philippic at the end of it, upon the forgetfulness of chamber-maids.—I have but two reasons for thinking otherwise.
>
> First, Had the matter been taken into consideration, before the event happened, my father certainly would have nailed up the sash-window for good an' all;—which, considering with what difficulty he composed books,—he might have done with ten times less trouble, than he could have wrote the chapter: this argument I foresee holds good against his writing a chapter, even after the event; but 'tis obviated under the second reason, which I have the honor to offer to the world in support of my opinion, that my father did not write the chapter upon sash-windows and chamber-pots, at the time supposed,—and it is this.
>
> —That, in order to render the *Tristra-paedia* complete,—I wrote the chapter myself. (V, 26)

I have no intention of making a complete analysis of Sterne's novel because I am not interested in it but in plot theory. A few words now concerning the profusion of quotations. Of course, it is possible to delve more deeply into the quoted materials, since no device appears in its pure form, but this would have made of my work an interlinear commentary of grammatical observations. Such a method of analysis would have smothered the material, making it difficult for the reader to see it.

I had to follow in my analysis the course of the novel in order to show its lack of "consecutiveness." The novel's characteristic trait is precisely the unusualness of the pattern of deployment often even of its typical elements.

In conclusion and as proof of the self-consciousness of Sterne's work —the method of slowing down, the disruption of the normal plot scheme —I reproduce his own graphic depiction of the progression of Tristram Shandy's story.

> I am now beginning to get fairly into my work; and by the help of a vegetable diet, with a few of the cold seeds, I make no doubt but I shall be able to go on with my uncle *Toby*'s story and my own in a tolerable straight line. Now,

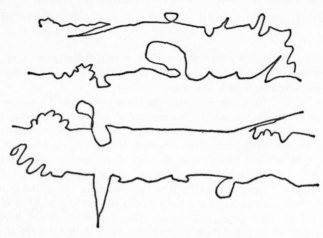

These were the four lines I moved in through my first, second, third, and fourth volumes.—In the fifth volume I have been very good,—the precise line I have described in it being this:

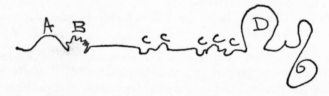

By which it appears, that except at the curve, marked A, where I took a trip to Navarre,—and the indented curve B, which is the short airing when I was there with the Lady *Baussiere* and her page—I have not taken the least frisk of a digression, till *John de la Casse*'s devils led me the round you see marked D—for as for *c c c c c* they are nothing but parentheses, and the common *ins* and *outs* incident to the lives of the greatest ministers of state; and when compared with what men have done,—or with my own transgressions at the letters A B D—they vanish into nothing. (VI, 40)

Sterne's charts are approximately accurate, but they do not take into account the interruptions of motifs. The concept of plot is too frequently confused with the description of events—with that which I suggest that we call *story*. Actually the story is only the material to be shaped by plot.

Art forms are to be explained in terms of the laws of their artistic orientation and not in terms of their motivation to exhibit a mode of life. By delaying the action of a novel without an introduction of disrupting motifs, for example, but through a simple transposition of its parts, the artist shows us the aesthetic laws which lie behind both compositional devices.

It is commonly insisted that *Tristram Shandy* is not a novel; those who say this maintain that only an opera is music and a symphony is a disorder.

Tristram Shandy is the most typical novel of world literature.

The Revolt of Sterne

by A. A. Mendilow

It was clearly high time to do again for the English novel what Furetière and the other realists had done so effectively for the French: to flout the conventions of plotting, with its special and arbitrary requirements of the beginning, middle, and end; of the chronological sequence of action which denied artistic form altogether, of the principle of causality, which involved rigid selection and economy of incident in the interests of an artificial patterning of the action. Sterne was very deeply interested in the problems these conventions raise, namely the relationship between reality and fictional illusion. Above all, he wished to arouse his readers to the realization that these *are* conventions, that they should not be taken for reality, not even for valid symbols, let alone transcripts of reality, that, as Thomas Warton wrote of the early romances, "reality is disguised by the misrepresentations of invention." [1] At the very outset he had determined not to confine himself "to any man's rules that ever lived," and more truly than Fielding he could claim the right to say:

> I shall not look on myself as accountable to any court of jurisdiction whatever; for as I am, in reality, the founder of a new province of writing, so I am at liberty to make what laws I please therein.[2]

The great aim of Sterne was to give as true a picture as possible of real human beings as they are in themselves, not as they imagine themselves to be, nor as others judge them to be by their actions and outward behavior alone. This meant the shifting of emphasis from the external to the internal event, from the patterned plot artificially conceived and imposed on the characters, to the free evocation of the fluid, ever-changing process of being. It also brought him face to face with the problem of the limitations of language to convey all this; he had to investigate the ways

"The Revolt of Sterne" by A. A. Mendilow. From *Time and the Novel* (London: Peter Nevill, Ltd., 1952; New York: Humanities Press, Inc., 1965), pp. 158-99. Copyright © 1952 by A. A. Mendilow. Reprinted by permission of the author. Notes have been shortened or dropped without notice.

[1] *History of English Poetry, 1774-81*, Sect. III.
[2] *Tom Jones*, II, 1.

by which a sequential medium could be manipulated to express simultaneity and the flow of human consciousness.

Though the idea of trying to indicate the inner as distinct from the outer man reached the fullest expression in Sterne, it was of course far from new in fiction, as, in their way, the "romans de longue haleine" and the novels of Richardson had shown. The claims of the two diametrically opposed schools of writing were put very clearly and forcefully, both in practice and theory. The followers of the French anti-Romance realists sided with the view of Fielding that:

> The only ways by which we can come at any knowledge of what passes in the Minds of others, are their words and Actions; the latter of which hath by the wiser Part of Mankind been chiefly depended on, as the surer and more infallible Guide.[3]

His sister, on the other hand, discussing Virgil's use of plot, declared that

> when we stop at those outward Circumstances, and perceive not the further Intention, we read as children see Tragedies, who place their chief Delight in the Noise of the Kettle-drums and Trumpets;[4]

and again in another of her critical prefaces:

> The motives to actions, and the inward turns of the mind, seem in our opinion more necessary to be known than the actions themselves; and much rather would we chuse that our readers should clearly understand what our principal actors think, than what they do.[5]

Mary Mitford was even more explicit:

> With regard to novels, I should like to see one undertaken without any plot at all . . . without any preconceived design further than one or two incidents and dialogues, which would naturally suggest fresh matter, and so proceed in this way, throwing in incident and characters profusely, but avoiding all stage tricks and strong situations. . . .[6]

Sterne's awareness of the degree to which the accepted conventions limited the expression of this greater inwardness in fiction, and of the discrepancy between reality and fictional illusion is what makes him so strikingly akin to modern novelists.

> The excellencies of Sterne [said Coleridge] consist in bringing forward into distinct consciousness those minutiae of thought and feeling which appear

[3] *Champion,* December 11, 1739.
[4] Preface to *History of the Countess of Dellwyn,* 1759.
[5] Preface to *The Cry,* 1754, written in collaboration with Miss J. Collier.
[6] Letter to Sir William Elford, May 13, 1815. *Letters of Mary Russell Mitford,* ed. Brimley Johnson.

trifles, yet have an importance for the moment, and which almost every man feels in one way or other.[7]

When an author is trying to give an impression of a character, not in terms of a melodic progression of actions or descriptions, but as "a system of harmonic vibrations," to use a phrase of Sterne himself;[8] when he becomes involved in those levels of the mind that lie below the rationalizing, conscious plane of being, he is drawn into many new linguistic and literary problems. He must try to devise novel techniques and conventions to convey the illusion of simultaneity in spite of a consecutive medium, and to find some way of equating the mind's flickerings backward and forward in time with the forward movement of language. He must somehow overcome the effect of discreteness made by words which chop up into separate units the indivisible flow of experience. He must consider whether he should not substitute a loose rhythm for the tight metre of the close plot which tries to force into a pattern that which is not amenable to any such conventions of structure and time.

> Life does not . . . present that combined plot, (the object of every skillful novelist), in which all the more interesting individuals of the *dramatis personae* have their appropriate share in the action and in bringing about the catastrophe. Here, even more than in its various and violent changes of fortune, rests the improbability of the novel.[9]

The innovations by virtue of which Sterne merits in a double sense the title of "first of the moderns" were not the outcome of mere chance; they were not struck out by the author in ignorance of what he was about. It is only on a cursory reading that *Tristram Shandy* gives the impression of being haphazardly constructed. In fact it is built to a very deliberate plan worked out in detail by a writer who was aware of the technical possibilities of the novel and was consciously experimenting in new principles and conventions. The validity of his approach is shown by the fact that the modern novel has followed the path he blazed rather than in the footsteps of his sedater contemporaries. Like Sterne, the writer of today is preoccupied with the problems of time in fiction; what the associationist psychology of Locke with its corollary of the "time-shift" technique was to the one, Bergson's *durée* and theory of intuition is to the other. Alike, they have been led to challenge the formal princi-

---

[7] Lecture on *The Nature and Constituents of Humour*, etc. *Literary Remains* (1836), I, 142.

[8] Letter to Mrs. Vesey, June 1761.

[9] Review of Jane Austen's *Emma*, published December 1815, in the *Quarterly Review*, October 1815.

ples of narration based on the sequential relating of successive events. Alike, they have abandoned the close and closed pattern of the plot imposed on the novel by the principle of limited selection, a principle determined by tradition rather than by the desire to get closer to the truth of life. Alike, they have tried to develop a less arbitrary kind of selection on a qualitative rather than quantitative basis, chosen for its power to convey an illusion of reality, rather than for artistic shapeliness or adequacy to prove or illustrate some thesis. In particular, they are concerned with psychological time and duration rather than with chronological time and separated moments. They aim at conveying the effect of an all-pervading present of which past and future are part, in preference to an orderly progression in time of separated discontinuous events.

Although Sterne flouts the principle of chronological succession in fiction so flagrantly, he astonishes us by the accuracy with which the dates, scattered as they are in scores of so-called "digressions," are nevertheless made to cohere. In the usual single-thread and parallel plots moving forward in a straight line, this would not be remarkable. The adherence to the rule of sequential narration is sufficient to place events in their relative temporal positions, and any calendar dating that may be required is comparatively simple. Even where an expository passage is intercalated, the difficulties are not great, for such exposition is presented in a single block which is in direct temporal relation to the main forward-moving issue. Where however the principle of time-shift based on the free association of ideas is followed, the relative positions in time of events is not easy to determine; and where, as in *Tristram Shandy,* the "digressions" are so numerous and so short and are themselves so often broken up by yet further digressions, and furthermore where the fictional time of the novel covers so long a period (on the shortest reckoning three quarters of a century), and where the scope of action is so elastic and the characters and incidents so varied, to maintain and control the chronology consistently is a feat reminiscent of a juggler keeping a large number of balls in the air at the same time. Not the smallest incident but its date is given or can be deduced or, at the very least, can be fitted into its chronological order: Aunt Dinah's lapse with the coachman (1699), the imprisonment of Trim's brother by the Inquisition (1704), the death of Le Fever (1706), the cow breaking into my Uncle Toby's fortifications (1718), the marriage of Obadiah (1712) and the birth of his first child (1713), the death of Yorick (1749). There is scarcely an incident, no matter how slight, no matter where it occurs in the book, no matter how often it is interrupted and taken up again, but falls into its correct place in time in relation to every other incident. Slips in dating are very rare, one or two at most.

Many of these incidents, especially those relating to Uncle Toby, can be checked against historical events. Every piece in the jigsaw puzzle is found to fit into its place. This is itself evidence against unplanned writing, demanding as it must have done an intricate system of cross-references. We know that Sterne was a careful and deliberate writer who constantly worked over his manuscripts time and again until they finally satisfied his fastidious taste and judgment.

Noteworthy, too, is the naturalness with which this chronological dating is worked into the substance of the novel. The times are not paraded but are slipped in quite casually in the course of other matters. They are often revealed, not by the specific mention of a date, but as taking place at some certain time before or after some other event the date of which can perhaps be deduced from a chance reference to some historical event. The remarkable thing is that all these times and dates fall in their correct places when checked against each other. They do so because, instead of being presented, as it were, outside the characters, as a background against which these characters are plotted, they form part of their consciousness and emotional experience, and are in consequence readily called to mind, naturally and without effort, through the working of association.

What interests Sterne much more than chronological dating however is the discrepancy between duration in terms of chronological and psychological time. His main interest lies in the states of mind and the character of the protagonists rather than in their actions, in what they are and think and feel, not so much in what they do. The true duration therefore is subjective, measured by values, not by the clock; it consequently varies in length with each individual, having regard to the circumstances and frame of mind in which he happens to be. The external, objective, unvarying duration as measured by the pendulum has little place in the novel, except as presenting a contrast to psychological duration, for it has in itself no validity in the sphere of feeling and thinking. This is the principle which Sterne owed as he told Suard,

> à l'étude de Locke, qu'il avait faite au sortir de l'enfance, et qu'il refit toute sa vie. . . .[10]

This principle he was the first to apply deliberately to fiction:

> It is about an hour and a half's tolerable good reading since my Uncle Toby rang the bell, when Obadiah was ordered to saddle a horse, and go for Dr. Slop, the man-midwife;—so that no one can say, with reason, that I have not allowed Obadiah time enough, poetically speaking, and considering the

[10] *Mémoires Historiques sur le XVIII siècle, et sur M. Suard,* par Dominique-Joseph Garat, 2nd ed. (1821), II, 149.

emergency too, both to go and come:—though, morally and truly speaking, the man perhaps has scarce had time to get on his boots. If the hypercritic will go upon this; and is resolved after all to take a pendulum, and measure the true distance betwixt the ringing of the bell, and the rap at the door;—and, after finding it to be no more than two minutes, thirteen seconds, and three fifths,—should take upon himself to insult over me for such a breach in the unity, or rather probability of time;—I would remind him, that the idea of duration, and of its simple modes, is got merely from the train and succession of our ideas,—and is the true scholastic pendulum,—and by which, as a scholar, I will be tried in this matter—abjuring and detesting the jurisdiction of all other pendulums whatever.

I would therefore desire him to consider that it is but a poor eight miles from Shandy Hall to Dr. Slop, the man-midwife's house;—and that whilst Obadiah has been going those said miles and back, I have brought my Uncle Toby from Namur, quite across all Flanders, into England:—That I have had him ill upon my hands near four years:—and have since travelled him and Corporal Trim in a chariot-and-four, a journey of near two hundred miles down into Yorkshire—all which put together, must have prepared the reader's imagination for the entrance of Dr. Slop upon the stage, —as much, at least (I hope) as a dance, a song, or a concerto between the acts. (II, 8)

In this passage, Sterne is, as elsewhere in *Tristram Shandy,* playing on the several different kinds of time that operate in the novel. Firstly, he jocularly correlates the time taken by the reader to read, with the time that the events related in the novel take to happen. This chronological measurement of the act of reading is furthermore effectively contrasted with the reader's sense of the passage of time; that is, his psychological time as judged by values as distinct from the other measured by scales outside him. These questions naturally involve the technique of narration which to be effective must reduce any sense of discrepancy between the different kinds of time and so give an illusion of reality and truth.

But Sterne is concerned with the distinction between chronological and psychological duration not only as it affects the reader. He is equally interested in the relationship between the two as experienced by the characters themselves, and as it affects *their* sense of the passage of time.

It is two hours and ten minutes—and no more—cried my father looking at his watch, since Dr. Slop and Obadiah arrived,—and I know not how it happens, brother Toby—but to my imagination it seems almost an age. . . . Though my father said, "he knew not how it happened,"—yet he knew very well how it happened;—and at the instance he spoke it, was pre-determined in his mind to give my Uncle Toby a clear account of the matter by a meta-physical dissertation upon the subject of duration and its simple modes, in order to show my Uncle Toby by what mechanism and mensurations in the brain it came to pass, that the rapid succession of their ideas, and the eternal scampering of the discourse from one thing to another, since Dr. Slop had come into the room, had lengthened out so short a period to so inconceivable an extent.—"I know not how it happens—cried my father,—but it seems an age."—'Tis owing entirely, quoth my Uncle Toby, to the succession of our ideas. [Walter Shandy continues a little later]: To understand what time is aright, without which we never can comprehend infinity, insomuch as one is a portion of the other—we ought seriously to sit down and consider what idea it is we have of duration, so as to give a satisfactory account how we came by it.—What is that to anybody? quoth my Uncle Toby. For if you will turn your eyes inwards upon your mind, continued my father, and observe attentively, you will perceive, brother, that whilst you and I are talking together, and thinking, and smoking our pipes, or whilst we receive successively ideas in our minds; we know that we do exist, and so estimate the existence, or the continuation of the existence of ourselves, or anything else, commensurate to the succession of any ideas in our minds, or any such other thing coexisting with our thinking—and so according to that preconceived—You puzzle me to death, cried my Uncle Toby.—'Tis owing to this, replied my father, that in our computations of time, we are so used to minutes, hours, weeks, and months—and of clocks (I wish there was not a clock in the kingdom) to measure out their several portions to us, and to those who belong to us—that 'twill be well, if in time to come, the succession of our ideas will be of any use or service to us at all. Now, whether we observe it or no, continued my father, in every sound man's head there is a regular succession of ideas of one sort or other, which follow each other in train. . . . (III, 18)

This exploitation of the principle of psychological duration allows Sterne to vary his tempo by expanding or telescoping the time by the clock to accord with the artistic effect he is concerned with producing. In an early fragment Sterne wrote

Glasses can make an inch seem a mile. I leave it to future ages to invent a method for making a *minute* seem a *year*.

In *Tristram Shandy* he was to invent the method himself. By playing the different values of psychological and chronological time against each other, and by emphasizing the difference between them, he can at will convey a sense of urgency and hurry, or of relaxation, waiting and suspense.

Judged chronologically, *Tristram Shandy* has neither beginning, middle, nor end.

The novel starts in the year 1718 and ends in the year 1713, and in the interim goes as far forward as 1766 and backward to the time of

Henry VIII. It is built up of a large number of interwoven and inter-related episodes, of "digressions" as critics commonly call them. The term is inapt. "Digression" implies a minor divagation from what is discernible in the novel as the strict line of forward moving narration. Where a book begins with some "constituted scene" or "discriminated occasion" [11] which forms the first of a consecutive series leading to some fixed time-point, strictly speaking, any chronological departure from the series, such as retrospective or anticipatory flashes or inserted exposition, constitutes a digression. Such a novel is to be distinguished from that where more than one thread of action is followed; there the alternated transfer of interest from one to another of a parallel series is inevitable, and provides the chief means of arousing suspense. In pattern-plots based on causality, any departure from the main issue by the introduction of episodes such as do not contribute to the catastrophe may likewise be held to be digressive. Richardson proudly claimed in his preface to *Sir Charles Grandison* that

> There is not one episode in the whole . . . but what tends to illustrate the principal design.

The ideal for this kind of plot had been concisely put by Addison who said of the epic:

> . . . nothing should go before it, be intermix'd with it, or follow after it, that is not related to it.[12]

In the thesis novel, elements irrelevant to the central idea or not contributing to the general view of life which it is the author's intention to expound, constitute digressions. In every case, digressions must digress —whether from some clearly defined pattern, purpose, or line of action. They could be dispensed with and leave no vital break or flaw in the main structure. A novel cannot consist of nothing but digressions. But in *Tristram Shandy* there is no forward-moving line or architechtonic plot from which to digress. There is no point of departure from which the line could start, for Sterne realizes that, as Mme. de Staël observed:

> Human life exhibits but a series of commencements, in which no precise line or limit is discernible.[13]

Like the school of writers hit off by Butler, Sterne can therefore

---

[11] Henry James's terms for a scene presented dramatically as "present."

[12] *Spectator*, January 5, 1712. The theory, deriving from Le Bossu, is expounded more fully by Blackmore: *Preface to Prince Arthur*, 1695.

[13] *Essay on Fictions*, prefaced to *Zulma*, English trans. 1813, Vol. I, p. 9.

Make former times shake hands with latter,
And that which was before come after.

He moves at will backward and forward in time without regard for
chronological logic, and whatever temporal point he deals with, he
treats as a constituted scene in its own right, that is, as a dramatic
present, and not as past or future relative to some major event in the
story.

In his description of his method as working forward and backward
along the line of his story,[14] Sterne is misled into using the word "line"
by the common practice of limiting the narration to one or more main
characters followed chronologically along single or parallel lines from
one period to another. An apter description of his method might be to
say that he worked in stipple on a broad canvas. Proust adopted what
is essentially the same method, save that he expanded the episodes or
"discriminated occasions" into large time-blocks to which he devoted—
it might be a whole section or even an entire volume. His scenes, like
those of Sterne, are presented in temporal sequence but are linked by the
association of ideas and lengthened or shortened (usually lengthened) by
being conceived in terms of psychological duration. Nor are any of his
episodes digressive. In both, the picture grows, not part by part but as a
whole, into an indivisible unity out of the multitude of scattered strokes
of the brush distributed in no fixed order; these strokes finally are seen to
cohere and blend into a single, wider whole. This whole can only be
guessed at in *Tristram Shandy,* which is incomplete and therefore appears
fragmentary; had Sterne lived to finish his book, and as he carefully
proves to himself with the aid of mathematics it could never be finished
(IV, 13), it might theoretically be possible at the end to piece out a full
picture of the Shandy *ménage,* possibly even including the hero himself.

By breaking up the story and every little episode and scene in it into
small disjointed fragments presented, chronologically speaking, in pell-
mell disorder, Sterne has evolved a technique that allows of several
different effects at once. He can trace the fleeting impressions and associations that float in the minds of characters, including Tristram himself
as a quasi-autobiographer during the act of writing. He can bring an
effect into high relief by artfully relating it to some other contrasting
effect. He can build up a climax by an accumulation of several incidents,
or create a single emotional impression by bringing together elements
selected from many stages in the life-story of the various characters. He
can give rein to his fancy for the ludicrous, or create suspense by break-

---

[14] "Provided he keeps along the line of his story,—he may go backwards and forwards
as he will,—'tis still held to be no digression" (V, 25).

ing off at some crucial moment and switching over to some other incident. He can also give the equivalent of empty spaces, intervals of waiting and *longueurs* by his "digressions."

Sterne shows himself an adept at expanding the moment and contracting the years at his pleasure. Especially, he can create an impression of all the parts of the story proceeding simultaneously, each at its own pace and in its own direction.

> When a man is telling a story in the strange way I do mine, he is obliged continually to be going backwards and forwards to keep all tight together in the reader's fancy. (VI, 33)

Removal or transposition of the episodes in *Tristram Shandy* would leave gaps in the picture or snap the delicate links which bind part to part, for every episode has its right context from which it cannot be wrenched. Not only does he achieve effects of simultaneity when dealing with events that are going on at the same time, but he even telescopes together the two journeys Tristram made to Auxerre, one as a young man with his father and uncle, the other in search of health some twenty years later, bringing himself up with the rueful comment:

> I have been getting forward in two different journeys together, and with the same dash of the pen—for I have got entirely out of Auxerre in this journey which I am writing now, and am got halfway out of Auxerre in that which I shall write hereafter—There is but a certain degree of perfection in every thing; and by pushing at something beyond that, I have brought myself into such a situation, as no traveller ever stood before me; for I am this moment walking across the market-place of Auxerre with my father and my uncle Toby, in our way back to dinner—and I am this moment also entering Lyons with my post-chaise broke into a thousand pieces—and I am moreover this moment in a handsome pavilion built by Pringello, upon the banks of the Garonne, which Mons. Sligniac has lent me, and where I now sit rhapsodizing all these affairs. (VII, 28)

Sterne is, in this passage, hinting at the fundamental limitation of language as a symbolic medium for expressing experience; the inevitable conflict that must arise when a consecutive "horizontal" time-form is used to express simultaneity of impression and the "vertical" sense of the process of living. In this and similar passages, he can give cross-sections of life at one moment at different places and with different people, or open up long temporal perspectives of one character, or telescope the temporal perspectives of several characters into one overwhelming present in which all of them are, at the same time and for each of their individual times, whether past, present, or future, in relation to one another, simultaneously involved. Every part is a dramatic present. As he puts it, this technique saves him dramatically, even if it damns him biographically (II, 8).

Not only is the novel as a whole constructed without regard for chronological beginning, middle, and end. Even the digressions, or more truly, the episodes related by the device of the time-shift, share the same characteristic, and jump back and forth and interweave in the most surprising fashion. Thus Walter Shandy's prostration on learning of the mishap to the bridge of his newly born's nose is interrupted by the contretemps over the jointure between Tristram's great-grandfather and his wife. This in turn is broken into by Tristram's defeat of Eusebius's intention to define the word "crevice," and so goes back naturally to his grandparents and his father and their feelings in the matter of paying the same jointure to the long-lived great-grandmother, with a short discussion on heredity. Into all this enters the dispute between Tristram, Didius, and Tribonius on the question of proprietary rights in the opinions of others, and so by way of Slawkenbergius on noses back to Walter Shandy's prostration (III, 29 to IV, 2).

Sterne was fully conscious of what he was about. He goes out of his way to meet objections to the technique he has evolved, and insists that there is a method in his seeming madness, and that definite principles of composition underlie his apparent vagaries. He commends himself on "a master-stroke of digressive skill," namely that

> tho' my digressions are all fair, as you observe—and that I fly off from what I am about, as far, and as often too, as any writer in Great-Britain; yet I constantly take care to order affairs so that my main business does not stand still in my absence.
>
> I was just going, for example, to have given you the great outlines of my uncle Toby's most whimsical character;—when my aunt Dinah and the coachman came across us, and led us a vagary some millions of miles into the very heart of the planetary system: Notwithstanding all this, you perceive that the drawing of my uncle Toby's character went on gently all the time;—not the great contours of it,—that was impossible,—but some familiar strokes and faint designations of it, were here and there touched on, as we went along, so that you are much better acquainted with my uncle Toby now than you was before.
>
> By this contrivance, the machinery of my work is of a species by itself; the two contrary motions are introduced into it, and reconciled, which were thought to be at variance with each other. In a word, my work is digressive, and it is progressive too,—and at the same time. . . .
>
> Digressions, incontestably, are the sunshine;—they are the life, the soul

of reading!—take them out of this book, for instance,—you might as well take the book along with them. . . .

All the dexterity is in the good cookery and management of them, so as to be not only for advantage of the reader, but also of the author, whose distress, in the matter, is truly pitiable: For, if he begins a digression,— from that moment, I observe, his whole work stands stock still:—and if he goes on with his main work,—then there is an end of his digression.

This is vile work.—For which reason, from the beginning of this, you see, I have constructed the main work and the adventitious parts of it with such intersections, and have so complicated and involved the digressive and progressive movements, one wheel within another, that the whole machine, in general, has been kept a-going. (I, 22)

The difficulty lies in understanding what Sterne means by his "main work." He is paying lip-service to his title: *The Life and Opinions of Tristram Shandy, Gentleman.* It has been pointed out that the life is largely that of Uncle Toby, and the opinions those of Walter Shandy; and Tristram is no gentleman in the modern sense of the word. Were his book what the title proclaims it to be, Uncle Toby's character would itself constitute a digression. Fortunately it is not a life of Tristram Shandy, and Uncle Toby and Aunt Dinah are not digressions, but take their place in the book in their own right. The greatness of Sterne lies precisely in this, that the different characters in it are not incidental to any hero. He gives roundness to every figure, implying that each one is, for himself the center of his own little world, and that each little world is relevant to the whole book. All these spheres, we feel, whether they are fully treated or no, exist. They intersect, forming segments of varying sizes common to each other. The main characters do not, as in many novels, live in a vacuum, isolated from everyone and everything that does not directly contribute to their progression toward some crucial point in their lives. Many apparently pointless digressions will be found to strengthen this effect of everyone living in himself at the same time and following his own path, irrespective of the part he may be playing in any major episode. Modern novelists aim at the same effect in their use of "breadthwise cutting"—temporal cross-sections of a group of people or even of a whole section of society. Sterne's method is the forerunner of the polyphonic technique, as contrasted with the melodic and harmonic techniques of his contemporaries, a system further elaborated in the contrapuntal experiments of de Quincey, Conrad, Joyce, Gide, Huxley, and others.

The episodes in *Tristram Shandy* fall into two main categories. Those linked to one another by the association of ideas in the minds of the characters, and those linked in the mind of the quasi-autobiographer himself. These so-called digressions contribute to the use by Sterne of the device of time-shift a century and a half before Conrad and Madox Ford adopted it as a principle of composition under the name of impressionism.

> We agree [writes Ford] that the general effect of a novel must be the general effect that life makes on mankind. A novel must therefore not be a narration, a report. Life does not say to you: In 1914, my next door neighbour, Mr. Slack, erected a green-house and painted it with Cox's green aluminum paint . . .

Here follows a short series of incidents in strict chronological sequence.

> If you think about the matter you will remember, in various unordered pictures, how one day Mr. Slack appeared in his garden and contemplated the wall of his house. You will then try to remember the year of that occurrence and you will fix it as August 1914 because having had the foresight to bear the municipal stock of the city of Liège you were able to afford a 1st class season ticket for the first time in your life. You will remember Mr. Slack—then much thinner because it was before he found out . . . etc.

He continues in this strain, bringing in a large part of his life in the process of describing Mr. Slack's greenhouse. He maintains therefore that the interrupted method of the time-shift is invaluable for giving a sense of the complexity that is life.

> In the pre-war period the English novel began at the beginning of a hero's life and went straight on to his marriage without pausing to look aside . . . such a story was too confined to its characters and too self-centeredly went on, *in vacuo*. If you are so set on the affair of your daughter Millicent with the young actor that you forget that there *are* flower shows and town halls with nude statuary your intellect will appear a thing much more circumscribed than it should be.[15]

He claims elsewhere that

> that technique is identical with that of all modern novelists, or of myself . . . or Proust.[16]

He might have added—or of Sterne.

One essential feature of the time-shift technique is that the author does not describe or summarize for the reader events occurring in the

---

[15] Ford Madox Ford, *Joseph Conrad, a Personal Remembrance* (1924), pp. 191-92.
[16] Ford Madox Ford, *It was the Nightingale* (1934), p. 194.

intervals between constituted scenes. Knowledge of the relative position in time of the scenes is pieced together from internal evidence within them. No matter how interrupted or broken up an episode may be by inserted or intervening events, between the breaks there must be no author's links such as summaries, temporal explanations, or expositions. This is the method used by Sterne in *Tristram Shandy*. With rare exceptions, every full action is presented directly as happening; nothing is reported as having happened. The impression is of direct as opposed to reported action and speech, and the extensive use of dialogue strengthens this effect of dramatic present. The book consists almost exclusively of constituted scenes and discriminated occasions, presented without introduction or reference to their calendar relation to preceding or succeeding scenes. This is the true time-shift, and it emphasizes the effect of every part as a present, not as relatively past or future.

The result is that there are no fixed time-points to which episodes bear reference, no beginning from which everything proceeds sequentially and to which events are relative in time. The nearest approach to such a time-point is the birth of Tristram, given as the fifth day of November, 1718 (I, 5).

> It is from this point [the death of my brother Bobby that occurred actually a few weeks later] properly that, the story of my Life and my Opinions sets out,

he says at the end of the fourth volume. But the bulk of the book deals with events that took place long before this date, events that are not presented in the form of exposition but on their own merits as deserving a place equal to any others. On one other occasion, while dealing with Uncle Toby's amours, he writes that the armistice between Uncle Toby and the merry widow lasted till

> about six or seven weeks before the time I'm speaking of. (I, 32)

This refers likewise to Tristram's birth, the date of which was given about 180 pages earlier. On the next occasion when he mentions the date of the hero's birth, from which, in the regular novel, the fictional time of the action might be conceived to start, it is to mock at the whole convention of sequential narration:

> A cow broke in (tomorrow morning) to my uncle Toby's fortifications. . . .
> Trim insists on being tried by a court-martial. (III, 38)

Where every episode is presented as in a dramatic present, there can, strictly speaking, be no anticipatory passages or passages of exposition,

for there is no fixed line from which to divagate. Such passages when
they occur are retrospective or anticipatory only in relation to the time
of one incident, and the events the author looks forward to may have
been narrated already. Future and past are not future and past in time
but before and after in order of narration, which is a very different
matter. Thus, when in the course of recounting the circumstances surrounding the birth of the hero in 1718, Sterne promises an account of
the love affairs of Uncle Toby, it is a promise to tell of something that
occurred in 1713.

It is noteworthy that Sterne frequently gives the exact dates on which
he is engaged in narrating various episodes, that is, his own real time or,
if you will, the real time of the pseudo-autobiographer at the time of
writing. Attendant details relating to that real time are added—Jenny's
purchases, his cough, his surroundings, and so on. Sterne makes great
play with the contrast between the real time and the fictional time of
the events he is recording. The act of writing is chronologically consecutive, whereas the fictional time shifts constantly as he focuses his attention
onto some or other point in the whole of his past spread out at once
before him. This past grows as his real present moves forward, and this
presents him with the following dilemma:

> I am this month one whole year older than I was this time twelve-month;
> and having got, as you perceive, almost into the middle of my fourth volume
> —and no farther than to my first day's life—'tis demonstrative that I have
> three hundred and sixty-four days more life to write just now, than when
> I first set out; so that instead of advancing, as a common writer, in my work
> with what I have been doing at it—on the contrary, I am just thrown so
> many volumes back—was every day of my life to be so busy a day as this
> —And why not?—and the transactions and opinions of it to take up as
> much description—And for what reason should they be cut short? as at this
> rate I should just live 364 times faster than I should write—It must follow,
> an' please your worships, that the more I write the more I shall have to
> write . . . was it not that my Opinions will be the death of me, I perceive
> I shall lead a fine life of it out of this selfsame life of mine; or, in other
> words, shall lead a couple of fine lives together. (IV, 13)

A similar quandary confronts Walter Shandy as he writes his system
of education for his son:

> This is the best account I am determined to give of the slow progress my
> father made in his *Trista-paedia;* at which (as I said) he was three years, and
> something more, indefatigably at work, and, at last, had scarce completed,
> by his own reckoning, one half of his undertaking: the misfortune was, that
> I was all the time totally neglected and abandoned to my mother; and what

was almost as bad, the very delay, the first part of the work, upon which my father had spent the most of his pains, was rendered entirely useless,—every day a page or two became of no consequence. (V, 16)

Fictional and real time are continually brought into the closest relation, and the shifting points of reference in the narration are further complicated by the shifting points of reference in the real time of the narrator. The real and fictive presents are thus amusingly contrasted.

The frequent references in *Tristram Shandy* to the real time of the narrator are not evidence of the intrusive author such as leads to a division of interest between the author in his own person and his characters.

> . . . perhaps there is not a better Criterion of the merit of a book, than our losing sight of the author.

Such references to the writer's present are justifiable in a first-person novel, for the autobiographer is himself within the framework. What is fully permissible in *Henry Esmond* constitutes a blemish in *Vanity Fair* where it jars the reader out of the fictional time in which he is immersed back into the real time in which he is engaged in the act of reading. In *Tristram Shandy* the interpretations of events and the analyses of the character of Walter Shandy, Uncle Toby, Trim, and the rest come, not as from outside the novel, but to illustrate the character and opinions of Tristram who, as autobiographer, is himself a character in the novel. *Tristram Shandy*, it is true, is more biography than autobiography, but that may in a large part be attributed to its being a fragment and not a complete whole. The observations of Tristram are as much in place as those of Captain Marlowe and the other observers in Conrad's novels, where the device of refraction through intervening minds forms the basis of a highly complex technique.

It must be admitted, however, that Sterne, unlike Conrad, does stretch the truth considerably in making Tristram describe what he did not witness and could not possibly have learned from other sources. In spite of his protests, it

> render[s] my book from this very moment, a professed Romance, which, before, was a book apocryphal. (II, 8)

At first Sterne did try to give some degree of verisimilitude to his cognizance of such events as the contretemps between Walter Shandy and his wife at the begetting of Tristram

> in the night, betwixt the first Sunday and the first Monday in the month of March, in the year of our Lord 1718. (I, 4)

In this case, he gives his source of information:

> To my uncle Mr. Toby Shandy do I stand indebted for the preceding
> anecdote, to whom my father . . . had oft, and heavily complained of the
> injury. (I, 3)

Later, however, he abandons all pretence of coming by his information
as limiting his powers too seriously, and with unclipped wings he soars
into the convention of the omniscient author, a convention artificial in
itself and accepted as compatible only with the third-person novel. Sterne
might have learned from his predecessor Richardson how punctilious
the autobiographical novel could and perhaps should be in such matters,
but *Tristram Shandy* would have been fatally circumscribed and fettered
by the lesson.

Just as the comments of Tristram are not extraneous to the book and
are not therefore to be taken as from an intrusive author, the short
stories inset into the novel are not of the excrescent kind such as mar,
technically speaking, the form of so many earlier and later novels. The
tale of Le Fever or Trim's unfinished story of the King of Bohemia are
part of the fabric of the main narrative into which they are inserted.
Their removal would leave an irreplaceable gap in the structure. They
throw light, and are indeed the best comment on the character of Trim
and Uncle Toby; even Slawkenbergius's tale of the noses has the effect
of strengthening the impression of Walter Shandy's intellectual foibles,
and confirming a central *double entendre*.

These tales offer interesting examples of the technique of "Chinese
boxes." Sterne writes a book about Tristram Shandy writing his life
in which he, in the year 1760, relates how Trim in 1723 tells the story
of Le Fever's death in 1706; or how Walter Shandy translated for the
benefit of his brother the work of Slawkenbergius on noses in the course
of which there is given the story of Julia and Diego. One is reminded
of Gide writing a novel, *Les Faux-Monnayeurs,* about a novelist, Edouard,
who is writing a novel called *Les Faux-Monnayeurs* about a novelist
who is writing a novel the title of which, mercifully, we are not given, but
which perhaps we can guess.

Sterne was one of the earliest writers to realize that literature is one
of the time arts, and is therefore limited by the very nature of its medium,
language. The writing of a novel involves, in consequence, a number of
temporal factors and conventions which can be exploited in various
ways. Little wonder that Diderot, whose article on "Composition" for the
Encyclopédie furnished many of the ideas of Lessing's "Laocoön," was
so deeply impressed and influenced by Sterne; little wonder that Lessing

himself, the critic who first adequately analyzed the essential differences between the space and time arts, proclaimed that he would have given ten years of his own life to prolong Sterne's by one. Mrs. Montague wrote that Sterne "really believes his book to be the finest thing the age has produced." He was perhaps not so far out in his belief. Not till modern times do we find so intelligent an attempt to consider the aesthetic and philosophic implications of the novel. Not till Gide and Proust and James and Joyce and Virginia Woolf is there any comparable picture in fiction of the process of living, of life caught in the very act of being. Sterne, moreover, paralleled this with his picture of himself in the process of creating his book. There is in *Tristram Shandy* a threefold development: the characters as they evolve; the author as he works out his conception; and the reader whom Sterne is educating to understand fiction aright.

"A mighty maze! but not without a plan."

One of Coleridge's many unwritten masterpieces was to be an essay

on one who lived not *in time* at all, past, present, or future,—but beside or collaterally.[17]

He forgot that Sterne had anticipated his idea in *Tristram Shandy*.

[17] *Table-Talk*, August 4, 1833.

Laurence Sterne

by *Jean-Jacques Mayoux*

Recent critics, in reaction to Thackeray's vilification of Sterne, and indeed to the collective Victorian criticism which drew a parallel between the supposed degeneracy of the style and the heart of the wicked parson (who, according to malicious stories, allowed his mother to languish in debtor's prison and whose philandering drove his wife mad) have set about explaining his obscenity as an impish wish to purge men of hypocrisy and lies and to return them to the truth of their nature. Was there in this sickly and consumptive body a healthy, robust spirit, creator of a Shandyism parallel to Pantagruelism, though undermined slyly by sentimentalism? Does the author of *Tristram Shandy*, believing truth is health, dedicate himself to rubbing the noses of his readers in their forgotten truth? Is this healthy function the deliberate aim of Sternian obscenity? Well—was it really the soul of the English reader that Sterne was thinking of when in Paris in 1762 he agreed with Crébillon to exchange good specimens of their own pornography? Is it by accident that his best friend was John Hall Stevenson, a Crébillon *manqué*? Though there was one flame after another, from Kitty Fourmantelle to Eliza Draper, it appears that none of his relations with women was really carnal. What characterizes Sterne in these relations is what was to scandalize D. H. Lawrence: sex in the head. *The Journal to Eliza* seems to me not a single aberration but only a slightly more obvious example of a general and obsessional erotomania developing from nonsatisfaction of desire. I should think that the alleged curative aspect of Sterne's obscenity is the sort of thing psychoanalysis calls "justification." How curious that critics seem to shy away from psychoanalytic consideration in the belief that literary research has nothing to gain from it when it is psychoanalysis that throws out of court such pompous ethical judgments

"Laurence Sterne" (original title: "Laurence Sterne parmi nous") by Jean-Jacques Mayoux. From *Critique: Revue générale des publications françaises et étrangères*, Vol. 18, No. 177 (February, 1962), 99-120. Copyright © 1962 by *Critique*. Reprinted by permission of the author and *Critique*. The present essay includes minor revisions of the original. Translation by John Traugott.

as those of the Victorians. For psychoanalysis tells us that a man is what he is and invites us to admire him when he turns his misery into something of worth and genius.

A recent critic, for instance, makes of the obscenity of *Tristram* a "theme," turning into intention and conscious will what is first of all an irresistible penchant of the writer. Can one easily believe that because a polemic of obstetricians had recently been going on in York, the subject of generation plays such a role in the novel? Are we to believe with some critics that because the sexual symbolism is so obvious there is nothing to look for behind it? Obviously on the face of it, there is no suppression, but in such matters suppression need not be direct or simple. Finally, one must admit, it seems, a strange oscillation in Sterne between desire and disgust. Is that not a sufficient ground of his predilection for disguised salacity—a disguise that reveals all?

His malicious joy in throwing back upon the reader's dirty mind and lubricious imagination the responsibility for the smuttiness can scarcely be seriously presented as a design to create responsible awareness, or at least, or only, to confound hypocrisy. Whatever the critics may say, an anxiety shows through those interminable histories of noses, of enormous noses, of noses crushed to nothing, of accidental circumcision which is taken for castration, of the wound in the groin that reasonably disturbs the Widow Wadman, all this coming, as it does, after Tristram's maladroit conception. All this obstinately draws attention to the difficulty of sexual coupling, at the same time that the disdain and disgust of Walter Shandy for physical love, the distaste of which the Widow Wadman is the precise object, reinforce the inhibitions and emphasize the difficulty, while buttressing them by a capricious and false appeal to traditional and orthodox values. His jesting guise and curative obscenity is only a surface manifestation of the deeper emotions represented by the obsessive recurrence of these images.

Certainly, Rabelais was a priest and a humanist and, moreover, farcical and obscene. And the pastor Sterne chose to imitate Rabelais. But it is not sufficient to say that the times had changed to the point where obscenity must have become smuttiness; rather, times had changed to the point that such an undertaking as this imitation, though still warm and generous in its disorder, could not recapture the large and surprising unity of the original and had no other expedient, in truth, than to substitute for that unity the liveliness of contradictions. This discordant aspect is as characteristic of Sterne as boldly conceived correspondences are of Rabelais. The problem that Sterne's case posed in the dry clarity of 1760 was one of compatibility: could one, while still following a religion founded on sublimation, go on to a ridicule that strips the human animal naked? Nevertheless, taking this contradiction by the horns, Sterne baptized his pastoral self with the name of Yorick the jester. Moreover, he who announces so proudly that he writes not to eat but to gain fame, as was the style of his age, profited from the vogue of *Tristram Shandy* to push the printing of his sermons so as to eat well. These superficial and adventitious circumstances which ultimately had to be reconciled in a single psyche have without doubt helped make us aware of the possibly sickly, and certainly morbid, aspects of Sterne linked to the human demands of his diseased body. Why should it be necessary to defend him from such infirmities when everything in his nature confesses, and often professes, them, when it would be simpler merely to recognize a freedom founded upon cruel necessity, the greatest glory of man?

One of the really important aspects of Sterne's work is that it opens itself constantly to the reader and invites him to take part. Of course, one need not suppose that this imaginary dialogue, so involving and so constant, always goes forward with honest openness. More often what Sterne proposes to, nay imposes upon, the reader are relations of complicity. Everything that could possibly be annoying, indeed revolting, in his language is advanced with such equivocation that it takes on body and existence only after being thought out. *"Hypocrite lecteur, mon semblable, mon frère":* with Sterne this formula has all its meaning. One reads the account of the rubbing of Trim's knee by the Béguine, rhythmic, prolonged, increased until producing a sudden ecstasy, and one realizes with astonishment that the author has invited him to witness a scene of masturbation. But doubtless the shadow of our pastor will exclaim, "Now, go along with that imagination of yours! Must you be so impure? Kindly remember that to the pure everything is pure!" For myself, I must say that this solicited participation and invitation to complicity are the mark of a curious and subtle exhibitionism, furtive and delicate, requiring of the reader-spectator that he compromise himself to the point of becoming a responsible actor. This bawdy trickery, falsely naïve and wearing the mask of innocence, thus takes on the trappings of humor, but in truth both smut and humor, for humor does require for its effect such participation—but in a concealed presence—a complicity, but with a gesture pretending unawareness. With this nonchalant insistence, humor comes back to an original subjectivity, veiled and unveiled by subtle alternations, and passes likewise from one subjectivity to the other without having taken on an objective solidity.

The difference between the smutty humor which prevails in *Tristram* and the smutty sentimentalism of the *Sentimental Journey* is essentially

the difference between an intellectual satisfaction—the idea of the thing
—and a more or less open sensuality—of glances, of hands, febrile and
feeling, those fugitive contacts which will set the traveler afire. As for
the glances, they are obviously already part of the atmosphere of *Tristram,*
particularly associated with that sentimental duo, my Uncle Toby and
Corporal Trim. The author, always teasing, becomes a voyeur, his roving
eye now on us, now on a tender scene. In the spirit of sentiment we are
invited to an imaginative complicity. The witness is necessary to the
triangulation of the sentimental scene. And the author-witness involves
the reader as witness, whether of the pathetic suffering of Le Fever, or
the generous emotion of Trim about it, or that of Toby in regard to
Trim, or that of the author concerning the gushings of the tender
marionettes he has conjured up for us.

One thus comes back by all paths to the problem of Sterne's sentimentalism. How mistaken to take this sentimentalism as an external aspect of the Shandean, as a merely fanciful variant of the Epicurean tradition. For how opposite is the self-concern accompanied by gentle benevolence, which is the character of Epicureanism, to this sentimentalism
resting on a lacuna, a doubt, a want, needing for its fulfillment a rather
artificial communion, an opening-up of a reciprocal tenderness. But if
one considers Shandyism, the buffoonery included, as a constant appeal
to this psychic reinforcement which every understanding, every connivance affords an unstable and anxious personality, then one sees that the
jesting connivance and the sentimental communion have extraordinarily
close psychological links. The sentimental tone is brought to its highest
pitch well before the last books of the work. The Yorick of the beginning
of Book I, Yorick the jesting pastor—that is, Sterne the pastor playing
the jester—is he not from that point on the symbol of the blending of
the two elements? Yorick's teasing and imprudent language allows his
enemies to misunderstand his heart and wickedly to calumniate him, so
much so that he dies of the hurt. And by this trick Sterne commiserates
with himself, weeps for his beautiful, misunderstood soul: a playful commiseration certainly, since after all he is not yet dead, but in the very
expression of it, he ends by taking himself seriously: the death of Yorick
makes a tableau in the style of Greuze—and of Diderot. In every sentimental scene, there is the necessary intercessor, the tender witness: Eugenius, tears flowing down his cheeks, "with the tenderest tone that ever
man spoke," expresses a hope to which Yorick, eyes turned up to heaven,
responds by a gentle squeeze of the hand. "That was all, but it cut
Eugenius to his heart." And in his last breath, Yorick makes a Cervantic
jest about himself. There he is at last dead and buried under the black

page with the epitaph, "Alas! poor Yorick," reminding us that if Sterne chose to identify himself with a jester, it is with a dead jester, in fact the only one of all the empty skulls that moves Hamlet. As Sterne would say, let us remember this incident: it will be of use.

Doubtless the highest pitch of the sentimentalism comes in Book VI in the episode of the death of Le Fever: here once again and more clearly, the agency of the onlookers, the grouping of the characters, the sympathy of gestures and their echo gives the scene its character. For as sadness wants solitude, so sentimentalism wants this grouping and this reciprocal witnessing. Trim with that innocence of what he says that also characterizes humor, recalls that he had a mind to cry with the son of the dying man. "What could be the matter with me," cries Trim. "Nothing in the world, but that thou art a good-natured fellow," says my Uncle Toby. And he knows what's what, and so does Sterne about these three.

Farcical, sentimental, with his affectations, his grimaces, his poses set up for the public, Sterne is deliciously rococo: he is old-fashioned, and even, one must say, in one respect out-of-date.

Nothing is more noteworthy, nor more typical in a certain phase of humanity than Sterne's sort of ambivalent outlook on culture. As soon as there is a humanism—witness Erasmus and Rabelais—there is mockery of culture generally. And we are not finished with that: Joyce and Ionesco have taken it up again. But Sterne's "anti-culture" is a different thing from ours; his is amused where ours, in the uncertainty of what we have left, is the sign of anxiety and bitterness. A science too sure of itself, a philosophy too self-satisfied, both tending to crazy system-making and showing the seed of madness that awaits as soon as one cuts himself off from living reality—this sort of thing is after all the traditional and ordinary butt of that common sense which ridicules, threatens, and represses adventure, particularly spiritual adventure. The peculiar note of Sterne here is that the seduction is felt but held at a distance, the acceptance turned into jest and game. Even more, it is the opposition, so subtle and profound, of intuitive thought, the language of the heart, to discursive reason. This friend (from time to time) of Diderot and the Encyclopedists would be much closer to Rousseau, if his self-mockery did not make such an enormous difference, if his very scepticism did not throw him back into the camp of the intellectuals, if the endlessly protracted debate of scepticism and sentimentalism did not define a particular playfulness. And yet (for Sterne catches us up in his zig-zag), despite appearances, here the heart wins the day, sentiment predominates, with the attitudes of the sentimental voyeur simply given the guise of comic game. The sentimentalist is or pretends to be an actor who plays at being sentimental; thus does the sweetness of the thing season itself with a light piquancy.

But just here, beyond the poses of the author, anxiety returns: where is the real, outside the beating heart? What reality can be mixed (or not at all mixed) with the feigning of parody? If every representation is in some degree parody, is not every parody in danger of becoming in some degree representative? We never quite touch absolute reality. We come close to it only by signs more or less inadequate, of which the most immediate, the most powerful, correspond precisely to our intuitions, and the most hackneyed are frozen in the code we call culture. Culture masks what would perhaps be reality; and the nostalgia for reality is one of the liveliest of Sterne's sentiments. Hence his reaction: "I will lock up my study door the moment I get home and throw the key of it ninety feet below the surface of the earth into the draw-well. . . ." "Shall we be destined to the days of eternity . . . to be showing the relicks of learning, as monks do the relicks of their saints—without working one— one single miracle with them?"

As could happen in that time, the critical spirit in Sterne is in service to the requirement of living truth. In giving himself to an attack upon all the layers of illusion of which we have constructed an "objective" pseudo-reality, he becomes truly a creator. In locating reality he discovers it. "Man cannot dress himself but his ideas get clothed along with him." Here we are at the heart of human reality. Here it is that of course Sterne not only passes the Locke he swears by, but profoundly and obstinately opposes him. For Locke, the man who lets himself lapse into subjectivity, he who abandons himself to the associations of ideas, is already the prey of a mild delirium. That man who uses rational processes belongs to the world of human intercourse which is for all practical purposes sufficiently objective. This rational communication Sterne transforms into a crazy ratiocination: it is one of his favorite games. Walter Shandy, the obstinate reasoner, has less good sense in his head than his brother Toby behind his sweet manias. The *Essay Concerning Human Understanding* liberated in Sterne a vein of fantasy that would have been blocked by Descartes' *Discourse on Method*.

An effect of droll surprise and absurdity becomes the visible aspect of the intersections of the subject with the nonsubjective, and accompanies the kind of collision that occurs when the interior life emerges in the middle of the outside world. The comic that results is the comic of misunderstanding and disillusion. Where indeed was Uncle Toby wounded? At Namur, he replies. Was it really in the groin? the Widow asks herself. Thus Sterne's humor attaches itself to the hint of ridicule which comes

from the play of circumstances with intention, from the perpetual surprise of finding oneself in these circumstances, of being shut up in a
postchaise with Mme. de L., of feeling the pulse of the grisette, and of
being in the process greeted by her husband. The humor here is, in fact,
simply in the salt of the discovery of oneself in contact with the world,
as it will be with Proust. It is a mental country where fleeting humors
pass like clouds and shadows, where impulses and interferences succeed
one another, where chains of ideas alternate with cross-purposes, where
the accommodation of the soul to reality is made and remade with a
nimbleness particularly manifested in the fade-outs (which literature discovered long before the cinema). The constant shift from material existence—with its heaviness and density—to the momentary, the impal-
pable, to darting lines of thought—that is what gives to this work its
extraordinary suppleness of texture.

The subject of man is man: it is not only Pope's formula but that of
his century. And the merit of the sharpest minds of this century, such as
Sterne's, is to have seen that that is also the greatest mystery and includes
all others. But if every man remains a mystery to himself, all the more
is he to others. One of Sterne's strangest and most striking images, born
of this nostalgia for a true meeting of minds, asks us to think of what the
inhabitants of Mercury might be by reason of their bodies of fine crystal
—namely, *transparent;* but "our minds shine not through the body, but
are wrapt up here in a dark covering of uncrystallized flesh and blood."
Virginia Woolf, who owed much to Sterne, could recall, at least uncon-
sciously, this formula when she in her turn spoke of "the semi-transparent
envelope surrounding us." To communicate in the face of this opacity
we have constant recourse to systems of signs. The words of language
represent without any doubt the most treacherous and equivocal of them,
but gestures are hardly more reliable, and if Walter and Toby nod their
heads together, Sterne can write that "never did two heads shake together,
in concert, from two such different springs."

Certainly, while our pastor, like Swift before him, understands the
subtleties of theology as no more than inane confrontations among men,
while Christian revelation does not seem to have concerned him in any
way, he received the Lockean revelation with a singular force. We make
up the world from our sense data but without ever communicating with
anything that is other than ourselves, anything objective which can re-
strain us, anything clear that can guide us. It is perpetual invention, and
how could one better, more comically, show it than to put side by side
several characters, a Walter Shandy, an Uncle Toby, a Mrs. Shandy, a

Doctor Slop, each living in his or her peculiar universe and every minute feeding an irresistible peculiarity at common springs?

Pope had defined the individual by his ruling passion; Sterne announces his intention to define him by the hobbyhorse he rides, the cap and bells he shakes. They are found at the heart of his personal vision of the world, and they become the resource of his activity, the heart of his existence. The subjectivity of man is another name for his solitude. When he formulates the propositions which he holds valid, he is the victim of an illusion of which Sterne learnedly, lovingly, sketches the grotesque and ridiculous side. The century in whose course modern science developed mocked science, or rather an idea of science that had, two centuries before, confused the ideas of a Paracelsus, but which had ceased to exist. Sterne's caricature is essentially Swift's, and his philosopher and his obstetrician would have their place among the monomaniacs of Laputa, the most memorable of whom, smeared with a disgusting and stinking yellow stuff, devoted his life to turning excrement back into its original food. The century in the course of which crucial inventions opened the way to the industrial revolution produced for the amusement of the Sternian public the forceps of Dr. Slop.

But here is the novelty: where Swift saw only grotesque lucubrations, the stuff of satire, Sterne sees fragmentary images of the world, fragments of the world, the stuff of parody. Parody pervades *Tristram Shandy* because nothing that has been constructed and formulated by man escapes subjectivity, nor ever loses, in consequence, its personal coloring. It is this coloring that Sterne heightens by parody. Nothing escapes, not even Locke, and in many a passage one finds the propositions of Locke on the associations of ideas or on duration very nearly reproduced, and yet changed by a bizarre intonation, presented with a wink of the eye. The "documents" scattered through the work, such as the sermon of Yorick, the curses of excommunication of Ernuphus, the dissertation of the Sorbonne theologians on prenatal baptism, the contract of marriage, are sometimes heady realities which it has sufficed Sterne to reveal as having a parodic nature and sometimes as pure parodies. These foreign bodies are part of this very particular attack that Sterne makes at once against reality and fiction. The border zone of reality and fiction they mark out naturally encourages parody, an element which has a larger literary importance in the work as a whole and as it is caught here and there in the Sternian style.

This element of parody represents a remarkable intuition which was to be taken up and developed by Joyce in *Ulysses*: that all representation,

by the very fact that it is at a distance from the reality represented, uti-
lizes a certain style, takes its place in a certain cultural tradition, is, of
its nature, half-parody. Sterne is fascinated by the intangibility of the
real, by the fact that there can never be more than partial and many-
colored images of it. But on the other hand, if one is content to with-
draw to a distance, he is struck by the possibility of a relative apprehension of the real by means of technical language. Sterne has his fun but
constantly returns to it. There can be no doubt: factual precision, detailed and minute, in the description of objects, attitudes, movements
seemed to him a not inconsiderable factor of representation. It is the
age of the encyclopedias, and in reading him one often thinks of the
naïve precision of the dictionary or treatise. By nature he has the relish
of seeing things in detail: to know this, it is enough to read his letters
of advice to his wife and daughter leaving for a trip. But rather than
his love of objects taking the form of effusion, it takes that of inventory
—although inventory with ultimately a striking effect of actual presence
of the object. One has only to read the description in Book I of Yorick's
saddle: "quilted on the seat with green plush, garnished with a double
row of silver-headed studs, and a noble pair of shining brass stirrups,
with a housing altogether suitable, of gray superfine cloth, with an edging
of black lace, terminating in a deep, black, silk fringe, *poudré d'or* . . ."

At every moment we come to this fascinated standstill before a reality
transformed into geometric structures, into movements split up until
they seem made of a series of immobilities. Trim reading the sermon is
a figure set in space on a certain number of planes. His body is bending
forward "just so far as to make an angle of 85 degrees and a half upon
the plane of the horizon." Walter, prostrated by the disasters which accompany Tristram's birth, appears to be a body become a stranger to
itself, and material, in contact with other bodies: bed, chamberpot, at
fixed points. Bridget the maidservant pins Widow Wadman's nightgown
according to a ritual custom but equally according to the exigencies of
the obtruding objects. It is not Joyce, but perhaps Beckett among our
own people—the *nouveau roman* would furnish only coincidental re-
semblances—who has inherited this taste for geometries and mechanics,
while accentuating again a little the ruthless obliteration of human
autonomy which such geometries and mechanics constitute when they
are applied to man. This absurd and alienating realism, which knows
nothing in the world but pure matter, is completed by a burlesque fantasy which is unaware of all specificity of beings and phenomena, and
which imparts to that which it describes a metaphorical transfiguration

like that which transforms the meeting of Obadiah and Dr. Slop into a collision of meteors.

The parody is not only in the detail of expression; it penetrates even to the conception of the characters; and particularly of the famous pair of my Uncle Toby and his faithful orderly, Corporal Trim. Much more deeply than France, eighteenth century England was impressed and at times dominated by the figure of Don Quixote. If one pays attention to the fact that Don Quixote is already a parodic figure, one will see that Uncle Toby is parodic to the second degree. He is a Don Quixote clear-headed enough not to risk putting dream in contact with life, but to be satisfied with a very small dream. Whereas Don Quixote imitated an idea with an intrepid originality of interpretation, Uncle Toby permits himself no leeway in his imitation of the tactics of a war or siege. The attentive and even tender, docile, and passionate care with which, movement by movement, day by day, gazette in hand, Uncle Toby reproduces on the scale of his bowling green the sieges conducted by the generals of the alliance, the complete absorption of his activity by this ridiculous game, and the constant suggestion throughout the amused narrative that this game is worth quite as much as another, and perhaps seriously is worth as much as what it imitates—all this gives the character his meaning and makes of him quite another thing than a fancier of tulips in the style of La Bruyère. In this subtle relationship established between Uncle Toby and Prince Eugene, it is Prince Eugene who has more to lose. ("When the Duke of Marlborough made a lodgment,—my Uncle Toby gained a lodgment too. . . .") A strange parodic dimension governs the life of the character. "The siege of Termond was conducted so quickly [by the allies] that my Uncle Toby hardly found time to dine."

From this problem of representation—should one say *of reality,* or rather, *as* reality?—one passes naturally to problems of aesthetics, or rather of aesthetization. Sometimes the metaphoric translation of the episode retains the identity of the event and of the characters, sometimes the musician that Sterne is leaves only a modulated allusion to them, the indication of a mood in the form of *pizzicati*. Through these diverse manifestations what one seems to discover is Sterne's instinctive sense, developed perhaps into a clear awareness by his reading of Locke, of the merciless separation between the world of objects and the unique subject. He is the only one of his time and almost the only one before our time to have received this shock, and having received it, his agile spirit will pass ceaselessly, by leaps and bounds, from the one to the other.

An element of teasing is mingled in everything having to do with Laurence Sterne. Nothing is ever made easy for his reader. He promises *The Life and Opinions of Tristram Shandy*; Tristram, however, will always be the one who presents the others. The "I" who prevails from start to finish gives an inkling of an autobiography—one discovers that it is indeed there and superabundant—but most of the time manifested in characters other than this "I." "My father," for example, for Walter is essentially the portrait-caricature of that bizarre mind that he recognizes in himself, while Uncle Toby represents at the same time the transcript of our author's *bizarrerie* in the register of humor, and the evocation, underneath the game, of the tender and innocent temperament of his father; and Yorick likewise represents a transcription of himself, this time in self-pity and sentiment; "my mother," finally, is very clearly his wife Elizabeth. But if it were enough to realize that the labels of various flasks were maliciously changed and that it was necessary to rearrange them to correspond with the contents, this would be too simple: and if the title shows itself as true on second examination, as true as it had appeared false on the first, it is so in another sense, on another plane.

Sterne realized that one could talk only about oneself. Every text is a pretext to do so, every description of the world is a revelation of self. There, the speculation of the empiricist philosophers had its most direct and intense reflection in the domain of the creative imagination.

We must underscore how much the work owes to this fundamental "I" present throughout, dominant throughout, which brings about its true unity. "I" in search not of time past, but of an absent world, in search of a definition of itself. "I," or Tristram, is at first a series of necessities, pre- and post-natal, which make nose, name, the asthma that you have— this "asthma" from which you will die and which you got from skating against the wind in Flanders. Between what is done without you and what you have done without thinking about it or at least without wanting to do it, it seems that all is determined. But you are the subject, you are the unforeseeable content and form of each moment of existence, the series of your discoveries and finally your microcosm, the total image of a world. "I" is the particular form that one gives to all one perceives, all that one feels, all that one thinks, each movement, each joy, each anguish, in contact with what is not "me." *I*, then, covers, as images, "my father," "my mother," "my Uncle Toby," Trim, Slop, Susan, Bridget, Obadiah, the Widow Wadman, a very untidy interior theater, not tied down to the exigencies of practical life. Fatal disorder, mechanical incoherence, out of which, however, the game of the creative intelligence can make a freedom, the only one which can oppose itself to the drift of all things toward death, the only one which will count likewise in Proust's eyes. The world interiorized—the world as image—is raw material for the creative spirit, a treasure to draw upon. The liberty to make use of this as it seems right to him fascinates Sterne so much that not only does he draw upon it continually, but also he constantly makes himself seen drawing on it.

Here again, Sterne is one of us, in that the illusion, the deception, the creation of a pseudo-objective do not interest him, but rather the reduction of these former figments of art, once taken as objective, to the thought-in-process where they adhere. "You see, it's only a game," Sterne seems to be saying, "there are the puppet strings, I pull, it moves." But look, it seems to move now of its own accord. Just when one has noticed that everything has come down to representation, one is tempted to confer existence on it. The image detaches itself, seems to liberate itself. The microcosm will show itself to be haunted. With Beckett anxiety will mark the determination of these puppets-become-phantoms to manifest themselves. With Sterne the game remains a game. But all the same: ". . . take care that the poor woman should not be lost in the mean time;—because when she is wanted we can no way do without her."

The liberty that counts, whatever the illusions of the action, is that of shifting oneself as one wishes in the world of the memory and the imagination. Sterne is the first to show us, among other ambiguities, the creation of the artist and of the universal human condition of man, while pretending to explore *at random* this inner world and to take advantage of the happy accident of encounters and chains of ideas which are knotted up with their occasions. The world turned into image of the world acquires the suppleness, the malleability, the protean quality proper to the image. People have sometimes wondered what literature owed to the cinema. The boldness of a Sterne does not need the real and materialized presence of the moving image to exert its freedom and invent the fade-out, which is linked with the motion of the subject, with living duration, with the unreality of time swallowed up in the memory and become a thing without depth. Take, for example, the passage in which he celebrates Nanette, the girl from Languedoc with the tattered petticoat: "Capriciously did she bend her head on one side, and dance up insidious —Then 'tis time to dance off, quoth I; so changing only partners and tunes, I danced it away from Lunel to Montpellier—from thence to Pesças, Beziers—I danced it along through Narbonne, Carcasson, and Castle Naudairy, till at last I danced myself into Perdrillo's pavilion."

Here we are at last facing what appears as one of Sterne's great themes: time. Do not critics tend to put excessive stress on the play of duration and of memory and on certain showpieces such as the passage set in Auxerre in Book VII? A passage nevertheless very important, not so much because it superimposes two past tenses one on top of the other in the apparent confusion that gives Sterne such joy, but because it emphasizes that there is truly, outside of the fantastic and unreal crisscrossings of the memory, only one real time, which is the present of the living being who remembers: not at all what might be called Auxerre A or Auxerre B, but today at Toulouse where pen is put to paper.

It is, one must say, in this sector of time that one is the most dazzled by Sterne and the most exasperated, as one can be by one's favorite authors, such as Joyce, when they end up with *Finnegans Wake,* when their ingenuity which was the admitted price of their subtle intelligence makes itself cumbersome, insistent, and excessively self-satisfied, and prevents all absorption of the creator in his creation.

Critics also stress in Sterne the abolition of chronological time in favor of subjective duration, measured, according to Locke's analysis, by the succession of ideas. But Sterne achieves more singular effects from the continual superimposition of one measurable time upon another, the time of the occurrence of the primary event which is the object of the narration, and the time of the secondary representation which he gives of it, of the account he makes of it. In the episode of Obadiah being sent in quest of Dr. Slop, he pretends that the moment of the Doctor's arrival could have been accounted for (if in actual fact he had not set out on the way of his own accord) by the time that it has taken him, the author, to narrate the matter while mingling abundant digressions with it.

To test for fun the possibility of bringing together the time of the representation and the time of the thing represented, is this not to rediscover in his own very novel fashion the obsession of the classical drama? But with Sterne it is not quite the same, for neither order of time is simple: the author presents the inner world as well as the existential chronology in a variety of absurd relations. "No more could my uncle *Toby,* after passing the French lines, as he eat his egg at supper, from thence break into the heart of France."

One sees by this example that inner time—that of Uncle Toby—running parallel to actual time, can assume an essentially parodic character. In fact one can no longer speak of personal time in this truly extreme and pathological case. Uncle Toby has had none since the beginning of his neurosis. It is a very curious analysis of a real or imaginary case that Sterne has made here: he has shown the wounded, nailed to his bed of sorrow, powerless, humiliated, taking a new lease on life by dwelling on his last battles, and passing from this pleasure to a new dimension—from the repetition of the past to the identification of it with a fictive present. His personal time becomes absolutely stagnant—until the day when the Widow Wadman bustles in. Then the invalid's impatience, his *need* of time, puts time back in gear.

Sterne manipulates time like the musician in love with virtuosity that he is. One sees him, more serious than he thinks through his bantering, pursuing like a mirage the pure reality of time. If at first he brings the time of the thing represented toward the time of the representation, ultimately he mingles with the past, in make-believe, not only the present but also, on occasion, master of time that he is, the future: "A cow broke in (to-morrow morning) to my uncle Toby's fortifications." In the burlesque magic of one single sentence is all *Helzapoppin* and more. But Sterne bypasses this burlesque magic in pursuit of a more authentic reality and a purer time, that of the very book in the process of creation, carrying its movement across the temporal structures that it absorbs. "The door opens in the chapter after next." The pseudo-reality of the story dwindles while the reality of the writer and the process of writing increases proportionately and much more.

On the way he discovered still another thing. This breaking apart of what had used to be linked up by literary imposture liberates and releases not only an author come alive for himself and for us; it liberates the work also. Freed from rational control the work shows an unaccustomed and, one might say an autonomous, vitality. This imaginary world, in fact, takes responsibility for its own time. Once released, this time goes by its own logic. Alternately manifest and invisible to our eyes, it acquires a new property: it becomes continuous. This permits the author to begin a chapter by saying that, all his characters being asleep or occupied (Trim, in preparing the siege of Messina), he is going to turn his attention to his preface. It is this continuity which, in a complementary way, allows a particular mode of *suspense,* almost peculiar to Sterne and which we may call comic suspense. The time of the narrative is totally suspended. A gesture is stopped—a smoked-out pipe is held back at the moment when one is going to knock the ashes from it, a sentence remains unfinished: "I think. . ." The gesture, the sentence will be taken up again many pages further on, and the effect will be to reinforce the sense of time, of this unfolding that man cannot stop, which passes him by and flows around him on all sides to an infinite horizon.

Cannot one say indeed, beyond all these too-conscious games of digression with which Sterne amused himself, that he has grasped the importance for the creation of an imaginary world, beyond the time necessary to be given to the moments of the action, of losing time around the action, of weighing down the book with time, or more precisely, of *slowing it down*? Just so, in drama, no more in comedy, Melville knew how to weigh down and slow down *Moby Dick* with his numerous and copious digressive chapters. Sterne has, and he declares this explicitly, a sense of the interlude: "That which equals . . . a dance, a song, a concerto between the acts." There, it seems, is the idea that time, in whatever manner the author tackles it, reconstitutes itself, takes living form again in the reader's spirit, and that it is this time of the reader-interlocutor that must be prepared and constructed.

But here again, and whatever the clear volition, one finds that stimuli, attitudes, and effects are far from simple. Sterne plays tortoise and hare. He loiters about indefinitely at the first bushes, then all of a sudden proclaims his horror at not being able to make up the time, at not being able to hope to get back to the present, to make the time lived correspond with the time relived, which at the rate he is going is only too evident. Joking declarations follow each other. He left his father and his uncle thirty-five minutes ago. He was to rejoin them in half an hour. He has minus five minutes to say a multitude of things. In the midst of the fourth book, after a year of literary labor, he is at the first day of his life. "I shall never overtake myself." And certainly, that is teasing. But as un-Sternian as it may be, I recognize an insidious anxiety, perhaps completely unconscious, underneath these games. "Time wastes too fast," and certainly he could waste much less of it, but for what purpose? Here again there is a note of choice and of challenge. He decides by a free action to miss the chance, which in fact does not exist, to rejoin himself.

Time always goes too quickly. Sterne gives us here an inadequate but expressive image of our effort to live the present—always to discover that we have missed it, that it has gone to swell the past. In fact, the arts of time—literature or music—do the only thing possible by drawing a significant order from time's very flow, and Sterne, passionate musician, often has something of that genre present in his mind.

Whatever the ingenious and proliferating detail of the forms of time in Sterne, one can say that time has two opposite aspects: reversible and irreversible. On the one hand, from flashbacks to anticipations, the writer is master of time, and plays in every way with all the possible modes of succession. It is his liberty, his triumph. On the other hand, from book to book in the work we come upon that obsessive pursuit of a time which goes too quickly, that breathless pursuit, which, one would suspect, is not unrelated to the short, panting, feverish respiration of the tubercular writer. This pursuit, whose sham mockery and comic despair veil without suppressing its character of quest, seems to me in Book VII to take on all of its meaning, when, its rapid rhythm accentuated into a heroic scherzo, it has, like so many quests, become a flight, death pressing behind, time stealing away before. All the hints come together, become consistent, in Book VII where time assumes the form of a burlesque death in the manner of Rowlandson: certainly a scherzo, this Book VII, from sentence to sentence, from breath to breath, from stop to stop, from Calais to Paris, has no need of macabre onomatopoeia to create anguish more effectively than Bürger's *Lenore.* The entrance into Paris is naught but expressive rhythms, the noise of wheels, the cries of the coachman, the cracks of the whip, impressions clipped and syncopated by the speed which makes them follow one another; but if one looks over one's shoulder, all this takes on another meaning, its true meaning.

Is it then by chance that our author found under his pen just the formula to face all the nonhuman permanences, which will be that of Alfred de Vigny: "Love what you will never see twice." Let others be interested in churches. He is interested in Janatone. But "he who measures thee, Janatone, must do it now—thou carriest the principles of change within thy frame."

Yes, "time wastes too fast: every letter I trace tells me with what rapidity Life follows my pen; the days and hours of it, more precious, my dear *Jenny!* than the rubies about thy neck, are flying over our heads like light clouds of a windy day, never to return more—every thing presses on . . . whilst thou art twisting that lock,—see! it grows grey."

Pozzo says, "One day we are born, one day we will die, the same day the same instant. . . . Women come to childbirth astride a tomb, the sun shines a moment, then night falls again." It is more insistent but less heartrending, less upsetting than Sterne's extraordinary image, which pictures so well in its privacy this rush of time which makes all our moments like one and brings all to an end before we have properly begun.

"I have forty volumes to write, forty thousand things to say that no one in the world will say or do for me," says Tristram to Eugenius, with the thread of a voice that is left him. He knows himself now as the irreplaceable individual of Gide. How could he not feel the cruelty of time that consumes him and to which he refuses to submit, which he defies by this furious possessed rhythm that tries to triumph over change by going faster than change itself? "All this movement is so much of life, so much of joy," says he, even while he gallops toward Paris with death on his traces.

Let us notice as well that, save in the defiance that such scherzos represent, Sterne keeps to that reversible time which is always at his call in the concrete density of the present. By this definition, this book devoted to all the time-games is almost entirely written in the present, and constantly reaffirms the here and now against the traditional past tenses of narration. The here and now is the sole reality, living amid the concrete that it absorbs, reducing all things to itself. More than the formulas good for flabbergasting the bourgeois, one is struck by the starkness of such a small formulation as this which expresses the eternal instant: "The very day I am now writing this book, which is the ninth of March 1759," ". . . that observation is my own,—and was struck out by me this very rainy day March 26, 1759. . . ." "And here I am sitting this 12th day of August, 1766, in a purple jerkin and yellow pair of slippers, without cap or wig. . . ."

What makes such a present time special is that it does not leave the writer shut up within the separateness of the creator—he is always open to any reader who becomes a listener. The narrator himself has become a conversationalist; the reality, which finally is in neither an objective, geometric, "scientific" precision of detail, nor the intuition of the heart, is a contact, a spark, a current which is established between two separate imaginations that the "word" brings together. It is a matter neither of grand tales nor of imposing persons, but of daily life, of hinges and windows, of pillows and chamberpots, of the narrow borders of consciousness, of little madnesses and little idlenesses, of little impulses and little intentions, of hesitations and *aporiae*.

But in the end it all comes down to Sterne's craft—no, his genius as a writer. There, in the genius itself, ends the unacknowledged quest of the absolute or the real—beyond the jesting and anxiety. All the writer's experiences have their place in constituting together a sort of real presence. They bring us up sharp, for example, against the irreducible object such as Yorick's saddle or Mrs. Shandy's "blue, pellucid, chrystal" eye. If Sterne gives the eye a singular importance, not as object but as organ, it is not, however, the purely visual that is his end but the creation of something like the presence, at once actual and parodic, of the stage by a precise, humorous, coldly impassive image of a gesture, a pose, a slight movement of the body. Trim gravely lets his hat fall as if he were illustrating the fall of bodies, and this gesture indicates, better and more eloquently than a speech, irremediable and pitiless death. With his cane Trim describes aerial flourishes which are "more expressive than a thousand syllogisms" and with which the author decorates his page. The visual and scenic hieroglyph, dear to Diderot, has its place everywhere. Widow Wadman, transported by the force of her feelings for Uncle Toby, expresses them by making the pin with which her long nightgown is attached each night jump from Bridget's hand by a kick of the foot.

The eighteenth century ends with a Coleridge who oscillates between Hartley and Jacob Boehme, between a conception of thought as nervous influx and pure material movement, and as a universe of spiritual forces. Sterne, as little as one would expect it, takes part in this ambiguity— like his kindred spirit Diderot, another seeker for the real presence. Sterne also, like Diderot, knows that the creation of the real is a problem of language. And it is not so much in words that he looks for the language, as in the curious procedures of musical notation, of the spacing of imaginative thought, corresponding to what goes on ceaselessly between our bodies and the world. Such is the expression of movement at the beginning of Book V, helped out by the very characteristic Sternian punctuation—dash, long dash, double dash, triple dash. Or even more, chapter 15 of the same book, which is but a series of examples of musical onomatopoeia; not until the chapter about the sirens in Joyce's *Ulysses* will one find a similar experience of the shift from the language of discourse to the language of suggestion. Quasi-musical modulations are found constantly in the work, besides those other absolutes, the black page, the marbled page, and the white page—the last to allow the reader to paint the Widow Wadman according to his fancy. The play of the mind with the ocean of reality that must overcome it, pursued even while it sees itself tossed and carried away in the flood, could go no further.

The Shandean Comic Vision of Locke

by John Traugott

I

Any benign reader of *Tristram Shandy* accustoms himself to his own role onstage in adjusting the rigging with Tristram. "I beg the reader will assist me here, to wheel off my uncle Toby's ordnance behind the scenes . . . and clear the theatre, *if possible* . . ." (VI, 29). Impossible; the stage is never clear; the reader always finds himself viewing himself in character. How many personae are there? As many as the reader may care to discover. He discovers for one thing that even his sex is doubtful: "Madam," "Sir," "Your Worship." "Unmistrusting ignorance" may be shot from ambush "ten times a day . . . if nine times a day, Madam, had not served your purpose." And the reader will come to believe that not only his sex but his sexuality is in question. Is it a paradox that this man was a preacher? It was precisely as a preacher that Sterne insisted that his parishioners doubt themselves and discover themselves as all the personifications of his sermons. Walter Shandy congratulated the preacher on this rhetorical technique: "I like the sermon well, replied my father, —'tis dramatic . . ." (II, 17). Sterne knew that he had a vested interest in dramatic rhetoric, and this is why Tristram so often acknowledges the excellences of his own demonstrations in the jargon of the theater. In his wry development of the philosophy of John Locke, Sterne discovered a dramatic formula for the endless rhetorical inventions which demonstrate his conception of reality. These opinions of Tristram Shandy bespeak a philosophy; and it is with this philosophical content of Sterne's dramatic rhetoric that we are now concerned.

To speak of "philosophy" in a resolutely nonlogical work such as *Tristram Shandy* is of course a strain. Obviously every artist works on some hypothesis, if we consider a peculiar selection of phenomenal data as a hypothesis. But the artist "proves" nothing: he can only persuade by making his images descriptive of his peculiar selection or ordering. Thus he may by the "force and vivacity of the impression" induce a sort of belief (as Hume describes belief) in his system. The philosopher, on the other hand, at least pretends to apply abstract principles to experience, and pretends also to shun pure description with all its references to vague tastes and sentiments. Still, both Sterne and Locke had a hypothesis of communication and Sterne realized his by putting Locke's to the test of description in dramatic situations. Furthermore, they shared a passionate skepticism which started them worrying about communication in the first place.

Sterne chose a peculiar set of data. He chose creatures "heteroclite in all their declensions," pushed and swerved by *seemingly* casual ideas, creatures stalked by affections like Chastity, which, gentle enough usually, can become "ramping and roaring lions"—creatures, in short, determined in private and devious ways. Given this population, the world stands in need of an ingenious rationale. So far as Sterne could contrive an order for this world of his, he was, in the broad sense noted above, a philosophical artist. Yet he stands accused (he is always on trial) of creating exquisite tableaux in which meaning begins and ends with the niceness of the pictures. Even the nastiness is nice. Goldsmith's catechizing Chinaman received an evaluation of *Tristram Shandy* that until recently was pretty much standard: "The author had nothing but the jest in view; no dull moral lurking beneath, nor ill-natured satire to sour the reader's good-humour; he wisely considered, that moral and humour at the same time were quite overdoing the business." [1]

Now if there is a philosophic vision of order—and where there is order, morality must be—in *Tristram Shandy*, there is also an inevitable and just question: why does the vision of order not appear to many readers, some of them honest enough? A rhetorical question, this, which logically must hang by while there is a try at finding what philosophy means in the conception of Tristram's rhetoric. As we consider the difficulties of understanding the order of the book, the question may find an answer.

The reason's work in the proofs of philosophy is arduous and always frustrated *somewhere* in every system. If the display of gymnastics and machines used to clear a way is wondrous enough, the display itself becomes a proper subject for satire. But such display is *not* Sterne's primary reference; for involuted and exfoliated as they are in the wreathing, his jests on the snares of belief and philosophy, were they not part of a

---

[1] Quoted by Wilbur L. Cross in his *Life and Times of Laurence Sterne,* new ed. (New Haven: Yale University Press), I, 214.

larger purpose, could scarcely supply the tension requisite for evoking a dramatic situation or realizing a character. *Scriblerus,* for example, a mere satire on systems, is small addition to the stock of humanity. *Tristram Shandy* uses philosophical snarls for more than a satire on systems; it uses them as a dramatic device displaying human motives and for creating a world of human relations. And satire verges into comedy when it begins to consider the inescapable human situation. "Everything in this world, said my father, is big with jest,—and has wit in it, and instruction too,—if we can but find it out" (V, 32). And so, too, at that inevitable *somewhere* of philosophical frustration, big with jest as the situation may be, lies a dramatic engine—if the artist can but find it out. Now Locke, like all philosophers, had a vision of order that satisfied a passion in him. And although *Tristram Shandy* is not a slight and fantastical exegesis of Locke's *Essay,* it evolves on the energy of the same passion of skepticism and comes alive with the drama implicit in Locke's failure to find a convincing relation between two worlds, real and ideal. Locke will have it—Berkeley, one of Locke's best critics, will not have it—that there are two worlds. We can know only our ideas, says Locke; we can never know the substantive reality of existence exterior to our own minds. But even accepting Locke's fundamental hypothesis, almost any careful reader is likely to feel uneasy in considering Locke's paradox that there can be a "proof" of "*unknowable*" substance and its primary qualities. Poets have always found a quickening dolefulness in the reminder that we are here as on a darkling plain; but an especially peculiar—in Sterne's consideration of Locke a comic—sort of agitation arises when the fact is "proved" philosophically. Of course, while Sterne's talents were purely mundane, he yet found in certain aspects of this so worried problem of world-splicing, ideal to real, and the consequent problem of communicating ideas, as these problems find form in the rationale of the *Essay,* a real energy. Since the truth is, if the test of truth is ridicule, that Sterne's characters are utterly limited to their human fallibility—when they are set down on Locke's ontological vast abrupt, the abysm between ideas and reality, they perfectly display the worldly problem of Locke's *Essay.*[2]

---

[2] The one direct comment by Sterne on Sterne and Locke is reported at second hand, but sounds plausible enough. Dominique-Joseph Garat, a Boswell for Jean-Baptiste Suard, tells of Suard's enquiry of Sterne (*Mémoire historique sur la vie de M. Suard, sur ses écrits, et sur le XVIIIe siècle* [Paris, 1820], T. II, p. 148). He wanted to know "quels etaient . . . les attributs naturels et acquis de ce génie qu'on aime autant que les plus beaux, et qui leur ressemble si peu?" The solemn response cannot be literally Sterne's but it is credible in outline: "Sterne attribuit la première cause de ce qu'on appelait son originalité, à une de ces organisations où prédomine le principe sacré qui forme l'âme, cette flamme immortelle qui nourrit la vie et la dévore, qui exalte et varie subitement toutes les sensations, et qu'on appelle *imagination, sensibilité,*

From the traditional material of Locke's philosophy with a talent fantastically original, he constructed an order. What follows, therefore, is an attempt not to match lines from Locke with some from Sterne, but to demonstrate Sterne's peculiar use of the formal elements of Locke's philosophy.

II

Locke's *Essay*, despite the professional plainness of the author, is not wanting in the ambiguity that is useful for varying interpretations; the particular interpretation used here, therefore, carries no authority except that of *Tristram Shandy*. It seems to develop from and answer to Sterne's references to Locke, and it seems to fit a critical scheme which imports meaning to those references. Nothing heterodox, I believe, is involved in this interpretation; in fact, it is an interpretation of only certain aspects of the *Essay*. The emphasis given those aspects is, I think, not correspondent to that of the *Essay*, but the concern here is with *Tristram Shandy* and not with Locke.

As general guides to this discussion of Locke two propositions are useful. First, both Locke and Sterne found primary energy in reflection on learned trumpery and its utter success in the world. So annoying a spectacle led Locke to nearly twenty years of investigation of the origin and extent of human knowledge. His awful conception was no less than to banish error. Still, although he could not abide men of lore and although he wanted to smash the all-knowing who would have tribute of the blind, Locke was a genuinely humble man, and he conceived the *Essay* as a guide for sweet reasonableness. Secondly, where our knowledge of the secret nature of reality, of substance cognitive and noncognitive, is frustrated, both Locke and Sterne suggest a method for finding our way. Locke's is a rational system for comparing ideas and determining

suivant qu'elle représente sous les pinceaux d'un écrivain ou des tableaux ou des passions; la seconde, à la lecture journalière de l'ancien et du nouveau testament, livres de son goût à la fois et de son état; la troisième, à l'étude de Locke, qu'il avait faite au sortir de l'enfance, et qu'il refit toute sa vie; à cette philosophie que ceux qui savent la reconnaître où elle est, et où elle dirige tout secrètement, retrouvent et sentent dans toutes les pages, dans toutes les lignes, dans le choix de toutes les expressions; à cette philosophie trop religieuse pour vouloir expliquer le miracle des sensations, mais qui, avec ce miracle dont elle n'a pas la témérité de demander raison et compte à Dieu, développe tous les secrets de l'entendement, évite les erreurs, arrive aux vérités accessibles; philosophie sainte, sans laquelle il n'y aura jamais sur la terre ni vraie religion universelle, ni vrai morale, ni vrai puissance de l'homme sur la nature." Let us, then, look "dans toutes les pages, dans toutes les lignes, dans le choix de toutes les expressions."

language. Sterne's is something else, but by developing the possibilities of confusion or absurdity in Locke's rational system Sterne has created a dramatic engine which controls situation and character. The characters are so made that, operating on Locke's premises, they completely foil his rational method for communication. And in the consequent isolation of personalities the vitality of situations is maintained by the comic gropings of those personalities for some sort of concourse. The excitement of *Tristram Shandy* lies not in its whimsical view of man's nature, but in its rhetorical demonstration that what is easily called odd, whimsical, and eccentric *must* be related to the basic motivations of Everyman; that the reader must know the difficulty not only in communication with foreign minds but also in discovering his own.

The final doctrine of sympathy or sentimentalism which Sterne offers us depends upon our ability to understand the relations of ideas and words as they appear in human situations; he had always emphasized the pathetic proof [3] in his sermons, but Locke in affording a dramatic situation based upon the isolation of minds gave a use for the pathetic or sentimental (though not in the word's modern invidious sense) that is artistically essential to the Shandean world of conception.[4]

As he begins to invent his Uncle Toby, Tristram laments elaborately the pains of character drawing: If "the proposed emendation of that arch-critick," Momus, had taken place, he says, nothing more would have been wanted in order to have taken a man's character (I, 23). The proposed emendation was a window in the breast through which to look on the interior machinations of your subject. Certainly the interiors of both characters and readers (for they too are performers in this book) are offered to view so often that this display can only be described as the principal work of the book. But "interior" almost always means the odd but not abnormal ideas and affections of characters and readers as they are revealed in activity which is made part of a probable human situation. That is, ideas are never analyzed according to Locke's rational rubric,

---

[3] Traditionally, rhetorical proofs, i.e., methods of persuasion, are three: logical, ethical, and pathetic. Today we should call this pathetic proof an appeal to emotions, or, prejudice. The modern understanding of pathos is not necessarily involved. What is involved is a play upon certain dispositions which the normal mind can be expected to have.

[4] Another treatment of Sterne's use of Locke will be found in Kenneth MacLean's *John Locke and English Literature of the Eighteenth Century* (New Haven, 1936). Whereas MacLean argues that Sterne simply follows Locke's philosophy, my view is that he exposes and exploits certain philosophical problems in Locke having to do with mind and language. I should say, further, in distinction to MacLean's argument, that Sterne's *Tristram Shandy* is not only a criticism of Locke but a development of a notion of mind and language wholly antagonistic to Locke.

but are made part of a context which permits us to see what those ideas mean in terms of normal human activity. Of course, it is obvious that had Sterne followed Locke we might have had a sort of Scriblerean satire on eccentricity (though a feeble one), but no drama, no personalities. Locke suggested, merely by way of warning, the possibilities of the isolation of minds, and Sterne carried his suggestions logically as far as they would go.

This lack of access, one soul to another, was certainly a controlling fact of life for both Sterne and Locke; for Sterne, I say again, it served as a basis for dramatic and comic development; for Locke it was a principal torment urging him to develop his rational system for the analysis of ideas and language. Of course, among Walter, Toby, Trim, Slop, Mr. Shandy, and the Widow Wadman no determinate idea ever lodged at a time in any two breasts, or perhaps not even in one. Whole conversations are *performed* without a single participant's understanding or having the least desire to understand. After a prologue by Tristram on Locke's directions for the rational comparison of ideas, Walter and Toby are put on the scene to run an empirical test of the philosopher's method (III, 40-41). Walter in earnest preface to his mighty metaphysic of noses announces a rival scholar's "solution." Walter wants no more of Toby than a small gasp of metaphysical wonder. But, "replied my uncle Toby, shattering a conceptual world, 'Can noses be dissolved?' " (We later find that Toby's naïveté is prologue to Walter's more profound naïveté in arguing the scholastic quiddities of the being and reality of Slawkenbergius' stranger's nose.) One more "determinate" idea is dissipated into the Shandean air, untasted, uncompared. And the nocturnal terrors of Mr. and Mrs. Shandy's bed of council are well known (VI, 17-18). Never an idea crossed the marital couch. Just so, the Widow Wadman must abandon language and engage her puissant eye to make Toby realize the possibility of breaching her fortifications (VIII, 23-25). And so it goes—or, rather, doesn't go.

Such a total want of rational correspondence, such a self-preserving instinct, on every hand, to follow a fixed set of ideas, such utter inharmony, Mr. J. B. Priestley has carefully observed, "deal death to philosophies and sciences and all reasonable intercourse and call up a horrible vision of humanity as a set of puppets worked on the wires of a few instincts. A satirist, loathing his species, could have taken such tragicomical little creatures, each in the separate mechanical box of his mind, and made out of them a scene or narrative that would have jangled the nerves of a dozen generations. Sterne, however, . . . preserves the balance by emphasizing what we might call the kinship of his people. If the Shandies cannot share one another's thoughts, they can share one another's feelings. . . . [We] would be rather taken aback at the bleak satire of the narrative . . . if the unity in feeling, the mutual trust and affection, of the Shandies were not so broadly and so often emphasised." [5]

If any one form shapes Sterne's work, it must be his sense of contrast, not the contrast of the world's affairs with a devoutly held moral conception, as with Swift, but a sense that can discover exceptions to any proposition. Such a need of exhibiting the dubious could not but be debilitating to artistic energy were it not contained by a constant contrast to the indubitable reality of social sympathy. Where he has exploited the skeptical possibilities of Locke's *Essay* in order to demonstrate the intellectual isolation of the Shandy people, therefore, Sterne has contrasted their absolute sympathetic correspondence. And, indeed, one may doubt that they are in the end even intellectually isolated, since all the hobbyhorses, though they often find expression in language that falls dead from the speaker's mouth, are yet understood. Are Walter's "thoughts," for example, his nonsense words? Or are they his passional needs to discover his life in rationally explicable systems? Toby *does* understand the latter.

Now Locke, as indeed everyone not an anchorite, understands that the first condition for communication is provided by the fact that we consider society among men as a real affair. Yet the very logic of his substrational hypothesis of substance[6] forces him to conceive men as having, each of them, a little world apart, shut up, self-regarding, and inaccessible to the vision of other, similar, worlds (4, 4, 1-3). For mind is substance (2, 27, 2), and if asked "what is substance," the ultimate generator of complex ideas, one would have to say, Locke almost sighs, "something, he knew not what" (2, 32, 2 *et passim*). But substance, that I-know-not-what, is reality, and reality, therefore, is beyond the possibility of rational conception. Consequently the effects of mental substance, ideas, and affections as perceived can be communicated only by the happy circumstance that minds may be caused to think alike by an exactly determined language (3). Even so, however, one mind can never hope to know how or why another may work. Hume's notion of the association of ideas through custom bridges this communicative gap, but Locke's system leaves it open.

Here, Locke's theory abysmally separates the individual from reality, including other individuals, and even himself should he forget his past ideas. Dr. Johnson might as well have booted the stone to rescue Locke as to refute Berkeley. It is Locke's doctrine that isolates the mind. "Since

---

[5] "The Brothers Shandy," *The English Comic Characters*, new ed. (New York: Dodd, Mead & Co., 1931), p. 156.

[6] *An Essay concerning Human Understanding* (6th ed.), Bk. II, chap. 23, paragraphs 1-37. All subsequent references to the *Essay* will be noted by book, chapter, and paragraph.

the mind, in all its thoughts and reasonings, hath no other immediate object but its own ideas, which it alone does or can contemplate, it is evident that our knowledge is only conversant about them" (4, 1, 1). Is this not the very chimera that exercised Boswell and stimulated Johnson's foot? Now hear Berkeley defending common sense: "You talked often as if you thought I maintained the nonexistence of sensible things; whereas in truth no one can be more thoroughly assured of their existence than I am, and it is you who doubt: I should have said, positively deny it. . . . Remember the matter you [Lockeans] contend for is an unknown somewhat . . . which is quite stripped of all sensible qualities and can neither be perceived by sense, nor apprehended by the mind." [7] This to Lockeans. To consider this matter analytically in relation to mind would certainly be to leave *Tristram Shandy* far behind, but this much pertinent to the Shandys may be said: Locke's theory denies any communication by public, nonanalytic activity of minds. Locke does not entertain any contextual view of communication; without determinate ideas signified by definitive words man is simply a beast who wants discourse of reason. The mind has no public character; it is not manifest in mere patterns of action or language, and so is not in any respect open to other intelligences. Berkeley makes himself merry with Locke's conception of communication and asks the reader to consider the understanding between children prating of sugarplums.[8]

The privacy of mind under these conditions is the ultimate fact with which a theory of communication must deal. Locke establishes this early: "Man, though he have great variety of thoughts, and such from which others as well as himself might receive profit and delight, yet they are all within his own breast, invisible, and hidden from others, nor can themselves be made to appear. The comfort and advantage of society n being to be had without communication of thoughts, it was necessary that man should find out some external sensible signs, whereby those invisible ideas which his thoughts are made up of might be made known to others" (3, 2, 1).

Communication, then, can proceed under Locke's theory only if those sounds which are words are the marks of the ideas of the speaker, as they are clearly understood by him (and to understand a complex idea is always to be able to analyze it into simple ones), and if the respondent has ex-

[7] Third Dialogue, *Three Dialogues between Hylas and Philonous.*
[8] *A Treatise concerning the Principles of Human Knowledge,* Introduction, § 14. Much of my discussion at this point derives from Albert Hofstadter's consideration of Locke's theory of communication in *Locke and Scepticism* (New York: Albee Press, 1935), pp. 115-24.

actly the same marks for the same ideas. Naturally, if the engaging of this communicative mechanism were dependent upon the mere coincidence that the same idea with the same word attached to it should appear simultaneously in two minds, the little candle which Locke allows human reason to be could illuminate nothing save a self-consuming void, with the few accidental sparks of human correspondence only limning the wastes around.

But this is a possible, perhaps necessary, implication of the logic of Locke's theory. (Locke did not entertain it.) Even ignoring the difficulty in knowing under Locke's hypothesis of knowledge that there is a reality of objects in nature which the mind's ideas may signify, or of other minds which may have corresponding ideas, frustrations are inevitable, certainly, in any attempt to analyze all ideas, to make them, in Locke's terminology, "determinate," and in "comparing"—as is necessary—all ideas rationally in order to import meaning to them in predications.

Here is Toby using Locke's method:

> Had the same great reasoner [Locke] looked on, as my father illustrated his systems of noses, and observed my uncle Toby's deportment,—what great attention he gave to every word,—and as oft as he took his pipe from his mouth, with what wonderful seriousness he contemplated the length of it, —surveying it transversely as he held it betwixt his finger and his thumb, —then foreright,—then this way, and then that, in all its possible directions and foreshortenings,—he would have concluded my uncle Toby had got hold of the *medius terminus;* and was syllogizing and measuring with it the truth of each hypothesis of long noses, in order as my father laid them before him. This by the bye, was more than my father wanted,—his aim in all the pains he was at in these philosophic lectures,—was to enable my uncle Toby not to *discuss* [compare],—but *comprehend*—to *hold* the grains and scruples of learning,—not to *weigh* them.—My uncle Toby, as you will read in the next chapter, did neither the one or the other. (III, 40)

Had Toby stood prepared to work *medii termini* as fast as Walter could form his philosophical sentences, he would still have encountered some little difficulty in analyzing the radical material of Walter's ideas. Clearly something outside the rational Lockean system is proceeding at both ends of this correspondence. Yet both Toby and Walter are but settling into their proper natures, and that, says Aristotle in the *Rhetoric,* is pleasure. Part of the pleasure is, in fact, that each understands the other's pleasure. This is a way of communication that depends upon the public character of our activity, mental or physical, and depends not at all upon the analysis of ideas. Is it not possible that Walter's principal strokes are merely to put his brother's mind in a disposition of wonder while he goes through his routine? It must be possible, for Tristram says just that. This end of language is suggested by Berkeley when he rejects Locke's insistence that communication means solely the transference of determinate ideas.[9] Indeed, Locke's view of mind, which prohibits public concourse of various mental activities, seems inadequate to explain the facts of the Shandy world, facts which Sterne does not allow the reader to forget. Anyone willing to stay at the job of reading *Tristram Shandy,* provided he is not an anti-Shandean (for all such are advised by Tristram to abandon it, in chapter 36 of Volume III), cannot fail to perceive the intellectual inharmony among the Shandys and the world of conception Sterne creates to achieve order in this potential wasteland. A realization of this conception has, incidentally, value as biography, and is necessary if we wish to understand this book as an example of how traditional materials can be used by an original talent. Moreover, and perhaps more important, when we scrutinize a book so often passed down to readers with critical assurance of its chaos, a study of its formal elements should be a slight balancing of the critical account. And finally, the critic, by appreciating Sterne's formal conceptions, can speak with objective reference and not merely quiver or shudder as personal impressions become pleasure or pain or, even, pleasing pain.

Such is the formal content of the dilemma of Locke's rationalism with which Sterne has constructed one control for his comedy. It concerns at bottom, of course, one universal of existence: the will to communicate. With Locke's hypotheses Sterne obviously has wrought something that is not Locke.

III

In that psychological room where most men keep obvious muniments, Sterne stored oddments, and it is with this maggoty area of his conception, his sally against the gerund-grinding windmills of learning, that we are now concerned. Locke tells us (and tells us again and again throughout his *Essay*) that his philosophical quest to discover the limits of reason was stimulated by his dismay at the utter success in the world of learned quacks. Sterne shares this passionate skepticism, and it energizes his own conception. But while Tristram's incidental satire echoes so often Locke's flings at the lumberyards of learning, it is in the trivial satiric play with odd scraps of lore of his Augustan exemplars

---

[9] *Principles of Human Knowledge,* Introduction, § 20.

and the long tradition of learned satire[10] behind them that Sterne discovered a manner for turning his skeptical notions to creative account.
Since we are not here concerned with influences per se, but with the
more significant matter of an artist's original use of traditional materials,
we shall try to understand the organic place of this bagatelle, this use of
the most trifling trifles, in the comedy that is Sterne's world of conception. Bagatelle is traditional ornament to the mask of the professional
fool—a figure, Sterne reminds us, formerly honored, now unemployed.
And Tristram Shandy is an atavistic original showing the ancient leer
of the professional fool. Like Montaigne and Rabelais, like Burton, like
the Scriblerians, like Walter Shandy, Sterne was a snapper-up of considerable trifles, and in a mask of as subtle modality as that of Erasmus'
Folly he spoke his mind. Like Walter he had a "thousand little sceptical
notions of the comick kind to defend." He warns the reader in elaborate
mock horror that Walter had these notions at first "upon the footing of
mere whims, and of a *vive la Bagatelle*" (I, 19), but that finally that
madman had run them down into perfect systems. Sterne too ran his
bagatelle down into a perfect fool's system, but unlike Walter he was
a fool of Folly's sort, an artist who controlled his form. If his wry development of the ontological dilemma of Locke's rationalism afforded him,
as we have seen, a controlling scheme for dramatic situations, so did
Locke's passionate skepticism concerning the pretensions of human reason
stimulate his imaginative conception of a fantasy world of chaotic lore
in which to display the Shandys. And in considering this desultory,
fragmentary, carping satire, the material labeled "trivial" by the collective voice of criticism, we shall have to appreciate the complication of
Sterne's apparent adoption of the Scriblerian manner, and particularly
the manner of Swift, in his use of trivia.

Stouthearted wonderers at the bland majesty of Swift's intellectual
will have so inured themselves to the irony that calls up the final horrors
of this world—the King of Luggnagg's grace, for example, to the page
who forgot to remove the poison from the floor when a young lord of
promise was granted the honor of licking the dust before the royal foot-
stool—that the cry *"vive la Bagatelle"* cannot be appreciated save as
just another bitter spasm. But Swift loved trivia—learned junk, chambermaids' prattle and all vulgar idioms, the formless shows of things—
perhaps because trivia suggested to him a guilelessly insane world useful
to juxtapose to the guileful insanity of perverted reason and will which
he saw around him. Sterne's stock of urbanity, his moral assurance, was

[10] See D. W. Jefferson, *"Tristram Shandy and the Tradition of Learned Wit," Essays
in Criticism*, I (July, 1951).

certainly deficient for affecting this grand hauteur of Swift's. Yet large portions of *A Tale of a Tub* and *Tristram Shandy* seem almost interchangeable, so exact is Sterne's feeling for certain aspects of Swift's style and tone.[11] A good portion of *Tristram* is a texture of by-the-way ridicule of learned lumber, of systems, of foolishly innocent poseurs. In Swift's manner (and in the manner of the other Scriblerians) he sets up equivocations, allows us to hear the hum of etceteras from critics, voices of minute philosophers and academicians, indulges in comic and ironic digressions of learned bric-a-brac. But Sterne's bagatelle is finally not a debilitated posturing in Swift's manner. Nor is it merely a cloudy adumbration of Locke's skepticism rhetorically expressed in the *Essay* by constant sneers at "learned rubbish." Sterne loved bagatelle for his own aesthetic reasons, though both Locke and the Augustan satirists stimulated his imagination.

Locke's skepticism, his passion for doubting, shows everywhere in the *Essay* as an emotional rhetoric, not a logic, intended to convince the reader of the need of studying his formula for finding light where our reason fails. The eighteenth century, despite the textbook tag which labels it the Age of Reason, generally shared Locke's skepticism, and especially did the Augustans and their follower, Sterne. His incidental satire is the working of a skeptical mind. Sterne politely despised critics and they have had their revenge upon him with such labels as "trivial," but perhaps this material can be shown more to the credit of Sterne's artistic judgment than can the label to the critics' insight. The Sorbonne doctors, the schoolmen, the law, the Church, the gentry, in short, almost any typical dignity—this is the material good for a passing jibe in any paragraph. How many times does Tristram open a sentence to insert a seemingly irrelevant comment on systems and system builders. One difficulty in appreciating Sterne's bagatelle as a responsible technique is that, unlike Swift, he appears often to go out of his way to mask himself in resolute foolishness, to make all subjects trivial.

It is surprising, for example, how little about Sterne we can learn from his letters because of this very effort to speak in the voice of a character (Yorick, Tristram, a zany, a sentimentalist) and thus avoid a downright statement of anything. He seems to have been sure of himself only when he was being determinedly casual. This device covers well. Except in a few casual remarks, never a mention is there of his creative desires or of his comments on social matters. His background,

---

[11] The elusive narrator, his sudden shifts in tone, attitude, and topic, his similarity to Erasmus' Folly, the addresses to the reader, the subject matter, the hyperbolic expressions, digressions, and mad logic—all these Sterne shares with Swift.

of course, is precisely of the sort which would make him yearn for the manner of Swift and prevent his obtaining it. A poor relation, beholden to a powerful family, he was inordinately proud of his ancestry and contemptuous of his own station. A lousy prebendary, he called himself. The one thing that comes through the uneasy casualness concerning his creative inspirations is an intense admiration of Swift. There is evidence that he planned originally to travel Tristram through Europe (in the manner of Gulliver, perhaps) in order to make comments on men and manners.[12] He hopes that *Tristram Shandy* will "swim down the gutter of Time" with the *Tale of a Tub* (IX, 8). To Stella he compares Eliza. "Swift has said a hundred things I durst not say—unless I was Dean of St. Patrick's," he writes. One of his special delights in London was recognition by Swift's friend, Lord Bathurst,[13] as the first man of genius fit to follow the great Augustans. The odd prebendary of York Minster, in the mask of the fool, discovered for his own comic vision an odd synthesis of the satiric method of the Scriblerians with Locke's philosophical skepticism. Of course, Sterne's Augustan exemplars, Swift, Pope, Arbuthnot, and Prior, often found their own energy in skeptical thought. Prior, in fact, spares not even Locke. In attacking the schools Locke has only added another confounding system, says Prior.[14] Similarly, Martinus Scriblerus. But Prior's and Arbuthnot's strictures are exceptional, for Locke, who set down the limits of rationalism, was one of the eighteenth century's favorite weapons against learned quacks, and especially against mountebank rationalists of the scholastic stamp. Yet the Augustans are universally concerned with learned bagatelle because they are not finally removed from scholastic habits of mind. Nor is Sterne. Here it is that we discover an aesthetic rationale for his interest in this Augustan manner and in Locke's skepticism. Let us follow parallel (but finally different) devices of Swift and Sterne.

The scholastic habit of finding mystic significances in odd facts gathered by an omnibus learning, the scholastic ability to reason on an unlimited number of sides to any question, Swift turned to his own demonic uses in *A Tale of a Tub*. His anti-intellectualism is an obvious fact; and that the intellectual habits of scholasticism formed his mind is an equally obvious fact. Allegorical rationalism was in the grain. And fortunately, for since satire is a subversive activity and depends therefore upon the undermining of logical positions, a rationalism which finds

[12] So said John Croft in his anecdotes of Sterne. Quoted in *The Works of Laurence Sterne*, ed. Wilbur L. Cross (Cambridge, Mass.: The Jensen Society, 1906), VI, 13.

[13] *Letters*, No. 192, p. 319; No. 38A, p. 76; No. 185, p. 305.

[14] Matthew Prior, "Dialogue between Mr. Locke and Seigneur de Montaigne" and "Verse Intended for Locke and Montaigne," in *Dialogues of the Dead*.

symbolic significance on various levels can be turned to the service of a very complex satirical intention. Just as the scholastic mind interpreted phenomena in fourfold significances, so Swift's allegoric satirical method achieves multilevel significances. We may think, for example, of the passage from *A Tale of a Tub* on the sect of tailor-worshipers (sec. II). Here within the allegory of Peter, Martin, and Jack is the allegory of a clothes-religion, and the satirical levels of significance range over religious history, theological tenets, the penchants of human beings for supporting their extravagances with reason, the superficiality of moral attitudes (conscience is a pair of breeches, easily slipped down for lewdness or nastiness), human worship of appearance (a bishop is an apt conjunction of lawn and black satin), etc. Swift's skepticism always employed the tools of the enemy. Similarly eighteenth century philosophy reasoned to undermine reason. Locke would banish error by reasoning away most of the early bases of reason; Berkeley would settle the "learned dust" by pointing to the reality of reality, perceptions as perceived, and the impossibility of knowing substance; and Hume sardonically "manages to chevy Christian mystics and atheists into the same camp," by undermining the presumptions of both to a common skepticism.[15] The subversiveness of the eighteenth century philosophers is accomplished by rational subversion of reason; often they are quite as satirical as the satirists.

Locke, said Sterne, had rid the world of the lumber of a thousand vulgar errors. "Heat is in proportion to the want of true knowledge," Sterne can say, echoing Locke, in moral application to the school-divinity debates on Slawkenbergius' nose, and at the same time he can use allegory in Swift's manner. On various allegorical levels the Slawkenbergius epic involves the reader's own assumptions in a satire on rationalism (can God make two and two five?), on Locke's scheme for determining ideas, and on anyone's logic ("it proved the stranger's nose was neither true nor false. This left room for the controversy to go on"), on pedantry and that scattered and crazy memory of the race which is scholarship, on religious polemics and practices, on sexual prudery (and by suggestion there again appears one of the book's fundamental themes, sterility, the alien worlds of uncoupled minds, bodies, and ages), and finally, on Walter Shandy's pretension that he is any different from Toby Shandy, that his rationalism is more than an odd rhetoric by which he expresses himself (precisely as Toby's military excursions are his rhetoric). In the tradition of scholasticism the story has various

[15] Carl L. Becker, *The Heavenly City of the Eighteenth-Century Philosophers* (New Haven: Yale University Press, 1932), p. 68.

levels of apprehension. But organically in the whole conception of *Tristram* the Slawkenbergius story represents by all these allegorical levels a kind of fantasy world in which one of the principal facts of existence is that we live in a whirl of incoherent and contradictory shards of all the ages' learning. Any stance in such a world is subject to the undermining force of a skeptical sensibility. E. M. Forster[16] has suggested keenly that *Tristram Shandy* is a fantasy in which a fantastic God called Muddle works chaos in ordinary life. Sterne has adapted Swift's technique to call up a chaotic fantasy world in which reason may alienate, confuse, and obfuscate. Slawkenbergius' fable becomes a kind of surrealistic epitome of all the implications of learned jumble in *Tristram*. Sterne calls the reader to an ironic awareness of this darkling plain, and, through his characters, to the way of sympathetic correspond- ence. It is in such passages as this that Sterne's conceptual use for bagatelle calls both Locke and his Augustan exemplars into service.

But *Tristram Shandy* is a comedy, not a nerve-jangling satire on the human situation, and its incidental satire only makes its doctrine of sympathy artistically necessary. For the Shandys find their way blind in the noon of Enlightenment. (One of the complications of literary history is that the modern term "Enlightenment" is applied to a period which produced so many satirists whose principal study was to deni- grate the human reason.) Sterne is in this skeptical tradition, but he also wrote a comedy which is as salutary to the life force as it is deadly to the reason. But the satire is necessary to the comedy, not extrinsic bagatelle. As a rhetorician Sterne had to subvert the reason so that he could persuade his reader of the moral substance of that ultimate sym- pathy which reconciles the eccentric egos of the Shandy world. Another effort of rhetoric demonstrates that those egos indeed are not eccentric at all, or are at least very similar to that of His Worship the Reader. The undermining skeptical arguments of Hume (which recommend his doc- trine of sympathy) find almost a descriptive statement in *Tristram*.

Locke's effort (which Sterne so often reflects) to define the grounds and limits of human knowledge is an expression of an attitude that amounts to a real passion; yet, unlike Sterne's, it is an acerbic passion predicated as a rhetorical proem to his rational solution for man's diffi- culties in communicating. Sterne, on the other hand, undermined Locke's solution and exploited its absurdities. His sympathy with Locke's skepticism, then, is only *his* rhetorical proem to a solution, very different from Locke's, for man's difficulties in communicating. The solution is the comedy of the Shandys' real sympathetic correspondence in the midst

---

[16] *Aspects of the Novel* (New York: Harcourt, Brace & World, Inc., 1927), p. 165.

of their misunderstandings. Thus the incidental satire in the Augustan manner was made to serve the general comic scheme built upon a subversion of Locke's philosophy. Adopting the skeptical attitude of Locke, Sterne pursued it to a total reduction of Locke's scheme.

In Sterne's peculiar use, the scraps of incidental satire which reflect both Locke's skepticism and the Augustan manner do suggest a lurking fantasy world of mad rationalization and private systemization. In this fantasy world the antics of the Shandys are comedy; in the genteel decorum of the Enlightenment, they would be only an unrelieved satire such as the *Memoirs of Scriblerus* or the third book (considered in isolation) of *Gulliver's Travels*. Sterne's very detachment from the vortices of eighteenth century society enabled him to recreate the ironic but sympathetic world of Erasmus' Folly. To say, then, that the ubiquitous remarks on systems, on scholars, on churchmen, on gravity, on scraps of odd philosophies—all the apparent bagatelle—are trivial and puerile is to say that we need no fantasy in which to see the mad philosopher Walter, the crazy little military logician Toby, Trim his mechanical man, and the popish medicine-man Slop. The fantasy, of course is universal, for everywhere men's schemes fail of closure. Such schemes can be the death of society; for Sterne, this was so only when men refused to recognize themselves as fools. His rhetoric, like that of Erasmus, invites the reader to acknowledge himself as fool. Always he suggests that the Shandys and their world are not wholly eccentric.

Of course the world of learning means to Sterne, as it does to Rabelais, the drama of man's effort to make sense of things. Things are more than merely things when they become metaphors and allegories of the orders that men will make. "What hindrance, hurt, or harm doth the laudable desire of knowledge bring to any man, were it from a sot, a pot, a fool, a stool, a winter's mitten, truckle for a pulley, the lid of a goldsmith's crucible, an oil-bottle, or an old slipper," says Pantagruel, in urging Panurge to consult a new voice in his long investigation of the marital problems of individual identity, who is who, how many joys there are and aren't, and force and faith and cuckoldry.[17] This very sentence Sterne echoes in defending metaphor and wit—and as Rabelais displays in comic paradoxes all the world's learning on Panurge's problem and thereby reduces to its essential absurdity any manly posture that denies or forgets that women are involved in human nature, satirizes the sixteenth century hothouse flower of *courtoisie*, but especially shows that men make of learning what they will to dramatize themselves, just so on the subject of Toby's instruction in the right end of a

[17] Rabelais, Bk. III, ch. 16.

woman by Walter and the reader's instruction by Tristram, or on almost any other subject cluttered with mock-learning in *Tristram Shandy,* Sterne uses learning to suggest both chaos and absurdity and by metaphorical transformation the drama of little men's passions. While the fantasy of total expression, of joyful wish-fulfillment and thirst-quenching by giants is of the essence of Rabelais's learned satire, Sterne, dealing essentially with alienation and comic insufficiency, turns the same material to the representation of interior dramas of small, Cervantic heroes. The fantasy is implied, is the measure of posturing in the probable world. Never does Sterne's use of learned bagatelle merely satirize pedantry. He loved Rabelais and the lesser French *conteurs* such as Bouchet, Bruscambille, De Verville, he rummaged in Burton, because these writers also had larger uses for learned satire.

Yet Sterne is accused of a certain lack of substance for the very reason that he sported with desiccated or nonexistent creeds. "Rabelais," Dr. John Ferriar observed in a prototypical criticism, "derided existing follies; Sterne laughed at exploded opinions." [18] But Sterne no more than Voltaire was attacking philosophy. *Candide* cannot possibly be construed as an assault on Leibniz. It is a mordacious comment on those who fret and fray life for the pleasure of canting, systematical strictures. Desiccated creeds and scraps of recondite knowledge were as good symbols as newly invented faiths for the attitude that Sterne reduced to its essential inanity. All the Shandys (and all the world) swear like madmen. Fortunately they (unlike the world) have a strange perception of their own ineffectualities.

Moreover, since Sterne's sympathy for the animal economy is real, the balance for this indulgence, the prevention of a fatuous mooniness in his own economy, is an elaborate contempt for "the stage-loads of chymical nostrums, and peripatetic lumber, with which, in all ages," quacks have "flattered" the world (V, 34). It was simply to his purpose on one level to pick here and there, for in this way he could ridicule solutions to speculative snarls that are unverifiable in the Lockean sense and at the same time could erect the fantasy world of dubious reality which, unlike Locke's philosophy, suggests man's responsibility to recognize himself as fool. Sterne's Panurgic spirit at sea in scuds of wind flew at more varieties of attitudinizing than did Locke, but a skeptical passion animates both. For Sterne, a bishop, a professional virgin, a critic, a sentimentalist like himself, anyone who bore a shield blazoned with the straight line of rectitude, in some aspect everyone, should be ludicrous; like Yorick he had an invincible dislike for gravity,

[18] *Illustrations of Sterne* (London, 1812), II, 42.

"a mysterious carriage of the body to cover the defects of the mind" (I, 11; cf. *Essay* 4, 16, 4).

Sterne's ridicule of learning, of academic word-play, and of large ideas is so parallel to Locke's opinions in the *Essay* that it is instructive in understanding the original turn of Sterne's skepticism to follow the philosopher's reasoning. Locke liked to explain to the reader the goads he felt to set up his system. He announces, rather often, and with passion, his disdain for scholastic subleties (3, 10, 6). Words, for Locke, are signs of ideas (3, 1, 2), and ideas come from experience (1, 1-3); something founded in substance or in an affection is the object of the mind in raising ideas (1, 1, 8; 2, 2, 3). But the ultimate generator of ideas, substance, is the familiar "I-know-not-what." So the effects of substance, not substance itself, may be known surely in their simple or compounded manifestations, but we can never know more than this (2, 23). Thus Locke knows what is the proper object of knowledge, and what is not. His world is circumscribed. He knows the place of revelation (4, 19, 14): it reinforces reason, and it assures us of what is "beyond" rational conception, that is, resurrection, heaven, hell, and the realm of spirits. He knows the place of reason: it can discover a true moral system (3, 11, 16-17). He knows the grounds and limits of skepticism and the degrees of probability (4, 15-16). And, assured of God's sun, the steady small glow of his own candle is sufficient to man.

Nevertheless, the use of a candle with aplomb requires efficiency, and it is for that reason, Locke tells his reader, that he wrote the *Essay*. In another metaphor: "It is of great use to the sailor to know the length of his line, though he cannot with it fathom all the depths of the ocean" (1, 1, 6). After he and his friends had come to a stand in their consideration of a subject, they determined that the only way to clear their befuddlement was to "examine our own abilities, and see what objects our understandings were or were not fitted to deal with" (Epistle to the Reader). This, of course, would not solve a problem, but it would prevent charges into the unknowable by philosophical gymnasts. It was a theory of knowledge rather than knowledge itself that Locke sought; his system is critical (and hence useful to a satirist) rather than constructive. Therefore, his purpose: "to inquire into the original, certainty, and extent of human knowledge" (1, 1, 2). So did his skepticism take rational form.

Locke is a rationalist at least in the sense that he thinks reason a completely reliable source of a limited knowledge and the only infallible guide for certainty. The restriction on reason is that it has to concern itself with materials given to the mind in a sensory or reflective experience (1). We can know only our ideas and their relationships to one another. This being the human situation, the spheres in which certainty is possible are indeed very limited (4, 3). Particularly where we most need it, in the world of real entities, both physical and mental, certain knowledge seems impossible. As a consequence, we cannot know (*a*) any necessary relations within things, i.e., how qualities cohere in a thing, or (*b*) necessary relations between things, e.g., the causal relation, if there is such. Perhaps most important, for a consideration of Sterne, we are ignorant of the true inner nature of that immaterial substance which we call mind, and have no way of knowing, indeed, that any mind other than our own exists. Locke's only concession to reality is that despite our lack of ideas we intuitively feel that it exists (4, 2, 1). This is a rationalization, a stray thread in his system, and the one most vulnerable on his own principles. But Locke reasons thus concerning the limits of human reason so that he can heap elaborate scorn on those whose reasoning is out of bounds. His philosophy authorizes his contempt for total rationalists.

It is perhaps too much to say that Locke disliked "learned rubbish" so much that he discovered this system to disenfranchise it; but whichever came first, the philosophy or the affection, the two elements are often blended. Certainly this constant spitting at "learned rubbish" which decorates Locke's *Essay* must have been a joyful little drama for Sterne. Though Locke was a sober man, he could hypostatize other men's chimeras as devils in his road. For all his pride in the "historical plain method" and plotted rationalism, and despite his stated intention of ignoring the odd ramblings of the animal spirits, Locke had a passion which exhibits itself everywhere along the history. He wrote for those "not content to live lazily on scraps of begged opinions" (Epistle to the Reader), for those who with him would be content to work as underlaborers "in clearing ground a little, and removing some of the rubbish that lies in the way to knowledge." For knowledge "certainly had been very much more advanced in the world, if the endeavours of ingenious and industrious men had not been much cumbered with the learned but frivolous use of uncouth, affected, or unintelligible terms . . . [which] have so long passed for mysteries of science . . . [and which] with little or no meaning, have, by prescription, such a right to be mistaken for deep learning and height of speculation, that it will not be easy to persuade either those who speak or those who hear them, that they are but the covers of ignorance, and hindrance of true knowledge."

Since the use of the reason in society depends upon a language that determines ideas precisely (so runs the argument) (3, 1, 1), Locke became particularly heated when he considered something called "subtlety" in philosophical snarls. Book III, "Of Words," is dotted with flings at the schoolmen, who invented a nomenclature "the apter to produce wonder because it could not be understood." "These learned disputants, these all-knowing doctors" somehow had made their "gibberish prevail with grave and subtle rhetoric." He hawks at any pompous metaphysician with fancy, erudite, recondite names unattached to ideas—"from whence commonly proceeds noise and wrangling . . ." (3, 10, 22).

The passional life of man Locke considered out of his road. He treats the passions in one short and uneasy chapter (2, 20), with an apology that he might have been more discursive. He might, for example, he says, have said something about the "pain from captious, uninstructive wrangling, and the pleasure of rational conversation" (2, 20, 18). Such is Locke's passionate dispassion.

Noise and wrangling and rectitude and gravity were a single pannierload of devils to Sterne, which in Lockean cant he proclaimed insupportable, although we know they served him well—served him as form. Obviously it is Sterne's opinion, considered as it is in a hundred passages, that the world is tolerable only when we at last settle down with the fact that the human reason is only a shadowy image of God, is weak and imbecile (VIII, 5). Locke, too, of course, tends in the same direction, but pulls himself up short. A little candle Locke allows us, and then erects such a system that he can say, near the end of the *Essay*, "Reason must be our last judge and guide in everything" (4, 19, 14). On the other hand, nowhere does Sterne suggest any such steady, though small, illumination of chaos. Wherever Locke's skepticism searches out a source of obscurity, Sterne settles, and develops the possibilities of that obscurity into a jibe at system makers or at length into a Toby or Walter. Indeed, he stops not there, but continues, as we have seen, to reduce even Locke's rationalism to confusion. "Professing themselves to be wise, they became fools," is Sterne's text in the profane as well as sacred pulpit. On this text he preaches "The Advantage of Christianity to the World." To convince his parishioners that although reason may of itself discover the first cause and a consequent but perhaps imperfect moral system, human passions never suffer it to remain dominant. Consequently, Christianity offers a guide which the well-disposed may, by their will, follow. We need not see this as especially a Lockean derivative or as a dilution of deism: Paul says quite unequivocally that Romans have no excuse for denying God since "the invisible things of him from the creation of the world are clearly seen . . ." (Rom. 1:20). The point is that Sterne is concerned much less with Christianity, if we are to judge from the space allotted it, than with describing pretenders to wisdom, and less with describing pretenders to wisdom than in making a rhetorical and satiric demonstration of human passions. *Clearly, Sterne's capacity for doubt is his capacity for expression.* Locke was simply a device for amplifying that expression. Locke too is often concerned much less with philosophy than with a rhetorical assault on pretenders to wisdom; but, unlike Locke, Sterne sees a dramatic life-force in the text: "Professing themselves to be wise, they became fools."

What rational account can be rendered of the sudden inflammation of Uncle Toby upon perceiving the Widow? (VIII, 5-6). Tristram runs through old medical lore. But nothing fits. "One would think I took pleasure in running into difficulties of this kind, merely to make fresh experiments of getting out of them." But "the whole is an equivocation; it shews the weakness and imbecility of human reason."

"Reason is half of it sense; and the measure of heaven itself is but the measure of our present appetites and concoctions" (VII, 13). Against Locke's dictum that, weak though it be, reason has its proper activity in the study of morality, this statement displays Sterne's radicalism from the Lockean view. However, whenever Locke's formulas fit the purpose of reinforcing an empirical observation of the passions, and of deprecating the rational-passional antithesis, they are offered up as unquestioned assumptions. Walter's eccentric manners in bearing up under his various vexations need an explanation, says Tristram. Unless the reader has a great insight into human nature, he will expect standard reactions from Walter. Explanation? "But mark, madam, we live amongst riddles and mysteries—the most obvious things, which come in our way, have dark sides, which the quickest sight cannot penetrate into; and even the clearest and most exalted understandings amongst us find ourselves puzzled and at a loss in almost every cranny of nature's works . . ." (IV, 17). At this point Walter's mind is inscrutable, though we learn in a volume or two to read it. And we learn, without a single determinate idea, from a context of situations.

And this sort of skepticism is a refrain that is sung whenever a learned disputant is to be considered. "It is the nature of an hypothesis," says Tristram, ". . . that it assimilates everything to itself as proper nourishment; . . . it generally grows the stronger by everything you see, hear, read, or understand. This is of great use" (II, 19). It unriddles the observations of "monstrous heads,—shewing *a priori,* it could not be otherwise." Schoolmen and Walter, for example, know all about noses—including their allegorical significance. Does a nose have a soul, can it think? Can matter think? (IV, Slawkenbergius' Tale).

The remedy, Locke conceives, for our blind gropings after knowledge is a sedulous application of the principles of judgment. Here is the empirical side of his philosophy, concerned with probabilities. "Probability is the appearance of agreement [of ideas] upon fallible proofs" (4, 15, 1). The proofs being not constant and immutable, or at least not perceived to be so, predications from them must be based upon a diligent examination of all probable agreements or disagreements among ideas. This technical use of judgment, Locke opposes to wit, which is a mere recognition of superficial congruence among ideas, without exhaustive analysis. Obviously, then, wit is no guide in "this twilight state" of life.

But when "the judgment is surprised by the imagination," Tristram says, "I defy the best cabbage planter that ever existed . . . to go on coolly, critically, and canonically, planting his cabbages one by one, in straight lines, and stoical distances, especially if slits in petticoats are unsew'd up . . ." (VIII, 1). So was Phutatorius' judgment subverted upon his reception of the hot chestnut. In such overwhelmings of the judgment, wit may tell us something of the phenomenal chaos. As wit for Sterne is a description of experience in terms of unlikely relations, Locke's judgment is not exclusively the light in the probable world.[19]

[19] The present essay, being only a part of a larger study, does not include my discussion of other important relations of Sterne to Locke—his associationism, his theory of time, and his emphasis upon sense experience.

Tristram Shandy and the Tradition
of Learned Wit

by D. W. Jefferson

I

Tristram Shandy, though a much-loved work, is in many respects misunderstood. It is a pity to have to quarrel with Mr. E. M. Forster's engaging description of it:

> There is a charmed stagnation about the whole epic—the more the characters do the less gets done, the less they have to say the more they talk, the harder they think the softer they get, facts have an unholy tendency to unwind and trip up the past instead of begetting the future, as in well-conducted books. . . . Obviously a god is hidden in *Tristram Shandy* and his name is Muddle, and some readers cannot accept him.[1]

Tristram Shandy certainly does not satisfy the usual expectations as to how a novel should be organized, but that is because it is not the usual sort of novel. The tendency among critics has been to comment on its structural oddities without first discovering to what literary kind it belongs and what its author was trying to do. Some attempt will be made in this essay to show that it has traditional form and a thematic pattern. Perfect fidelity to an artistic scheme would be too much to claim for Sterne, but it is important to realize that he had one. The view that *Tristram Shandy* is a muddle is related to a tendency to approach Sterne in the light of his affinities with certain later writers, exponents of the eccentric or the nonsensical. Mr. Graham Greene says that "his whimsicality was inherited by the essayists, by Lamb in particular." [2] Whatever his relations with the whimsical school—"whimsicality" is rather a dam-

"*Tristram Shandy* and the Tradition of Learned Wit" by D. W. Jefferson. From *Essays in Criticism*, I (1951), 225ff. Copyright © 1951 by *Essays in Criticism*. Reprinted by permission of the author and *Essays in Criticism*.

[1] *Aspects of the Novel*, 1927, p. 146.
[2] From an essay on Fielding and Sterne in *From Anne to Victoria*, ed. B. Dobrée, 1937, p. 282.

aging word today—he differs fundamentally from these writers in being also of an older and better school. He belongs to a tradition of wit to which they had no access. It is in relation to this background that we must place *Tristram Shandy,* if we are to appreciate fully its point and structure.

II

We are confronted not with one kind of wit but with several related kinds. They are sufficiently related to be seen as one tradition, though the points which unite them would be difficult to state with absolute precision. It is also difficult to give the tradition a suitable label. The word "scholastic" covers certain examples and could, with a little elasticity, be extended to cover others, but as the tradition moves further and further away from scholasticism without ceasing to be a tradition the problem of terminology becomes increasingly embarrassing. Donne's use of Thomist metaphysics in "Air and Angels" is scholastic wit in the strictest sense. Where he uses materials which were not actually taught in the schools but which belong to some branch of medieval learning, as in his exploitation of legal expressions in "Lovers' Infiniteness," the term is perhaps permissible. But the ratiocinative ingenuity which writers of the Renaissance and later inherited from the schoolmen was liable to be applied to all kinds of ideas, even to those of the new science and philosophy; and the result, for our purpose, is a species of wit essentially similar to that based on scholastic ideas. Some of Sterne's material may be labeled scholastic, but he also used ideas from Descartes and Locke.

There is something in the scholastic approach to intellectual issues— a speculative freedom, a dialectical ingenuity—which lends itself to witty development. And there is something in the empiricist's approach—a puritanical restriction on speculation, a plodding regard for truth—which is alien to wit. We do not look for jokes among the serious students of Newton and Locke, but a person brought up in the old tradition of wit might well find that some of the new ideas of Newton and Locke suited his purpose. When this happens the spirit of scholastic wit is still alive, though whether it is convenient to use that term is another question. Some of the most interesting types of wit which concern us have no direct connection with learning. It may be claimed that they are traceable ultimately to a mentality formed under scholastic or quasi-scholastic influences, but it is in the field of imagery not of ideas that the indebtedness is revealed. Here again, the term "scholastic wit" might cause misunderstanding, though not much more perhaps than the term "metaphysical image."

By way of summing up, it may be said in general that the types of wit which come within our survey owe their character to intellectual habits belonging to the pre-Enlightenment world of thought, and that the habits were those against which the Enlightenment set its face. This kind of wit is found in considerable quantity in Augustan comic and satirical writing: for example, in Swift's *Tale of a Tub,* in Pope's *Art of Sinking in Poetry,* and in the *Memoirs of Scriblerus.* Sterne is perhaps the last great writer in the tradition. It is not enough to argue that the comic use of old-fashioned ideas or ratiocinative techniques is merely a symptom of satirical reaction against them. That they should have been matter for comedy is a sign that they were not dead. To be matter for comedy they had to be matter for the imagination. We know that Swift despised the old pedantic learning, but it provided him with excellent comic material, and the discipline of the disputation did much to mould his art. No writer has ever excelled him in the exploitation of dialectical stratagems.

The survival of this type of learned wit in the eighteenth century may be attributed partly to an isolated event in literary history: the publication of the English Rabelais. The first two books of Urquhart's translation appeared in 1653; but the wonderful third book, which we shall find most significant in relation to Sterne, was not published until 1693. The remaining books appeared in the following year. Rabelais was known to English writers before he appeared in translation, but Urquhart and Motteux made an enormous difference to his influence. It is noteworthy that the completed work was a new book when Swift began to write his early satires. Rabelais was the greatest of all masters of the comic use of scholastic wit.

I propose to review the main types of wit belonging to this tradition. When we have the tradition as a whole to refer to, we shall be in a position to concentrate on *Tristram Shandy.*

It is not to be expected that all the materials of medieval thought should survive as themes for wit into the eighteenth century. The outer framework of the medieval world-picture, the cosmological system, survived less well than other elements.

The "determinate, humanly comprehensible universe" of medieval and Renaissance man gave opportunities to the imagination which are not afforded by the "unrepresentable, inconceivable, affrighting universe of contemporary science." [3] There was an all-embracing scheme of facts and meanings in which any particular matter for inquiry could always be placed. It was possible to pass from the particular event to the general

[3] J. L. Lowes, *Geoffrey Chaucer,* 1932, p. 21.

cosmic pattern and *vice versa* with an easy, assured sweep of the mind such as modern man can never enjoy. This opened up huge possibilities to a comic genius. Thus with a single stroke of facile logic Panurge invokes the entire cosmic order in support of borrowing and lending without which (he argues) the relations of the planets would fall into disorder, the sun would no longer give light, there would be an end to seasons, and within man's body there would be no cooperation of the different members. Comedy depends on pattern and order, on something which can stand distortion and yet retain its essential nature, like a human figure in a caricature. In some periods this is supplied by a social structure with its systems of manners and morals, but with a cosmic structure to play with comedy can attain to the colossal. Rabelais's comedy is of this order and it is more than comedy, for into Panurge's praise of the cosmic order he puts all his poetic sense of the goodness of creation.

Ideas relating to physiology and medicine survived better. Medieval learning gave the artist many things which modern learning, with its greater store and greater accuracy of information, cannot give. One of these was a rational, readily intelligible and complete conception of the nature of man. The Galenic physiology, which contained the elements of a psychology, was, from the modern scientific standpoint, quite inaccurate, but it was a considerable achievement of speculative intelligence. If it did not explain the workings of the human organism correctly, it explained them plausibly. And physiological theory was related to other parts of the medieval world-picture. One could pass quite naturally from the question of man's organic nature to that of his place in the Christian universe. The system did not burden the imagination with too much detail, and it left a great deal to rational conjecture. The problems of modern medicine are too technical for the nonspecialist, but it was open to anyone to discuss the influence of radical heat and radical moisture on bodily health. The points of the system lent themselves to ingenious handling. One could manipulate them to provide an amusing explanation for any eccentricity of character. This made the old physiology an excellent basis for theories of character: for example, the "Humours" theory of Ben Jonson.

A pleasing example of this exploitation of physiological ideas is found in the third section of *The Art of Sinking in Poetry*. Pope is explaining the process of creating bad poetry:

Farthermore, it were great cruelty and injustice, if all such Authors as cannot write in the other way, were prohibited from writing at all. Against this

I draw an argument from what seems to me an undoubted physical Maxim,
That Poetry is a natural or morbid Secretion from the Brain. As I would
not suddenly stop a cold in the head, or dry up my neighbour's Issue, I
would as little hinder him from necessary writing. It may be affirmed with
great truth that there is hardly any human creature past childhood, but at
one time or other has had some Poetical Evacuation, and, no question, was
much the better for it in his health; so true is the saying, *Nascimur Poetae.*
Therefore is the Desire of Writing properly term'd *Pruritus,* the "Titillation
of the Generative Faculty of the Brain," and the Person is said to conceive;
now such as conceive must bring forth. I have known a man thoughtful, melancholy and raving for divers days, who forthwith grew wonderfully easy,
lightsome and cheerful, upon the discharge of the peccant humour, in ex-
ceeding purulent metre.

Another characteristic of the old physiology is that it could be con-
cretely visualized. It could become material for poetic imagery. There is
a most eloquent account, in Panurge's defense of borrowing and lending,
of the cooperation of the members of the body in the work of making
blood (Book III, Chap. 4). As physiology and medicine became more
scientific and less speculative these subjects became less available for
imaginative treatment. Physiological wit, some of it based on old ideas
and some on new, is found in abundance in *Tristram Shandy.*

From the materials of medicine we turn to those of law. "Justice entangled in her web of law," writes an historian of English legal institutions, "is a familiar figure in poetry from Sophocles to Pope and in
philosophy from Aristotle to Kant." [4] But the idea of law as a kind of
net through which the undeserving, if sufficiently supple, may escape and
in which the deserving may be ensnared, has less point today than in
earlier periods. The old pedantic rigidity of the forms of action has gone,
and the reforms of the utilitarians have tended to make the legal system
correspond more to what ordinary human nature sees as reasonable and
just. *Ubi remedium ibi ius* has become *ubi ius ibi remedium.* Fewer
people need to go to law today, so we are all less legally minded; and
in becoming more efficient the law has become less picturesque. The
community has benefited from these reforms, but a theme for wit has
been lost.[5] Under the old regime the legal system, in real life as in literature, was a field for playful invention, some of the fictitious proceedings
which were used to manipulate the law, such as those involved in "bar-
ring the entail," having for us the qualities of ingenious farce. The

[4] C. H. S. Fifoot, *English Law and its Background,* 1932, p. 5.
[5] Sir Alan Herbert's *Misleading Cases* are a reminder that the legal quibble can
still be a source of light entertainment, but it no longer provides a major theme for
literature.

primitive concreteness of the law, as exemplified in such ceremonies as "livery of seisin" (the handing over by feoffor to feoffee of the symbolic clod of earth) made it also a natural source of poetic imagery.

The art of the legal quibble is one application of that art of logic-chopping for which the schoolmen were chiefly renowned. The power to use logic to give a show of plausibility to an absurd or unreasonable argument is, in general, one of the distinguishing marks of the writers in the tradition of wit which we are examining. Legal quibbles are common in seventeenth century literature. Donne, in "Woman's Constancy" cynically invents for his mistress a far-fetched excuse in legal terms for infidelity. Dryden's Almanzor, confronted with Almahide's betrothal to Boabdelin, seeks for a quasi-legal basis for his own claim to her.[6] *The Merchant of Venice* is a simple example of a story which turns on a legal technicality; but there is more play with the learned materials of law, more of the scholastic spirit, in Jonson's *Silent Woman,* where the bogus canonist and divine discuss the possibilities of a divorce for the unfortunate Morose. The impeachment of Bridlegoose in Rabelais, and the interpretation by the three brothers of their father's will in the *Tale of a Tub,* may also be cited as further examples of legal wit. It is hardly necessary to mention that *Tristram Shandy* is full of it: the "petite *canulle*" joke (IV, 29), the "in nomine patriae" (I, 20) dispute, the debate as to whether Mr. Shandy is of kin to his own child (IV, 29), are delightful examples.

If legal wit has declined it does not mean that law has ceased to provide comic situations. A distinction is necessary here between legal wit, which depends on the manipulation of the logic of law and is an intellectual thing, and what may be termed the comedy of the law court, which is simply a form of comedy of manners depending on human idiosyncrasies in a special setting. Legal situations, insofar as they are human situations, are always liable to give rise to comedy of this kind. The Bardell *v.* Pickwick trial comes mainly in the latter category.

Something must be said concerning the central subject matter of scholastic thought: religion. But religion comes too near to the thought-life of the common man to be typical material for learned wit. Learned jokes about religion can often be classified under some other subject, such as canon law. The medieval habit of referring to religion as the supreme arbiter on all matters, however secular and commonplace, continued among writers during and after the Renaissance. It was quite natural in

[6] *The Conquest of Granada,* III.

the *Compleat Angler* for Piscator and his friends to use scriptural arguments in defense of their favorite forms of sport, and convention allowed
them to do this without destroying the essentially social and practical
character of their discussion. It is a feature of conventions that they can
be accommodated to more than one level of attitude. A reference to
Christian doctrine could be a gesture of piety or of polite conformity,
or it could be a stroke of wit. The Wife of Bath quotes patriarchal
authority in defense of a promiscuous love-life and Panurge appeals to
Genesis in support of his theory of codpieces (Book III).

Under medieval Catholicism a good deal of joking on or near the
subject of religion was habitual, while the courtly love poet travestied
the materials of religion for serious purposes. Boldness in the treatment
of this subject is one of the general characteristics of those writers who
come within our survey: Rabelais, Swift, Sterne. Modern readers, especially those of puritan or rationalist mentality, often misunderstand this
freedom, because we have lost the idea of a Christian tradition within
which so much latitude is possible. Any view we take of Rabelais is incomplete if we forget that he had moments of tender piety, which give
way, however, almost without pause to his usual ribald gaiety. It is
characteristic of the tradition that the little company which sits waiting
for Tristram's birth should hear Trim's reading of a sermon as well as
Dr. Slop's reading of the Ernulphus curse.

This elasticity in moving from the serious to the flippant is parallel to
the capacity to alternate between the romantic and the improper in the
treatment of sex. The gradual encroachment in the eighteenth century
of a middle-class spirit in religion and morals destroyed both.

Certain types of wit within this tradition take their character not so
much from any specific materials of the prescientific era of learning as
from its procedures and habits. Modern science, with its more exacting
standards of certainty and accuracy, and its specialization, imposes conditions which did not exist for such studious inquirers as Sir Thomas
Browne and Mr. Walter Shandy, to whom the whole universe lay open
for learned exploration. There was no question for them which they
might not hopefully tackle by relying on their two principal methods:
abstract reasoning and the consultation of erudite authorities.

The "unbridled rationalism" (to use Whitehead's phrase) of the scholastic mentality, the complete absence of such restraint upon abstract
speculation as scientific principles impose, led to much eccentricity and
extravagance. Browne's *Vulgar Errors* is fertile in examples. On the ques-

tion of whether, "a Bear brings forth her young informous and unshapen, which she fashioneth after by licking them over," he concludes that it is, "injurious to Reason, and much impugneth the course and providence of Nature, to conceive a birth should be ordained before there is a formation." In Mr. Shandy this speculative freedom is carried to its limits.

The second method, the consultation of learned authorities, must be dwelt on rather longer. Under the regime of modern science it is not necessary to know all the views of one's predecessors; it is possible to say quite definitely that certain theories have had their day and can safely be forgotten. They remain of interest only as part of the history of science, a subject in which scientists are not always interested. For Sir Thomas Browne it was otherwise. In any learned inquiry—on the legs of the badger, for example, or of the elephant—reference would normally be made to a number of authorities, ancient and modern, the more the better. When one man's opinion might be quoted against another's without the question arising of a decision by experiment, it was honorable and useful to know all the best opinions. The list of authorities was the measure of a scholar's range of learning. Along with lists of authorities went lists of facts and materials culled from the authorities. Modern works of science and learning run to lists only for specific utilitarian purposes. The list has lost its rhetorical value. But in works like the *Anatomy of Melancholy* it is a thing of glory, the inventory of a treasure-house. When the facts are numerous, but not too numerous, there is some point in trying to know them all. There is a place for the gargantuan appetite of a Burton. Learning of this kind has a personal flavor: it represents individual achievement. Modern learning, with its infinitely greater array of facts and formidable mechanical organization of them, is inevitably more impersonal.

In Burton and other scholars and wits of his school we find two qualities combined: a pedantic thoroughness in the listing of authorities and facts, and a lively grasp of everyday things. The piling on of learned detail does not choke the human interest, while the materials of concrete experience are ordered with a learned thoroughness. In the following passage Pantagruel gives advice to Panurge on what to eat and what to abstain from in order to avoid fallacious dreams:

> You may take a little supper, but thereat must you not eat of a hare, nor of any other Flesh: you are likewise to abstain from beans, from the *Preak* (by some called the *Polyp*) as also from Coleworts, cabbage, and all other such like windy victuals, which may endanger the troubling of your brains, and the dimming or casting a kind of mist over your Animal

Spirits. . . . You shall eat good *Eusebian* and Bergamot-Pears, one apple
of the short-shank Pepin-kind, a parcel of the little plums of *Tours,* and
some few cherries of the growth of my orchard. (III, 13)

We are given the impression here that behind the choosing of Panurge's
supper lies a vast body of theory on the dietetic properties of all the
meats, vegetables, and fruits. Yet accompanying this is a personal knowledge of a particular fruit grown in a particular place. From an almost
limitless world of possibilities everything is most studiously hand-picked.

In Rabelais's third book, from which this passage is taken, stupendous
quantities of information, with authorities and *exempla,* are poured
forth, and one source of wisdom after another is consulted, all to the
end that Panurge—literature's most irresponsible figure—might be correctly advised about marriage. There is a huge comic disproportion,
which is also a noble disproportion, between Pantagruel's unflagging
helpfulness and its object. Only in an age which believed in princely
magnificence and courtesy (and, higher than that, in the overwhelming
bounty of God to undeserving man) could such a situation be created
and sustained. Only in an age which believed in the nobility of learning
could the materials of erudition be raised to such rhetorical heights.

A passage, similar to the last, may be quoted from *Tristram Shandy.*
It is from Mr. Shandy's letter to Uncle Toby, in which he recommends
a suitable diet for a wooer. It is hardly necessary to comment on the
solemn absurdity of the advice, which contrasts oddly with the sardonic
good sense shown earlier in the letter (". . . and thou knowest, dear
Toby, that there is no passion so serious as lust").

But thou must eat little or no goat's flesh, nor red deer—nor even foal's
flesh, by any means; and carefully abstain—that is, as much as thou canst,
from peacocks, cranes, coots, didappers, and water-hens. . . .

As for thy drink—I need not tell thee, it must be the infusion of Vervain
and the herb Hanea, of which Aelian relates such effects—but if thy
stomach palls with it—discontinue it from time to time, taking cucumbers,
melons, purslane, water-lilies, woodbine and lettuce, in the stead of them.
(VIII, 34)

The attempt to exploit the list for rhetorical or comic purposes is not,
as a rule, successful in modern writers. The list has almost ceased to be
an expressive form, and the mere piling on of words and names with
what is sometimes called "cumulative effect" is liable to become a cheap
trick.

All these types of wit hang together in that they depend for their
character on intellectual materials and habits belonging to what may be
roughly labeled a pre-Enlightenment world (pre-Utilitarian, in the case

of legal wit). In some cases the term "scholastic" may be used with differ-
ing degrees of justification. This tradition, as we have indicated earlier,
has no clearly marked frontiers and it is difficult to decide whether some
kinds of learned wit may conveniently be regarded as in it or not. Wit
based on the exploitation of rhetoric is a case in point. As rhetoric was
taught in the medieval schools, the case for including it would seem to
be strong. The possible objection that rhetoric was much more important
to the humanists than to the medieval educationists need not trouble us
at all: this is a case where differences between medieval and Renaissance
phenomena are less important for us than differences between phenomena
belonging to both the Middle Ages and the Renaissance on the one hand
and those due to the Enlightenment on the other. A more valid reason,
it may be urged, for excluding rhetorical wit is that it is concerned merely
with means of expression while the other types which we have considered
are all related to ways of thinking. The sort of wit which consists only
in the parodying of rhetorical figures (*Love's Labour's Lost* abounds in
it) would seem not to belong in spirit to the tradition we are studying.
But rhetoric does not deal only with manner; matter also comes within
its province. That branch of it which is called *inventio* is concerned with
the finding of the right things to say on a given topic. Panurge's defense
of borrowing is, among other things, a rhetorical performance. He follows the conventional recommendations relating to *inventio;* for instance,
in the passage where borrowing is associated with the Four Cardinal
Virtues, which are considered in turn. Insofar as the mock disputation
called for rhetorical as well as dialectical proficiency, rhetoric must be
regarded as part of our subject, though not perhaps very central to it.
The formal rhetorical handling of a theme meant an ordered copious-
ness, a systematic treatment of all the conceivable aspects, with tedious
consequences in many writers, but offering a genius like Rabelais scope
and warrant for a generous display of his powers.

There is a certain amount of play with the terms of rhetoric in
Tristram Shandy; for example, in the passage where it is left open to
dispute whether Uncle Toby had really finished a certain sentence or not:

> If, on the contrary, my uncle Toby had not fully arrived at the period's
> end—then the world stands indebted to the snapping of my father's to-
> bacco-pipe for one of the neatest examples of that ornamental figure in
> oratory, which Rhetoricians style the Aposiopesis. . . .[7]

[7] II, 6. Other examples may be found in I, 19; I, 21, and elsewhere. I am indebted
to Mr. F. W. Bateson for the suggestion that the blank pages, wriggly lines, patterns
of asterisks, etc., in *Tristram Shandy* are a parody of the poems in the shape of hearts
and other objects commended in some Renaissance handbooks of rhetoric.

Mention may be made in this context of Mr. Shandy's lamentation over his eldest son, with its Ciceronian and other borrowings. His use of a literary model in so personal a matter is akin to his use of learned authorities in other personal matters relating to his concrete problems as a parent. Both point to the same sort of intellectual eccentricity.

It was claimed earlier that the mentality formed by the old learning expressed itself in the treatment not merely of intellectual materials but also of concrete things. The result was metaphysical imagery in poetry and certain uses of descriptive detail in writers like Jonson and Swift and, as we shall see later, Sterne.

One of the accepted characteristics of metaphysical imagery is its ability to embody or at least to heighten ideas. The loss of this quality, attributed by Mr. Eliot to a "dissociation of sensibility," is obviously a complex matter, but the intellectual changes of the seventeenth century clearly have a great deal to do with it. The repudiation by the scientists of the study of final causes involved a splitting of the unity of reality: without metaphysics facts lose their roundness. The scientist ceases to be concerned with things as they enter into common human experience, but only with specific manageable aspects of things; a feat of abstraction which, affecting the general consciousness, imposes a serious deprivation on the sensibility of poets. Medieval thought knew no such schism: metaphysical principle had the ascendancy and the world of fact was kept in its place, the individual fact or thing being all the more solidly realizable for being clothed with a meaning which covered all its aspects. This harmony between the concrete and the abstract, the thing and the meaning, becoming a habit of the imagination, manifested itself in poetry; on the highest level in the imagery of Dante, the clear, living expression of the idea; on lower levels in the more mechanical type of allegory, that of Deguileville and others, in which every aspect of the spiritual meaning is given its corresponding concrete symbol *ad nauseam*. In both cases the quality which imagery acquires is that of *order*, which may be subtle or commonplace. The habit of ordered schematization of imagery and material detail was inveterate among medieval poets, in allegory or otherwise. It was natural for the medieval imagination to grasp the material world in terms of ordered patterns of particulars. An exciting play of idea and image is not common in medieval poetry: the well-designed scholastic universe tended to be accepted rather stolidly by an age which did not contemplate the possibility of losing it. Those effects in imagery which we call "metaphysical" are found mainly at a later period, when Renaissance thought was destroying the traditional world-picture, and the old integration was threatened. The inherited habit of coordinating the thing and the meaning served the poet well in an age when both things and meanings were in the melting pot.

When this use of imagery departed from poetry it was not altogether lost to other forms of literature. An excellent example in Swift is the episode of the spider and the bee in the *Battle of the Books,* where the argument as to which insect has the better way of life becomes, by a nice manipulation of terms, a debate concerning the relative merits of ancients and moderns. In replacing the two types of intellect by two types of organism Swift is able to operate on the imagination by imagery.

When we speak of imagery it is usually to the metaphor and the simile that we refer, but there are other ways in which ideas may take concrete shape: for example, in the laborious detail of medieval allegorical description, to which we have already referred. There are descriptive passages in Swift and Sterne where the selection and ordering of the detail play an artistic role oddly reminiscent of that of the metaphysical image: a pointedness, a sharpness of outline, seem to suggest an insidious intention. One of Swift's favorite devices is the use of the learned idea with the image, the pseudo-scholarly preamble providing the logical preparation for the embodied monstrosity. The account of the Aeolists is a most brilliant example of this technique, and a similar example occurs in the Introduction to the *Tale of a Tub,* where arguments are given in favor of an elevated position for an orator, and the posture of the hearers is described with an awful precision. These passages in Swift have features in common. A schematization is imposed upon the physical elements to create the appearance of ritual. But the grotesque position and grouping of the figures only *seem* to be significant: the suggestion of significance produced by the precision and pointedness of the description serves simply to give heightening to gross absurdity. It is Swift's imaginative response to the uncomely posturings of religious fanaticism.

Sterne's use of similar techniques will be more conveniently discussed when we examine *Tristram Shandy* by itself.

III

It is one of the good jokes of literature that we reach the third book of *Tristram Shandy* before the hero is born. But not all readers see why the joke is good. The entire structure of the work depends on the fact that the starting point is not Tristram's birth but his begetting. At the outset Sterne declares his purpose, which is to begin literally *ab Ovo:*

For which cause, right glad I am, that I have begun the history of myself in the way I have done; and that I am able to go on, tracing everything in it, as Horace says, *ab Ovo.*

Between begetting and birth much may happen. It is, from the point of view of medicine and psychology, a most important period in a person's life. But it does not offer the kind of material which the historian or novelist can normally handle. A modern novel dealing with so early a phase in the career of its hero would have to be something in the nature of a scientific fantasy, and although contemporary ideas could be exploited for such a purpose we should expect them to undergo a cheapening process. In the intellectual tradition available to Sterne ideas were not rendered crude through being familiar. *Tristram Shandy* breaks off before the hero is mature enough to become what in literature is recognized as a character. Of his history we know only what the influences of the prenatal period and early infancy have done for him. From the point of view of the ordinary historian or novelist very little has happened. But from the point of view of Mr. Shandy and the modern psychologist most of the really decisive things have happened. Tristram's character and fortune have been more or less settled by the sequence of events beginning with the unfortunate circumstances of his begetting and culminating in the sash-window tragedy. In this sequence of events lies the pattern of the novel.

We cannot accuse Sterne of not announcing his theme promptly. The first chapter is all about the perils which attend one's begetting.

I wish either my father or my mother, or indeed both of them, as they were in duty both equally bound to it, had minded what they were about when they begot me; had they duly considered how much depended upon what they were then doing;—that not only the production of a rational Being was concerned in it, but that possibly the happy formation and temperature of his body, perhaps his genius and the very cast of his mind;—and, for aught they knew to the contrary, even the fortunes of his whole house might take their turn from the humours and dispositions which were then uppermost;—Had they duly weighed and considered all this, and proceeded accordingly,—I am verily persuaded I should have made a quite different figure in the world, from that in which the reader is likely to see me.—Believe me, good folks, this is not so inconsiderable a thing as many of you may think it;—you have all, I dare say, heard of the animal spirits, as how they are transfused from father to son etc. etc.—and a great deal to that purpose:—Well, you may take my word, that nine parts in ten of a man's sense or his nonsense, his successes and miscarriages in this world depend upon their motions and activity, and the different tracts and trains

you put them into, so that when they are once set a-going, whether right
or wrong, 'tis not a halfpenny matter,—away they go cluttering like hey-go
mad; and by treading the same steps over and over again, they presently
make a road of it, as plain and as smooth as a garden-walk, which, when
they are once used to, the Devil himself sometimes shall not be able to
drive them off. (I, 1)

From this introduction we pass to the concrete scene: Mr. and Mrs.
Shandy are about to perform their function. At the critical moment
Mr. Shandy is interrupted by his wife's question about winding up the
clock, and so occurs the first of Tristram's misfortunes. The question,
coming at that moment, "scattered and dispersed the animal spirits, whose
business it was to have escorted and gone in hand with the HOMUNCULUS,
and conducted him safe to the place destined for his reception."

The misfortune takes place before conception, so the identity of the
victim would seem to be a rather delicate metaphysical problem. Sterne,
however, gives him metaphysical status and a living shape:

> The Homunculus, Sir, in however low and ludicrous a light he may appear,
> in this age of levity, to the eye of folly or prejudice;—to the eye of reason
> in scientific research, he stands confessed—a Being guarded and circum-
> scribed with rights.—The minutest philosophers, who, by the bye, have the
> most enlarged understandings, (their souls being inversely as their en-
> quiries) shew us incontestably, that the Homunculus is created by the
> same hand,—engendered in the same course of nature,—endowed with the
> same locomotive powers and faculties with us;—That he consists as we do,
> of skin, hair, fat, flesh, veins, arteries, ligaments, nerves, cartilages, bones,
> marrow, brains, glands, genitals, humours, and articulations. . . .
>   Now, dear Sir, what if any accident had befallen him in his way alone!—
> or that, through terror of it, natural to so young a traveller, my little Gen-
> tleman had got to his journey's end miserably spent;—his muscular strength
> and virility worn down to a thread;—his own animal spirits ruffled beyond
> description,—and that in this sad disordered state of nerves, he had lain
> down a prey to sudden starts, or a series of melancholy dreams and fancies,
> for nine long, long months together.—I tremble to think what a foundation
> had been laid for a thousand weaknesses both of body and of mind, which
> no skill of the physician or the philosopher could ever afterwards have
> set thoroughly to rights. (I, 2)

Tristram's second misfortune takes us into the sphere of legal entangle-
ments. It is because Mr. Shandy insists on the terms of his wife's marriage
settlement that Tristram is born in the country, not in London. Mrs.
Shandy, unable to have the best professional attendance, insists on having
the worst; and the result is the tragedy of Tristram's nose.

Mr. Shandy's theory, reached after much elaborate physiological speculation, is that, "the excellency of the nose is in a direct arithmetical
proportion to the excellency of the wearer's fancy" (III, 38). The flattening
of Tristram's nose is therefore a cruel blow to his parental hopes. He
falls back on the theory of names, and is again thwarted, by a mistake
which causes his child to be given the name which he has condemned
as the worst possible. He inquires into the possibility of changing it,
and this leads to a great orgy of legal quibbling ending in the decision
that the parents have no rights in the matter, not being of kin to their
own child! Opportunities continue to present themselves, however, for
applying learning to his parental responsibilities. He composes a *Tris-
trapaedia,* or system of education: he interests himself in theories of
bodily health: *à propos* of putting the child into breeches he makes
careful researches into the wardrobe of the ancients. Meanwhile Tristram
has encountered further disaster through the fall of a sash-window.

The theme of *Tristram Shandy* may be seen in terms of a comic clash
between the world of learning and that of human affairs. On the level
of theory Mr. Shandy makes formidable preparations for his child's wel-
fare, but partly through his own folly or inattention in practical matters,
and partly through unlucky accident, his schemes are frustrated. It is
Mr. Shandy's perverse insistence on legal principle that is responsible
for Tristram's being born in the country: he is therefore to blame for
the flattened nose. As for the mistake over the name, fortune is cruel in
making him just too late to prevent it: the finding and donning of a
pair of breeches causes the fatal delay. The sash-window accident is not
his fault directly; it is due to the intemperate zeal of Corporal Trim in
the service of Uncle Toby's hobbyhorse that, "nothing in the Shandy
household is well hung," but it is typical of Mr. Shandy's character that
he should be unaware, in his philosophical absorption, of what is going
on in his own house.

Was Sterne indebted for this theme to any of his predecessors in the
tradition to which we are trying to relate him? Cornelius Scriblerus's
grotesque application of pedantic learning to the education of his son
Martinus in the *Memoirs of Scriblerus* may have suggested something to
him, but the comedy here is not rich enough in human values to count
as a major inspiration. A more significant parallel is provided by the
third book of Rabelais, from which a number of passages were quoted in
the previous section. As these two works are, in certain obvious ways,
unlike, let us enumerate the points of resemblance. In each there is a
central human problem, for the solving of which an immense body of
knowledge is assembled: the question of how to give the infant hero the

best start in life, the question of whether Panurge should marry. In each there is unquenchable faith in the validity of learning in its application to life. In each there is a series of phases or episodes in which one form of learning after another is brought to bear on the problem. In each the well-meant efforts are frustrated, in the one case by a mixture of human frailty and the cussedness of things, in the other by perversity in its most pronounced form.

The comedy depends on the play between two things: a traditional order of ideas and beliefs, and human folly or mishap. It is essential to the effect that the ideas and beliefs should have a basis of seriousness in the mind of the author, though they are made to serve a comic purpose. The attitude of the author was, no doubt, rather mixed. We know that Sterne intended the theory of noses to be a piece of absurdity, but we cannot say the same of all the physiological lore in which *Tristram Shandy* abounds. Sterne was immersed in physiological ideas. It was a material which meant much to his imagination. It is appropriate that the Shandean philosophy should be stated in these terms:

> True Shandeism, think what you will against it, opens the heart and lungs, and like all those affections which partake of its nature, it forces the blood and other vital fluids of the body to run freely through its channels, makes the wheel of life run long and cheerfully round. (IV, 32)

The pattern of learned wit suggested above is not the only one to be found in *Tristram Shandy*. Wilbur L. Cross, the most eminent of all Sterne scholars, said that the whole work was organized in terms of Locke's doctrine of association of ideas. That this is an important structural principle is certainly true: it governs his use of digressions, and it manifests itself sometimes in the behavior of the characters; for example, when Mrs. Shandy inopportunely remembers the clock-winding ritual. Two comments need to be made on Cross's views. The first is that Sterne, unlike most eighteenth century writers who were influenced by Locke, exploited his ideas freely as opportunities for wit, playing with them in a manner quite unlike that of their original begetter. His was the old spirit at work upon new materials. The second is that Cross is untrue to the spirit of *Tristram Shandy* in saying that "Sterne assumes Locke's attitude towards scholastic and theological pedantry." Sterne's attitude was, to say the least, one of humorous interest; Locke's that of the serious reformer, the ideas he attacked making no appeal to his fancy.

The learned wit in *Tristram Shandy* would be all the less interesting if the intellectual tradition to which Sterne was indebted did not exert

some influence on the imagination, discernible in his treatment of concrete, everyday things. His descriptive passages are full of effects which
recall that pointedness in the ordering of detail which we noted in Swift
and for which kinship was claimed, at a humbler, prose level, with the
union of idea and image in metaphysical poetry.

Sterne had a curious feeling for order which expressed itself in a
number of ways. In one of its manifestations it is accompanied by what
would appear to be its opposite, a delight in confusion; but in Sterne
these things are not opposites. To dwell upon disorder, reducing it to its
particulars and bringing out its perversely twisted pattern, involves the
introduction of an element of order. The complicated description of how
Obadiah tied up Dr. Slop's bag of instruments is a good example (III, 8).
Another manifestation of his sense of order is an insistence on relating
happenings to their causes. Causation works in very odd ways in *Tristram
Shandy*, curious devices being used for holding the structure of events
together, so that one is reminded of some contraption designed by Heath
Robinson. Obadiah's entanglement is itself one of the obstacles to Tristram's smooth passage into the world. ("Sport of small accidents, Tristram Shandy! that thou art, and ever will be!") The sash-window disaster
is originally due to Uncle Toby's need for lead for his miniature field-
pieces. The first and aboriginal mishap is associated with the winding of
a clock. In a delightful passage illustrating the queer mechanisms of
family life in the Shandy household, Sterne dwells on the importance
of a faulty hinge on the parlor door (V, 6). Another of his habits is to
give a studied precision to descriptions of physical postures in scenes
where the composed effect is grotesque rather than dignified. The spot-
light is directed in such a way as to heighten the trivial. Mr. Shandy
prostrate with grief on hearing of his child's flattened nose (III, 24), Corporal Trim as he takes his stance to read the sermon (II, 17), are notable
examples of this type of effect. In another passage Sterne catches Mr.
Shandy trying to put his left hand into his right hand coat pocket, and
dwells with a connoisseur's finesse on the result (III, 2). Sometimes there
is the odd suggestion, or the parody of a suggestion, that the detail is
significant, that there is a meaning embodied in the pattern. If there is
any it is, perhaps, that of "order in disorder." It seems to be characteristic
of the Shandy world that the things belonging to order are sabotaged
by human muddle, while order and exactness are imposed quite arbitrarily
upon the unimportant and the incidental.

Uncle Toby's hobbyhorse is the most interesting example of Sterne's
idiosyncratic ordering of detail, but it is interesting for other reasons as
well. It brings us back to learned wit, for military science was a form of

learning like any other, and took similar forms to those of Mr. Shandy's intellectual interests. It had a relatively clearcut system, with an ordered grouping of particulars, but with just enough complication to provide a pleasing muddle. It had its lists of learned authorities and a terminology with rhetorical possibilities: *scarp, counterscarp, glacis, covered way, half-moon,* and *ravelin*. It was, in fact, good material for the kind of artistic exploitation which we have been studying.

In his discourse on hobbyhorses (I, 24), Sterne puts forward a theory of characterization, the point of which is that when a man becomes deeply attached to a favorite occupation, his character gradually takes on a shape and coloring derived from the materials belonging to that occupation. There is another side to this process, which Sterne does not mention, though his art illustrates it. If the man's nature is changed by the materials acting upon it, the materials themselves are changed by their association with the man. All organized pursuits or subjects for study may be said to have their abstract, impersonal character—their "textbook" character, let us say—and also a variable "human" character imposed upon them by the different sorts of treatment which they receive when human beings have to do with them. Whenever the human factor enters in there is modification and distortion. The materials of military science, entering so deeply into Uncle Toby's mind and giving him a medium through which to express himself, take on new shapes in the process.

Uncle Toby's hobbyhorse arises, as Sterne explains most fully, out of a difficulty he experiences in making himself clear when he tries to tell the tale of the siege of Namur, where he received his wound. Partly because his hearers do not understand the technical terms, and partly because the terrain was somewhat complicated, he gets tied up in his narration, and this (Sterne indulges in some medical speculation here) by irritating him, adversely affects his recovery from the wound. In his account of Uncle Toby's efforts (II, 1), Sterne achieves the effect of "order in disorder," the element of clear, circumstantial detail enhancing the confusion. The search for clarity leads Uncle Toby to the study of maps and textbooks. But now he becomes so full of his theme that he has to find other, more elaborate, ways of expressing himself through it, so he builds miniature fortifications on a bowling-green and fights mock battles with field artillery made from leaden gutters, a melted-down pewter shaving-basin, and the weights from sash-windows.

There is a quality about Uncle Toby's hobbyhorse which places it on a different imaginative level from other examples in fiction of make-believe and eccentric preoccupation. The difference is one of intensity. Sterne's art manifests itself in the transformation of the concrete objects so that they become completely assimilated to Uncle Toby's all-absorbing idea. A peculiar concentration and control of detail create the spell which we feel, as it were, objectively. The make-believe is not for us, there is no dubious invitation to fantasy:

> The corporal, who the night before had resolved in his mind to supply the grand *desideratum,* of keeping up something like an incessant firing upon the enemy during the heat of the attack,—had no further idea in his fancy at that time, than a contrivance of smoking tobacco against the town, out of one of my uncle Toby's six field-pieces, which were planted on each side of his sentry-box. . . . Upon turning it this way, and that, a little in his mind, he soon began to find out, that by means of his two Turkish tobacco-pipes, with the supplement of three smaller tubes of wash-leather at each of their lower ends, to be tagged by the same number of tin-pipes fitted to the touch-holes, and sealed with clay next the cannon, and then tied hermetically with waxed silk at their several insertions into the Moroccan tube, —he should be able to fire the six field-pieces all together, and with the same ease as to fire one. (VI, 26)

Uncle Toby's hobbyhorse differs from that of (say) Commodore Trunnion or Mr. Wemmick not only in intensity but in the fact that it refuses to keep within its allotted boundaries. It spreads, it gets mixed up with other parts of the novel. The toys, straying from their places, contribute to the complicated system of traps and obstacles in which the characters, bodily or mentally, are caught. There is the sash-window episode: the drawbridge broken accidentally by Trim is confused—only momentarily, but the explanation takes time—with the bridge of Tristram's nose: Mr. Shandy's mention of a train of ideas makes Uncle Toby think of a train of artillery.

The phrase "order in disorder" is also applicable to the external structure of *Tristram Shandy.* On the element of disorder it is unnecessary to dwell: it is this which strikes one most on a first reading. Sterne took pleasure in destroying the normal order of things and in creating an exaggerated appearance of disorder, but only to link up the pieces in another and more interesting way.

Sterne's treatment of sentiment is an example of the remoter operation of the "wit" tradition. The charge of false feeling, of indulgence in sentiment, has frequently been leveled against him. But may it not be said in reply that his indulgence is always allied to a self-knowledge, that an ironical consciousness of the limitations of his feelings adds just the right flavor to his presentation of them?[8] We understand this better

---

[8] Mr. Herbert Read has written well on Sterne's sentimentality in *The Sense of Glory,* 1929, p. 140.

when we are aware of the tradition of wit to which Sterne belonged, with its devices for keeping the comic and the serious worlds of feeling on the right terms with each other, and for allowing a writer to reveal the play of opposites in his own character. Sterne's suavely controlled treatment of a sentimental situation may have little in common technically with the blend of emotion and irony in Donne or Marvell, but both are examples of wit acting as a corrective to feeling or giving edge to it. It was Sterne's link with this tradition which enabled him to handle the new fashionable material of "sensibility" with adroitness and sophistication.

From "Yorick Revisited"

by W. B. C. Watkins

Being an invalid and somewhat neurotic, like Proust, Sterne was abnormally sensitive—partly because he was inevitably self-conscious physically to an abnormal degree. He was acutely aware of the very circulation of his blood and the beating of his heart, which most of us never feel or think of. This is evident even in *Tristram Shandy*—"I feel an abatement of the quickness of my pulse"; but it is especially true in *A Sentimental Journey*, written in the acute stage of his final dissolution. For example:

> In doing this, I felt every vessel in my frame dilate—the arteries beat all chearily together, and every power which sustained life, performed it with so little friction, that 'twould have confounded the most *physical precieuse* in France: with all her materialism, she could scarce have called me a machine—

> The pulsations of the arteries along my fingers pressing across hers, told her what was passing within me. . . .

> Would to heaven! my dear Eugenius, thou hadst passed by, and beheld me sitting in my black coat, and in my lack-a-day-sical manner, counting the throbs of it, one by one, with as much true devotion as if I had been watching the critical ebb or flow of her fever.

> . . . how sweetly dost thou mix with the blood, and *help it through the most difficult and tortuous passages to the heart*.

Indeed, it is only natural that Sterne's psychology should be to a large extent physiological, and that the importance of sensation in Locke's theories should so much appeal to him. No other English novelist has ever portrayed with such delicate skill the very nerve centers of the brain and spinal cord, the raising or lowering of blood pressure, the instinctive muscular reaction to mental and emotional agitation—in short, the intimate relation and interaction between body and mind.

The excerpt reprinted here is from the concluding pages of "Yorick Revisited," from *Perilous Balance: The Tragic Genius of Swift, Johnson, and Sterne* by W. B. C. Watkins, pp. 141-54. Copyright © 1939, 1967 by the Princeton University Press and reprinted by their permission.

And no one until Proust has equaled him. He considers humorously the effects which the passions and affections of the mind have upon the digestion, and he analyzes in detail the effect of Trim's inspiration on Uncle Toby:

> . . . this identical bowling-green instantly presented itself, and became curiously painted all at once, upon the retina of my uncle Toby's fancy;—which was the physical cause of making him change colour, or at least of heightening his blush, to that immoderate degree I spoke of. . . .

But the reverse procedure is also true. Sterne enunciates his principle thus:

> A man's body and his mind, with the utmost reverence to both I speak it, are exactly like a jerkin, and a jerkin's lining;—rumple the one,—you rumple the other . . . [unless] you are so fortunate a fellow, as to have your jerkin made of gum-taffeta, and the body-lining to it of a sarcenet, or thin persian.

"Why," he asks himself in his account of Maria's sad story, "does my pulse beat languid as I write this?" Because, he might have answered himself, of the intimate relation between moods and bodily functions:

> There are some trains of certain ideas which leave prints of themselves about our eyes and eye-brows; and there is a consciousness of it, somewhere about the heart, which serves but to make these etchings the stronger —we see, spell, and put them together without a dictionary.

He himself is a master of this translation, this "short hand," as he calls it, and is "quick in rendering the several turns of looks and limbs, with all their inflections and delineations, into plain words." Sometimes he uses it merely to cheat the expectation mischievously, sometimes to mark off the difference between appearance and reality and to bring home to the reader that the workings of the mind are too complex for any method to be infallible; but more often he uses this "translation" of behavior and expression as an important means of showing what is going on in the mind:

> Mrs. Wadman blushed—looked towards the door—turned pale—blushed slightly again—recovered her natural colour—blushed worse than ever; which, for the sake of the unlearned reader, I translate thus—
> "L——d! I cannot look at it—
> What would the world say if I looked at it?
> I should drop down, if I looked at it—
> I wish I could look at it—
> There can be no sin in looking at it.

—I will look at it."
. . . what little knowledge is got by mere words—we must go up to the first springs.

And when he is worried just how to address the Duke de C—— about the passport he counsels his alter ego to "see Monsieur le Duc's face first—observe what character is written in it—take notice in what posture he stands to hear you—mark the turns and expressions of his body and limbs—And for the tone—the first sound which comes from his lips will give it you."

His own reactions are instantaneous; no sooner has he thrown by mistake a fair sheet instead of the foul one into the fire than "instantly I snatched off my wig, and threw it perpendicularly, with all imaginable violence, up to the top of the room." He undoubtedly exaggerates the mobility of the average human countenance; he endows not just hands and arms but the whole body and even its periphery (since blushing is so frequent in his pages) with expressiveness. In other words, he imparts to most of his characters his own sensitivity; he attributes to them his mental consciousness of his bodily state, and conversely his physical reactions to his changing moods. But this explains the most telling and original effects which he achieves in his incomparable use of gesture, inflection, and pantomime—the subtle and vivid delineation of the flow of thought through the mind and the constant shifting of emotions. He was, of course, marvelously adept at getting inside the heads of his characters; he was just as skilful in portraying "rumples" in the "jerkin's lining" by means of these rumples in the jerkin itself.

We can understand why he comments that it was well that his father's passions lasted not long, for they led him a busy life, when we read this physical expression of Walter Shandy's shifting moods:

—My father thrust back his chair—rose up—put on his hat—took four long strides to the door—jerked it open—thrust his head half-way out—shut the door again—took no notice of the bad hinge—returned to the table—plucked my mother's thread-paper out of Slawkenbergius's book—went hastily to his bureau—walked slowly back—twisted my mother's thread-paper about his thumb—unbuttoned his waistcoat—threw my mother's thread-paper into the fire—bit her satin pin-cushion in two, filled his mouth with bran—confounded it. . . .

Walter's distress over the disaster to Tristram's nose, on the other hand, is portrayed entirely by the eloquent prostration of his body on the bed:

The palm of his right hand, as he fell upon the bed, receiving his forehead, and covering the greatest part of both his eyes, gently sunk down with his head (his elbow giving way backwards) till his nose touched the quilt;—his left arm hung insensible over the side of the bed, his knuckles reclining upon the handle of the chamber-pot, which peeped out beyond the valance—his right leg (his left being drawn up towards his body) hung half over the side of the bed, the edge of it pressing upon his shin-bone— He felt it not. A fixed, inflexible sorrow took possession of every line of his face.—He sighed once—heaved his breast often—but uttered not a word.

A more complex instance of this virtual mind-through-body-reading technique provides the charm of the little pantomimic comedy of Walter and Mrs. Shandy, when Mrs. Shandy—she said from curiosity, but he felt from a very different impulse—wished to peep through the keyhole at Uncle Toby and Widow Wadman. In *A Sentimental Journey,* there is not necessarily more subtlety but certainly more economy of method:

> The young girl made me more a humble courtesy than a low one—'twas one of those quiet, thankful sinkings where the spirit bows itself down— the body does no more than tell it.

The same delicate sensitivity which made him abnormally aware of the beating of his own pulse is evident in all the holding of hands, in the feeling of the precise degree of pressure in Mrs. Shandy's tap on her husband's hand, in Uncle Toby's laying down his pipe upon the fender as gently "as if it had been spun from a spider's web."

Tone of voice, too, is invaluable in "translation." Sometimes Sterne characterizes it as "that soft and irresistible piano of voice, which the nature of the *argumentum ad hominem* absolutely requires"; sometimes he establishes tone and mood—"Poor creature! said my uncle Toby, vibrating the note back again, like a string in unison." There is the same delicacy of discrimination and significance. Not only is meaning more subtly differentiated in this way, but the intention behind the remark, its mental background is clarified:

> A fiddlestick! quoth she.
>
> Now there are such an infinitude of notes, tunes, cants, chants, airs, looks, and accents with which the word fiddlestick may be pronounced in all such causes as this, every one of 'em impressing a sense and meaning as different from the other, as dirt from cleanliness—That Casuists (for it is an affair of conscience on that score) reckon up no less than fourteen thousand in which you may do either right or wrong.
>
> Mrs. Wadman hit upon the fiddlestick, which summoned up all my uncle Tody's modest blood into his cheeks.

Seldom has the devious comedy of mind and mood been carried to such lengths of hairbreadth discrimination.

Sterne, a psychologist and a writer who knows the full value of showing the unexpected reaction which is yet so true to character, also uses all of these elements of physical expression to portray emotional and intellectual shock:

> And what's the matter, Susannah? They have called the child Tristram —and my mistress is just got out of an hysteric fit about it—No!—'tis not my fault, said Susannah—I told him it was Tristram-gistus.
>
> Make tea for yourself, brother Toby, said my father, taking down his hat —but how different from the sallies and agitations of voice and members which a common reader would imagine!
>
> —For he spake in the sweetest modulation—and took down his hat with the genteelest movement of limbs, that ever affliction harmonized and attuned together.

A commonplace remark and a commonplace gesture, but made penetrating by the subtle portrayal of the quality of tone and movement. The taking down of a hat is enough for Sterne, not because he moves in a circumscribed small-scale world, though it is a world of relative values, but because, as he says elsewhere in the novel:

> There are a thousand unnoticed openings . . . which let a penetrating eye at once into a man's soul; and I maintain it . . . that a man of sense does not lay down his hat in coming into a room—or take it up in going out of it, but something escapes, which discovers him.

This is more than an adumbration of the nineteenth century use of *le petit fait significatif*, because it is far more than a mere technique; it proceeds from deep conviction. The famous serio-comic incident of the fly is too often pointed out as a purple passage, and the following paragraph ignored:

> I was but ten years old when this happened: but whether it was, that the action itself was more *in unison to my nerves* at that age of pity, *which instantly set my whole frame into one vibration* of most pleasurable sensation;—or how far *the manner and expression* of it might go towards it;— or in what degree, or by what secret magic,—*a tone of voice and harmony of movement,* attuned by mercy, might find a passage to my heart, I know not;—this I know, that *the lesson of universal good-will then taught and imprinted* by my uncle Toby, has never since been worn out of my mind. . . . I often think that *I owe one half of my philanthropy to that one accidental impression.*

Sterne's art and his beliefs are far more closely integrated than can be appreciated by those who persist in considering him only as an artist or a humorist; and his art would not be what it is without those beliefs.

Tristram Shandy and *A Sentimental Journey* are a dramatization of Sterne's whole integration—his own personality, his beliefs, his experience, his knowledge of his fellow man. Dramatization was conspicuous, as we have seen, in his daily life; it is the essence of his novels. "I like the sermon well," cries Walter Shandy, "—'tis dramatic,—and there is something in that way of writing, when skillfully managed, which catches the attention." In his own sermons Sterne employs all elements of surprise, of contrast, of action to galvanize attention. He analyzes psychological motive in Biblical characters; he puts soliloquies in their mouths; he creates vivid scenes, in which, as in his novels, he himself becomes the principal actor. Believing, as we have seen, in the close relation of body and mind, in the instinctive physical reflection of changing moods and thoughts, Sterne is naturally interested in the art of acting.

Consider this youthful sentimental letter to Elizabeth Lumley, written in 1739/40, before he married her:

> Fanny had prepared me a supper—she is all attention to me—but I sat over it with tears; a bitter sauce, my L. but I could eat it with no other— for the moment she began to spread my little table, my heart fainted within me—One solitary plate, one knife, one fork, one glass!—I gave a thousand pensive, penetrating looks at the chair thou hadst so often graced, in those quiet, and sentimental repasts—then laid down my knife, and fork, and took out my handkerchief, and clapped it across my face, and wept like a child.

At this time he had been little, so far as we know, in London, had most probably seen few plays. This passage was written twenty years before he began to make his yearly visits to town for the rounds of the theaters and salons. The tendency toward vividly visualized objective portrayal, self-dramatization, and pantomime was innate in Sterne, and would have been evident in his novels if he had never left York. His natural tendency toward a confidential, personal way of writing was strengthened and refined by his reading of Montaigne and Burton; and the first training ground, if we except the Swiftian imitation, *Tale of a Good Warm Watch-Coat,* for his novel technique was his sermons.

Sterne's apostrophe to Herod:

> Monster!—could no consideration of all this tender sorrow, stay thy hands? . . . but thou must thus pitilessly *rush in*—take the victim by violence—*tear it* from the embraces of the mother. . . .

is a forecast of the frequent and far more skilful use he makes of that device in his novels. In the midst of an elaborately detailed account of Uncle Toby's researches into the science of projectiles, Sterne suddenly bursts into one of his direct addresses, so vividly effective that the reader feels that Sterne and Uncle Toby are both in the room with him:

> . . . and that the semi-parameter,—stop! my dear uncle Toby—stop!—go not one foot farther into this thorny and bewildered track,—intricate are the steps! intricate are the mazes of this labyrinth! intricate are the troubles which the pursuit of this bewitching phantom Knowledge will bring upon thee.—O my uncle;—fly—fly, fly from it as from a serpent.—Is it fit—good-natured man! thou should'st sit up, with the wound upon thy groin, whole nights baking thy blood with hectic watchings?—Alas! 'twill exasperate thy symptoms,—check thy perspirations—evaporate thy spirits—waste thy animal strength,—dry up thy radical moisture, bring thee into a costive habit of body,—impair thy health,—and hasten all the infirmities of thy old age.— O my uncle! my uncle Toby.

Happening to mention that Uncle Toby would not hurt a fly, he suddenly dramatizes that trait of character into an actual incident. In the humorously plaintive address to the reader which opens *Tristram Shandy,* he explodes a disquisition on association of ideas with—

> "Pray, my Dear," quoth my mother, "have you not forgot to wind up the clock?"—"Good G——!" cried my father, making an exclamation, but taking care to moderate his voice at the same time—"Did ever woman, since the creation of the world, interrupt a man with such a silly question?"

Immediately Walter Shandy and his wife are there before us as if a curtain had just gone up on the first scene of a play. The long disquisitions and familiar essays which he explodes in this way really intensify the effect by the violence of the contrast, giving the illusion of suddenly breaking into life itself. More than any other novelist Sterne has this genius for making action appear to take place in the present.

Sterne visualizes his characters and his scenes, and he makes us visualize them as clearly as if they were before our eyes. This native skill in pantomime, gesture, inflection of voice he improved and refined as his acquaintance with painting and acting increased.

He was certainly familiar with painting, especially the caricatures of Hogarth, with their eloquence of pose, personality, and movement. Hogarth is his model in his portrait of Dr. Slop; and such a scene as this, in its frozen motion and exactness of detail, is like the pantomime of an Hogarthian drawing:

> Bridget stood perdue within, with her finger and her thumb upon the latch, benumbed with expectation: and Mrs. Wadman, with an eye ready to be deflowered again, sat breathless behind the window-curtain of her bed-chamber, watching their approach.

Both painting and the theater are drawn upon to do justice to one of Walter Shandy's poses:

> My father instantly exchanged the attitude he was in, for that in which Socrates is so finely painted by Raffael in his school of Athens; which your connoisseurship knows is so exquisitely imagined, that *even the particular manner of the reasoning of Socrates is expressed by it*—for he holds the fore-finger of his left-hand between the fore-finger and the thumb of his right, and seems as if he was saying to the libertine he is reclaiming—"You grant me this—and this: and this, and this, I don't ask of you—they follow of themselves in course."
>
> So stood my father, holding fast his fore-finger betwixt his finger and his thumb, and reasoning with my uncle Toby as he sat in his old fringed chair, valanced around with party-coloured worsted bobs—O Garrick!—what a rich scene of this would thy exquisite powers make! and how gladly would I write such another to avail myself of thy immortality, and secure my own behind it.

The influence of actual stage representation on Sterne is liable to overemphasis, but it must have sharpened his focus and reinforced his tendency to visualize action and scene. There are a few direct references in *Tristram Shandy:*

> A sudden impulse comes across me—drop the curtain, Shandy—I drop it —Strike a line here across the paper, Tristram—I strike it—and hey for a new chapter. . . .
>
> Now this, you must know, being my chapter upon chapters . . . that chapters relieve the mind—that they assist—or impose upon the imagination —and that in a work of this dramatic cast they are as necessary as the shifting of scenes.

Again, even more explicit:

> I beg the reader will assist me here, to wheel off my uncle Toby's ordnance behind the scenes,—to remove his sentry-box, and clear the theatre, if possible, of horn-works and half moons, and get the rest of his military apparatus out of the way;—that done, my dear friend Garrick, we'll snuff the candles bright,—sweep the stage with a new broom,—draw up the curtain, and exhibit my uncle Toby dressed in a new character.

It is doubtful that this is much more than a passing whim on Sterne's part to dramatize himself for the moment as a stage producer and scene shifter. We must remember that he did not serve an apprenticeship, like Fielding, in writing plays. His most effective changes of scene have no stage directions, no props to speak of. With Sterne you are one moment in Montriul, the next in Abdera; or you are sitting with him on the banks of the Garonne, and simultaneously walking across the market-square of Auxerre, and entering Lyons with a post-chaise broken into a thousand pieces.

The chief theatrical influence on him was his intimacy with Garrick. Judging from contemporary accounts of it, Garrick's acting must have been elaborately calculated and heightened; he must have run the whole gamut of gestures, tones of voice, and inflections, and significantly, he must have resorted frequently to deliberate silences. For example, consider Sterne's own satire on the dramatic critic:

> —And how did Garrick speak the soliloquy last night?—Oh, against all rule, my Lord,—most ungrammatically! betwixt the substantive and the adjective, which should agree together in number, case, and gender, *he made a breach thus,—stopping, as if the point wanted settling;—*and betwixt the nominative case, which your lordship knows should govern the verb, *he suspended his voice in the epilogue a dozen times three seconds and three fifths* by a stop-watch, my Lord, each time.—Admirable grammarian!— *But in suspending his voice—was the sense suspended likewise? Did no expression of attitude or countenance fill up the chasm?—Was the eye silent?* Did you narrowly look?—I looked only at the stop-watch, my Lord.—Excellent observer.

Clearly Garrick could have no complaint of Sterne's lively observation; in fact, as in the reference to Raphael's Socrates, the recreative, appreciative interpretation owes almost as much to Sterne as to Raphael or Garrick.

I have already considered the most profound significance of gesture in Sterne—that is, in portraying psychological states; but he also finds gesture of inestimable value in dramatizing action by making it pictorial. Gesture in his novels at times becomes mere gesticulation, or mannerism, or posturing. A casual count reveals thirteen laying of the hands on the breast, a number of laying of hands on the sleeve or to the side of the nose, and persistent clapping of hands to express obvious pleasure. Nevertheless, the importance of this visualization cannot be overestimated.

Frequently it is merely accompanying action, having little ulterior meaning, expressing only the natural, unconsidered movements of the body:

> The life of a family!—my uncle Toby would say, *throwing himself back in his arm chair, and lifting up his hands, his eyes, and one leg. . . .*
> My father reflected half a minute—*looked down—touched the middle of his forehead slightly with his finger*—
> —True, said he.

Tho' my father was a good natural philosopher,—yet he was something of a moral philosopher too; for which reason, when his tobacco-pipe snapped short in the middle,—he had nothing to do, as such, but to have taken hold of the two pieces, and thrown them gently upon the back of the fire.—He did no such thing;—*he threw them with all the violence in the world;— and, to give the action still more emphasis,—he started upon both his legs to do it.*

These are, in terms of the theater, far more than mere stage directions; they are equivalent to the consummate actor's interpretation of the part.

Sterne's careful description of the exact member or part concerned— the "third finger of the right hand," the "flat of the forefinger"—just like his giving time to a split second, acts as a sharpening of focus almost hypnotic. By such skilful detail he forces us to see bodily action in all its subtle fluidity of movement, with a perfection of timing. He does not give merely a number of static poses, though he achieves his effects frequently by these in rapid series, so that the result is cinematographic, producing a perfect illusion of the flow of action. His artistry is, as usual, absolutely self-conscious:

. . . every other limb and member of my father instantly relapsed with his nose into the same precise attitude in which he lay first described; so that when Corporal Trim left the room, and my father found himself disposed to rise off the bed—*he had all the little preparatory movements to run over again, before he could do it. Attitudes are nothing, madam—'tis the transition from one attitude to another—like the preparation and resolution of the discord into harmony, which is all in all.*

If he at times, as in the case of Trim's posturings during his reading of the sermon, goes to incredibly elaborate descriptive lengths for comic effect, this elaboration, nonetheless, explains his genius for making you feel bodily movement even from the first preliminary preparation of muscles for the effort.

This pantomime of Walter Shandy counting out the last fifty pounds of his grandmother's jointure would be just as effective on the stage:

. . . he generally gave a loud Hem! rubbed the side of his nose leisurely with the flat part of his forefinger—inserted his hand cautiously betwixt his head and the caul of his wig—looked at both sides of every guinea as he parted with it—and seldom could get to the end of the fifty pounds, without pulling out his handkerchief, and wiping his temples.

But he frequently achieves by his minuteness of method effects of pantomime far too delicate and subtle to be achieved, except in broad outline, on the stage, where the audience is necessarily at some distance from the player. For this reason he is often more akin to the cinema with its close-ups. No actor could do justice to the following superb pantomime on the stage; it would require the technique of a Charlie Chaplin close to the camera:

> My uncle Toby took the ivory pipe out of the corporal's hand,—looked at it for half a minute, and returned it.
> In less than two minutes, my uncle Toby took the pipe from the corporal again, and raised it half way to his mouth—then hastily gave it back a second time.
> The corporal redoubled the attack,—my uncle Toby smiled,—then looked grave,—then smiled for a moment,—then looked serious for a long time;—Give me hold of the ivory pipe, Trim, said my uncle Toby—my uncle Toby put it to his lips,—drew it back directly,—gave a peep over the horn-beam hedge;—never did my uncle Toby's mouth water so much for a pipe in his life.—My uncle Toby retired into the sentry-box with the pipe in his hand.—

The whole passage reads like a scenario.

Some of his pantomimes are too fragile even for the cinema; they could be achieved in no other medium than Sterne's prose. I shall choose one of the best, one which illustrates his astonishing imaginative power in portraying the body in repose and in movement, and also that hypnotic slow motion, giving the impression that momentarily time is in abeyance, that the swift flow of life outside in the world has virtually stopped while all attention is focused on a trivial transaction in a glove shop:

> The beautiful Grisset rose up when I said this, and going behind the counter, reach'd down a parcel and untied it: I advanced to the side over-against her: they were all too large. The beautiful Grisset measured them one by one across my hand—It would not alter the dimensions—She begg'd I would try a single pair, which seemed to be the least—She held it open—my hand slipped into it at once—It will not do, said I, shaking my head a little—No, said she, doing the same thing.
> There are certain combined looks of simple subtlety—where whim, and sense, and seriousness, and nonsense, are so blended, that all the languages of Babel set loose together could not express them—they are communicated and caught so instantaneously, that you can scarce say which party is the infecter. I leave it to your men of words to swell pages about it—it is enough in the present to say again, the gloves would not do; so folding our hands within our arms, we both loll'd upon the counter—it was narrow, and there was just room for the parcel to lay between us.
> The beautiful Grisset look'd sometimes at the gloves, then side-ways to the window, then at the gloves—and then at me. I was not disposed to break silence—I follow'd her example: so I look'd at the gloves, then to the window, then at the gloves, and then at her—and so on alternately.

When we reach the last paragraph, we, too, like people watching the ball at a tennis match, are looking sometimes at the gloves, then sideways to the window, then at the gloves, and then at her. It is not for nothing that Sterne made the clock so famous in another connection. Time in his novels is like a clock which he can stop, or speed up, or slow down at will merely by putting out his finger.

Chronology of Important Dates

1713	Laurence Sterne born, November 24, at Clonmel, Tipperary, Ireland, where his father, ensign Roger Sterne, was stationed.
1723-31	At school in Yorkshire.
1737	B.A., Jesus College, Cambridge.
1738	Ordained priest; vicar at Sutton-upon-Forest, near York.
1741	Married Elizabeth Lumley; preferred to prebend in York Minster.
1743	Preferred to Stillington, adjoining Sutton. Published "The Unknown World, Verses occasioned by hearing a Pass-Bell" in *The Gentleman's Magazine*.
1759	Published *A Political Romance (History of a Good Warm Watch-Coat)*. Published Volumes I and II of *Tristram Shandy* at York. London edition, January 1, 1760.
1760	Lionized in London. Presented with the living at Coxwold. Published *The Sermons of Mr. Yorick*.
1761	Published Volumes III and IV of *Tristram Shandy*, and later in the year, Volumes V and VI, in London.
1762	Travels in France.
1765	Published Volumes VII and VIII of *Tristram Shandy*.
1766	Published Volumes III and IV of *The Sermons of Mr. Yorick*.
1767	Published Volume IX of *Tristram Shandy*.
1768	Published *A Sentimental Journey*. Died in London, March 18.

Notes on the Editor and Contributors

JOHN TRAUGOTT, the editor of this volume, is professor of English at the University of California, Berkeley. He has been a Ford Foundation Fellow, a Fulbright lecturer, and is the author of *Tristram Shandy's World*. He has also written numerous articles on Swift, Sterne, and Restoration comedy.

D. W. JEFFERSON is Reader in English Literature at the University of Leeds, England. His studies of Henry James appeared in 1960 and 1964.

BENJAMIN H. LEHMAN is professor emeritus at the University of California, Berkeley. He is a novelist and author of critical studies of Strachey, Carlyle, and Emily Brontë, and of essays in fiction and comedy.

JEAN-JACQUES MAYOUX is professor of English literature at the Sorbonne. His studies, *Joyce* (1965), *Melville* (1960), and *Les Vivants Piliers* (1960), are well known.

ALAN DUGALD McKILLOP is professor emeritus of English at Rice University and the author of many studies in eighteenth century literature, among which are *Thomson's Seasons* (1942), *Richardson* (1936), and *Early Masters of English Fiction* (1956).

A. A. MENDILOW is professor of English literature and head of the department at the Hebrew University of Jerusalem. He is the author of *Time and the Novel* (1951) and other critical studies.

VIKTOR SHKLOVSKY, Russian literary critic and writer of fiction and film scripts, was a moving spirit of the Formalist and Futurist literary groups. He is the author of many critical studies of Soviet and other writers.

W. B. C. WATKINS, who died in 1957, taught at various times at Princeton, Louisiana State, and The University of the South. A gifted and original critic, he wrote in addition to *Perilous Balance,* studies of Shakespeare and Spenser (1950) and Milton (1955).

Selected Bibliography

Biographical and Bibliographical

Cross, Wilbur L. *The Life and Times of Laurence Sterne.* New York, 1909.

Curtis, Lewis Perry. *The Politicks of Laurence Sterne.* Oxford, 1929.

Fluchère, Henri. *Laurence Sterne, de l'homme à l'œuvre: Biographie critique et essai d'interpretation de Tristram Shandy.* Paris, 1961.

Hartley, Lodwick. *Laurence Sterne in the Twentieth Century: An Essay and a Bibliography of Sternean Studies, 1900-1965.* Chapel Hill. N. C., 1966.

Read, Sir Herbert. "Alas, Poor Yorick!" in *The Contrary Experience: Autobiographies.* New York, 1963.

Critical

Baird, Theodore. "The Time-Scheme in *Tristram Shandy* and a Source," *PMLA,* LI (1936), 803-20.

Burckhardt, Sigurd. "Tristram Shandy's Law of Gravity," *ELH,* XXVIII (1961), 70-88.

Connolly, Cyril. "Distress of Plenty," in *The Condemned Playground: Essays 1927-1944.* London, 1946. Pp. 21-26.

Dilworth, Ernest N. *The Unsentimental Journey of Laurence Sterne.* New York, 1948.

Erämetsä, Erik. *A Study of the Word "Sentimental" and of Other Linguistic Characteristics of Eighteenth-Century Sentimentalism in England.* Helsinki, 1951.

Fredman, Alice G. *Diderot and Sterne.* New York, 1955.

Hammond, Lansing Van der Heyden. *Laurence Sterne's "Sermons of Mr. Yorick."* New Haven, 1948.

Humphrey, Robert. *Stream of Consciousness in the Modern Novel.* Berkeley, 1954.

Landa, Lewis. "The Shandean Homunculus: The Background of Sterne's 'Little

Gentleman,'" in *Restoration and Eighteenth-Century Literature,* ed. Caroll Camden. Chicago, 1963.

Lockridge, Ernest H. "A View of the Sentimental Absurd: Sterne and Camus," *Sewanee Review,* LXXII (1964), 652-67.

Monk, Samuel H. Introduction to his edition of *Tristram Shandy.* New York, 1959.

Muir, Edwin. "Laurence Sterne," in *Essays in Literature and Society.* London, 1949. Pp. 49-56.

Priestley, J. B. "The Brothers Shandy," in *The English Comic Characters.* New York, 1925.

Pritchett, V. S. "Sterne's Temperament," *New Statesman and Nation,* XLI (1951), 41.

Putney, Rufus D. "The Evolution of *A Sentimental Journey,*" *Philological Quarterly,* XIX (1940), 349-69.

————. "Laurence Sterne: Apostle of Laughter," in *The Age of Johnson: Essays Presented to Chauncey Brewster Tinker.* New Haven, 1949.

Read, Sir Herbert. "Sterne," in *The Sense of Glory.* Cambridge, 1929.

Reid, Ben. "The Sad Hilarity of Sterne," *Virginia Quarterly Review,* XXXII (1956).

Stedmond, J. M. *The Comic Art of Laurence Sterne.* Toronto, 1967.

Stout, Gardner D., Jr. "Yorick's *Sentimental Journey:* A Comic 'Pilgrim's Progress' for the Man of Feeling," *ELH,* XXX (1936), 395-412.

————, editor, Sterne's *A Sentimental Journey through France and Italy by Mr. Yorick.* Berkeley, 1967.

Tave, Stuart M. *The Amiable Humorist: A Study in the Comic Theory and Criticism of the Eighteenth and Early Nineteenth Century.* Chicago, 1960.

Tuveson, Ernest. "Locke and Sterne," in *Reason and the Imagination: Studies in the History of Ideas, 1600-1800,* ed. J. A. Mazzeo. New York, 1962.

Van Ghent, Dorothy. "On *Tristram Shandy,*" in *The English Novel: Form and Function.* New York, 1953.

Watt, Ian. Introduction to his edition of *Tristram Shandy.* Boston, 1965.

Woolf, Virginia. "Sterne," in *Granite and Rainbow.* London, 1958.

————. "The 'Sentimental Journey,'" in *The Common Reader: Second Series.* London, 1932.